SHAKESPEARE SURVEY

SHAKESPEARE SURVEY

AN ANNUAL SURVEY OF
SHAKESPEARIAN STUDY & PRODUCTION

16

EDITED BY

ALLARDYCE NICOLL

Issued under the Sponsorship of

THE UNIVERSITY OF BIRMINGHAM

THE UNIVERSITY OF MANCHESTER

THE ROYAL SHAKESPEARE THEATRE

THE SHAKESPEARE BIRTHPLACE TRUST

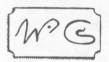

CAMBRIDGE
AT THE UNIVERSITY PRESS
1966

PUBLISHED BY

THE SYNDICS OF THE CAMBRIDGE UNIVERSITY PRESS

Bentley House, 200 Euston Road, London, N.W. 1
American Branch: 32 East 57th Street, New York 22, N.Y.
West African Office: P.O. Box 33, Ibadan, Nigeria

First edition 1963
Reprinted 1966

Printed in Great Britain at the University Press, Cambridge
(Brooke Crutchley, University Printer)
Reprinted by offset litho in Yugoslavia

EDITOR'S NOTE

Shakespeare Survey 16 has been planned as the first of a series of three related volumes. Its main theme is that of Shakespeare's impact on the modern world, and eight of its articles (those by L. B. Wright, R. M. Samarin, J. P. Brockbank, V. Y. Kantak, A. J. Axelrad, Wolfgang Clemen, Rudolf Stamm and Michel Grivelet) reproduce or are based on contributions made to the Tenth International Shakespeare Conference, Stratford-upon-Avon, in 1961.

In honour of the centenary year 1964 a special enlarged volume will be published, devoted entirely to the theme of Shakespeare in his own age. This book, designed to illuminate Shakespeare's environment, will dispense with the usual *Survey* features such as the 'International Notes' and the reviews, since it is intended to stand as an independent study of the Elizabethan period.

Survey 18 will revert to the established form, and it is hoped that most of its contents will be concerned with the topic of 'Shakespeare Then till Now', stressing the fortunes of the dramatist from his own period down to recent years.

CONTENTS

CONTENTS

LIST OF PLATES

AN OBLIGATION TO SHAKESPEARE
AND THE PUBLIC

BY

LOUIS B. WRIGHT

To assert that Shakespeare's position in the world of literature is universal and unique is to utter a commonplace. To assert that his significance as a writer and dramatist is increasing in our world, despite the divisions and difficulties of modern society, is also to reiterate what we all know and are constantly saying. The very convening of this distinguished body of scholars from many nations is proof of Shakespeare's importance in the cultures of each of our countries. We do not need to belabour the point that Shakespeare is of enormous interest to the peoples of every continent. But perhaps it might be profitable for us to contemplate for a few moments the problems, the responsibilities, and the obligations that this vast interest imposes upon us, an accredited body of scholars, whose presumed duty it is to make Shakespeare better understood and appreciated by the multitudes who read him or see his plays acted on the stage.

Since I represent the Folger Shakespeare Library, I inevitably find myself in the role of a kind of broker of information, and it is in that capacity that I, seeking help, want to appear before you. Like any other type of broker, whether his stock-in-trade is shares on the exchange or tangible commodities, we at the Folger have clients and customers who are inquisitive and clamorous for information. Some of our clients are professional scholars like yourselves; some are teachers; some are students; a surprising number can be classified as the general public. They are concerned with Shakespeare and his meaning on various levels of understanding. And they all ask questions that we find it hard to answer.

Although the Folger Library is primarily an institution devoted to research in the whole of Tudor and Stuart civilization, rather than just Shakespeare, the founder, Henry Clay Folger, had a profound interest in Shakespeare and hoped that his library would become a fountain of information about the dramatist, a place where scholars would come to study him and then make their knowledge available to the general public, who, he supposed, eagerly awaited the latest and most learned interpretations of the poet of Stratford. Folger, who had risen to wealth as president of the Standard Oil Company of New York, was himself not a professional scholar, though he acquired an amazing knowledge about Shakespeare and his times. It cannot be supposed that Folger intended to create a library which would become a temple for a special priesthood forever chanting litanies to themselves. As a business man and one of the general public— albeit a worshipper of Shakespeare—he hoped that his library would disseminate knowledge about Shakespeare and the history of that age and broaden the appreciation and understanding of Shakespeare and his contemporaries. It is natural therefore for the administrators of Folger's trust to feel a responsibility to a public that extends beyond academic walls. It is fitting that we ask ourselves whether we are achieving all that we ought in the illumination of an intelligent audience of non-specialists. It is also natural for us to inquire whether the specialists are achieving everything that they ought in this same endeavour, and whether we all might do more to enlighten one another and the lay brethren just outside our doors.

It may be objected that the specialist already has too much to do to become a 'popularizer'—an invidious term with which to damn a man. We all know how hard it is to keep up with the stream of scholarship today. But if scholars do not accept the responsibility for making knowledge available to non-specialists, they should not complain when the job is done badly by amateurs and the less competent.

The diligence and devotion of Shakespearian scholars in our generation probably cannot be surpassed in any period. Contemplation of the quantity and the quality of research focused upon Shakespeare always leaves me with a sense of awe and wonder. The activities of Shakespearian specialists are not confined to the English-speaking peoples, of course, but extend to most of the languages of the civilized world. This fact in itself raises a problem almost insuperable to the average scholar who worries along with two or three languages at most. Much of the scholarship in unknown languages must remain a closed book to him. Perhaps that is just as well, for he finds more than he can digest written in his own tongue.

At this point, I should like to pay a tribute that we must all feel to Allardyce Nicoll and the imaginative concept which led him to establish the *Shakespeare Survey*. It is hard to imagine how scholars managed in the period before this useful, informative, and stimulating instrument was available. The value of the special articles summarizing the state of knowledge on particular topics cannot be overestimated. For that extraordinary section in each volume, 'The Year's Contribution to Shakespearian Study', every harried and harassed scholar ought to sing hosannas. This section provides needed guidance to the student of literature or history who cannot devote himself exclusively to Shakespearian studies. From the beginning, the quality of this annual summary of Shakespeare scholarship has remained high, and we can all be thankful for the judicious and judicial appraisals that the authors of those essays have provided over the years.

The analyst of Shakespearian studies, however, must be haunted from time to time with the suspicion too that much of the stuff that he reads is rubbish, or at best, the printed result of misapplied energy. Nicoll himself in his excellent British Academy lecture in 1952[1] alluded incidentally to the pessimism that many scholars feel about the mass of minute and highly technical studies on Shakespeare that defy assimilation and coherent use. Recently Patrick Cruttwell, reviewing a mass of books about Shakespeare, commented with some asperity that 'We have too many Shakespearians. We have too few critics who can take Shakespeare in their strides as one writer among other great writers. My own prescription for the professional "Shakespearian" would be five years' reading of anything else. We are inclined to use our Shakespeare as a bible of texts from which to preach our religions. And we lack direction—the kind of direction which cannot come from Departments or Institutes but only from one great mind.'[2] Other scholars have suggested a moratorium on publication to provide a period of contemplation and digestion.

The realities of academic life being what they are, a period of quiet contemplation and assimilation has no more chance of success than the King of Navarre's academy in *Love's Labour's Lost*. Nor are we likely to persuade Shakespearians to turn to other subjects in order to broaden their outlook and deepen their perceptions, as Cruttwell recommends. That is not to say, however, that we ought to despair and resign ourselves to suffocation under a heap of jumbled off-prints. Nicoll and his colleagues of the *Shakespeare Survey* have at least provided an escape hatch.

As an individualist and an advocate of free enterprise, I would think it both unwise and impracticable to try to curtail or regiment the activities of Shakespearian scholars. They ought to be free to follow their own inclinations and to write as wisely or as foolishly as their capacities and judgements permit. But I believe that the wise men in the profession can and should exert a more vigorous influence to produce positive results of benefit to both the specialist and the non-specialist. This influence can be exerted in many ways and on several levels: by example and precept, by direction of graduate studies, by reviews, and by syntheses of knowledge that should be undertaken. We may also hope that the great minds desired by Cruttwell may emerge to provide the interpretation and criticism that each new generation requires. In my opinion the greatest need of Shakespeare today is first-class minds in each department of Shakespearian studies to sift the scholarship, appraise it with Olympian justice, and provide an analysis of its quality and usefulness. Let me hasten to say that in some of its essays, the *Shakespeare Survey* has made a beginning, but only a beginning. We need to go farther, for even the Shakespeare specialist finds himself wandering in chaos when he strays a mite beyond his own small field of penetration.

As a broker whose clients demand information that we cannot always supply, I hope you will permit me to make a few fairly specific suggestions of the kind of guides that we need. Someone is certain to remark: 'Why, that has been done by Professor *X*.' But Professor *X* may not have been entirely successful. I do not want to single him out for criticism. No good can come of treading on toes. Each Shakespeare specialist can supply his own footnotes for the paragraphs that follow.

Several years ago, the then American Ambassador to the United Kingdom telephoned me from New York with a request that I recommend a book about Shakespeare. He was flying back to London the next day and he had to make a speech at Stratford almost immediately on his arrival. He wanted a single volume that would explain to him the amazing appeal that Shakespeare retains for the mid-twentieth century and the significance that Shakespeare has for our generation. Perhaps it was my own ignorance, but not even the resources of the Folger Library enabled me to recommend a single book that would fully answer the Ambassador's needs. Since he was a Trustee of my own institution, I felt doubly embarrassed. Ever since then I have been wondering why, with all the energy that we have devoted to Shakespeare, somebody has not attempted that sort of book in language that an Ambassador of cultivation and intelligence could comprehend.

Of critical works about Shakespeare, our generation has been blest—if that is the word—with volumes unnumbered. We have works of excellence and learning that range from the general to the particular. A reading of Muriel C. Bradbrook's 'Fifty Years of Criticism of Shakespeare's Style: A Retrospect'[3] is highly instructive and reveals in a brief compass the amazing scope of the critical approach to Shakespeare in our time. Perhaps it is proper that most of the criticism should have been strictly professional, that is, written by scholars for scholars, for without such professional instruction, one of another, learning cannot make much progress. We should not expect each specialist in literature to reduce his findings to the level of the daily newspaper or even that of the popular magazine. That is a fallacy that hostile critics of scholarship in the humanities frequently voice.

Nevertheless, we ought to expect more criticism written to the understanding of scholars who are not technicians in the critic's particular corner of learning. It is also not too much to expect more criticism designed for the understanding of the cultivated and intelligent public that is concerned with literature in a non-professional capacity—my Ambassador, for example.

By now, I trust, we are all aware of the damage that has been done to literary study by obscurantist cults in a few academic communities, particularly in my country. For the most part, the obscurantists have been a priest-craft who, like other religions from time to time, have used a private language not always entirely lucid even to anointed members of the order. At least their commentary, even in praise of one another, has often been at cross purposes as if they did not quite comprehend what had gone before. Occasionally one has a hunch that some of this criticism possesses dark profundities, valuable if only an ordinary brain could plumb its depths. Much of it, of course, as Ben Jonson might have said, is writ in no language at all. As other literary fads had their day and vanished, so obscurantist criticism is no longer in fashion. A few ageing apostles in American academic communities still deliver their sermons, but disciples are few and less influential than their masters. For a number of years, however, this fad absorbed the interest and energies of young scholars, including many in the field of Shakespeare, who might have made useful contributions to interpretation and appreciation if they had had better direction. It remains for a new generation to repair a disaster that left a dearth of wise critics.

The field of Shakespearian criticism today is so vast and has such a ramification of specialized topics, from aesthetic appreciation to Freudian analysis, that non-specialist literary scholars, much less other folk, find it difficult to sort out the significant from the trivial. For scholars, we need a guide more explicit and more magisterial than any yet written that will analyse the work in print and give more extensive value judgements than are now available. Miss Bradbrook has made an excellent beginning and has pointed the way to further work in this area.

For the general reader, we need a simpler guide that will discover for him the critical works that have value and good sense, works that will not lead him astray to follow some will-o'-the-wisp of the critic's fancy. He needs an explanation without technical jargon of the place that recent critical works have in the stream of criticism from Coleridge to Bradley and beyond. He deserves some explanation of critical fashions from generation to generation and the part these fashions have played in the interpretation of Shakespeare in the study and on the stage. Such a book ought to be written by a scholar who has the gift of clarity and the wisdom not to be condescending.

Many battles have raged in our generation between the various schools of criticism, and in these wars during the last two or three decades, the historical critic has come off worst. He was vulnerable because of the excesses of some of his kind. Students complained that they lost sight of Shakespeare in the fog of background studies. They forgot, or never learned, for instance that *Love's Labour's Lost* was intended to be an amusing entertainment with a large amount of burlesque and slapstick, because they were so busy studying about the Elizabethan grammar school that Holofernes travestied. Such students were a little like the Latin pupils who spent their time building a model of Caesar's bridge across the Rhine instead of learning to read the *Gallic Wars*. A natural reaction followed, and we academics did what we frequently do: we threw the baby out with the bath. We gave over historical criticisms and rushed to something else, and presently one pedantry led to another, perhaps an even more barren pedantry: criticism

4

without a knowledge of the milieu from which a work grew often represented nothing more than a web spun from the critic's brain, and that was not sufficiently interesting to warrant our attention.

The time has come to adjust the balance and to realize that Shakespeare is infinitely richer in meaning if we know what he himself intended to say, not what we want him to say. Many fine monographs have been written in the past quarter of a century to show how Shakespeare's works reflect his infinite interest in the world about him, and how an understanding of that world helps us to interpret words, passages, and large significances of his plays. We should welcome continued probing into the social background of the Elizabethan period because all the information that we can gather helps toward a deeper comprehension of Shakespeare's genius.

Social history as an adjunct of Shakespearian study is a field that is attracting many students; it is small wonder that it should, for social history like archaeology brings us in contact with reality. For example, a study of medical theory and practice in the late sixteenth century is not a mere antiquarian pursuit for the Shakespearian. We forget that in Shakespeare's England, as in colonial America, a patient with an ache or pain frequently had to be his own doctor, and everybody had a wider knowledge of the medical theory of the day than we have of ours. A familiarity with medical theory and terminology enabled a scholar recently to settle neatly and conclusively, it seems to me, that Hamlet meant to say precisely 'too solid flesh' rather than 'sullied' or something else.[4]

An understanding of the social background that Shakespeare is reflecting removes his plays from the realm of the abstract to the concrete and gives them greater life and vividness. Why the literary scholar should object to this, as he sometimes does, baffles me. Perhaps realistic interpretation in the light of contemporary meaning is too destructive of pet theories that we would prefer to deduce out of thin air.

In the area of social history, the literary historian could profitably use guides, preferably written by someone above the tumult of argument that unhappily plagues certain historical quarters. One of the distressing developments in recent years is the substitution of controversy for truth among some of the younger historians—with a consequent deterioration of good manners. Why anyone should imagine that doctrinaire arrogance is a useful quality in a historian passes understanding. What the student of Shakespeare would like to have are discussions of current fashions and trends in historical research, with objective appraisals of the most enlightening works on such problems as the religious establishment in Shakespeare's England, the rise of Puritanism, the social structure and problems of class status, economic dislocations, and all of the variety of shifts and changes that affected day-to-day life when Shakespeare was producing his plays in London.

We should be mindful that history like criticism has its moods and fads, and what is cried up today may be scoffed at tomorrow. Social history is not an easy tool for the literary scholar to use, and he must be aware of its limitations. Shakespeare was an eclectic genius with an enormous capacity for assimilating this and that from the world around him. Yet we are inclined to see Shakespeare the dramatist as an image of ourselves, working as we would work. Let us remember that he was not a university professor. He did not go to the library and create *Hamlet* as a treatise on melancholy, however much he may have known about the contemporary medical theory of melancholy.

Textual criticism and scientific bibliography are fields in which we have seen enormous progress in recent years. Indeed, the ingenuity and skill demonstrated in this area have revolutionized older concepts of the preparation of texts. The annual descriptions in *Shakespeare Survey* by James G. McManaway of textual studies are an extraordinary and sometimes terrifying exhibition of human ingenuity struggling to get a glimpse of Shakespeare's manuscripts.

Modern bibliographic and textual studies had their beginning in the early work of those giants of our generation, Sir Walter Greg and R. B. McKerrow. We still miss their incisive criticism as well as their positive contributions to bibliographical knowledge.

In our country, Fredson Bowers at the University of Virginia has produced a group of younger disciples who have been trained to apply an exact and exacting method of textual analysis to the printed work of any author, but the emphasis has been on the Elizabethan period. Among the most constructive and useful studies that have come out of this school are the contributions by Charlton Hinman of the University of Kansas. Hinman, a brilliant technician, as all in this company must be aware, has completed the collation of all the First Folios in the Folger Library, and the publication of his findings by the Oxford University Press will be an event of the first magnitude for Shakespearian textual criticism. His work will settle definitively problems of the printing of the First Folio that have been a matter of speculation and conjecture. Though his discoveries may not alter substantially the readings of Shakespeare's text, his analysis of the quality of the work of each printer who set copy for the Folio will provide guidance for emendations. These discoveries will enable scholars in the future to give a better evaluation of the Folio text than has been possible heretofore.

In the hands of technicians as skilful, patient, and meticulous as Bowers and Hinman, textual and bibliographical analysis can be an instrument of enormous value to the Shakespearian scholar. In the hands of bumbling, careless, or second-rate practitioners, the method can be misleading and confusing because it may give the illusion of scientific accuracy which it actually lacks. It may also be deceptive because few will be willing to go through the labour necessary to check conclusions submitted with a panoply of data and statistics that on the surface may look convincing.

The principal danger in the excellent instrument that Bowers and Hinman have fashioned lies in too great a faith that the innocent and the naïve may put in it. Accurate as they are in some of their conclusions about printing practices, no analysis can be so detailed or accurate that it will answer all the questions that arise. When speculating about the actions of human beings, we should remember that they will not always react the same way under the same set of circumstances, or perform the same operation in the same manner each time. We shall only fool ourselves if we think we can reduce Elizabethan printing practices to an exact 'science'.

In my youth I was a professional proof-reader on a newspaper and dealt directly with a large group of printers. It was an instructive and revealing experience which I recommend to all textual analysts before they become too dogmatic about the invariable practice of printers in any period. The best printer in this particular outfit, the man who always set the leading editorials, had two distinct personalities: one drunk and one sober. Even one drink changed the quality of his work so that we frequently had to get someone else to set the editorials. Another printer whom I recall vividly did excellent work at the beginning of his stint, but occasionally, nearing the end of the day's run, his proofs were spotted with misread words and other typographical errors. Obviously his eyes tired or muscular fatigue took its toll. Because of the vast range of intangible influences that affect human behaviour, I am sceptical of too much certitude about what any printer saw in his copy when he picked up the type to fit in his stick. Much nonsense has been written by neophytes who have studied Elizabethan handwriting and can tell positively whether a printer saw an *e* or a *d*, let us say. Of all people in my experience, a printer is the last person about whom one can speak with assurance.

Valuable as have been the contributions of the best of the analytical bibliographers, they have not always given their gospel with the saving grace of common sense. We all now know that no two Elizabethan books may be precisely identical. But to tell the historian that he must spend years collating the texts of Bacon's *History of Henry the Seventh*, for example, before he dares quote from it, is to take leave of one's wits. It is true that in some instances collation of many copies of an edition will reveal the correction of a key word that might distort meaning in a critical passage, but to follow this technique to its ultimate conclusion is to achieve a *reductio ad absurdum*. It will be a pity if good scholars should be so terrified by the exactions of the new science of analytical bibliography that they will desert literature for mathematics or physics where the conclusions—and the rewards—may be more satisfying.

As in other fields of Shakespearian scholarship, we need a judicial appraisal of textual and bibliographical scholarship that goes beyond the annual surveys and gives value judgements on what it has accomplished, what it can accomplish, and what are its limitations. For the inexperienced and the naïve—and there are more than we might wish in this category—we particularly need an assessment of the limitations of this technique.

In recent years, textual critics have shown an increasing tendency to neglect linguistics and overlook the study of the language as a key to the solution of many cruxes. We suffer here from the general neglect of the study of language. Since the great period of philological investigation in the nineteenth century, we have fallen on evil days. Some incredible gaffes are being made by textual critics simply because they do not know enough about the structure of the language, about the fluidity of the language in Shakespeare's day, and especially about the variety of dialectal usage. If we could encourage a return to linguistic study we might ensure wiser textual conclusions.

In his British Academy lecture that I have already mentioned, Allardyce Nicoll yearned for a modern 'Authorized Version' of Shakespeare that would utilize the best of modern scholarship and supplant the old Globe, which has stood the test of time with such distinction. Obviously much new learning has become available in the time since the editors of the Globe prepared their text. Some new readings can and should be accepted. But in the present state of knowledge and opinion, it is doubtful whether an 'Authorized Version' would be desirable, even if it were possible. For one thing, what Sanhedrin of scholars could make their authority stick? We do not have a French Academy of Shakespearians who can impose their will upon editors. A convocation of textual critics would argue longer and louder than delegates to the United Nations—and arrive at solutions probably just as unsatisfactory.

The most acceptable modern text must be one that makes use of all the knowledge that can be mustered: literary, linguistic, historical, bibliographical, and analytical. In the end it must be subjective and represent the best intelligence of the individual editor or editors. It must be subjective because many of the solutions are not capable of scientific certainty. Our best efforts in many instances must remain educated guesses.

I wonder if this ought to make us grievously unhappy. Shakespeare, great as he is, did not compose Holy Writ. Our salvation or damnation does not turn on a word. Furthermore, we can never be sure that what we are reading represents the poet's own reasoned choice of diction. Anybody who has ever had anything to do with working playwrights and actors knows what happens to the most meticulously composed work. In production, passages may be changed, words altered, scenes slashed, characterizations modified, and a happy ending provided. Prompt copies are scribbled on and overwritten. The text is not sacred, even when the author is sitting on the sidelines objecting. When he is a manager and director, as Shakespeare was, he wants the play to succeed and he will not let a sacred word or scene come between him and profit. *Hamlet* as it stands in print is obviously too long for stage production. How the uncut version happened to be embalmed in print will remain a matter of scholarly conjecture and discussion.

My point is that we cannot be certain beyond peradventure that the surviving texts, even those texts selected by Heminge and Condell for the Folio, are precisely as Shakespeare wrote them down. Ingenious as our guesses are, they remain guesses about the method of transmission from playhouse to printer. There is no fool-proof method of knowing whether some of the passages over which we agonize represent the author's carelessness, the scribbling of a prompter, manager, or play doctor, the misreading of a printer, or heaven knows what chance alteration. Unless a miracle produces some of Shakespeare's manuscript or some revelation is vouchsafed us concerning the transmission of his texts, we are likely to remain in our present state of puzzlement.

In the past three decades, much ingenuity has gone into an exploration of the Elizabethan stage, and we have some excellent studies, a few of which have come to completely divergent conclusions. One scholar will defend the Swan drawing as a veritable representation of what the stage of the public theatres was like; another will submit good reasons to believe that the artist, sketching from memory, was inaccurate. One scholar will assert that Shakespeare's plays were designed for a stage 'in the round'. Another will point out the impossibility of this concept. Whether the public theatre had an inner stage, doors set at an angle or flat against the wall, what properties were available and how used, and sundry other problems of the physical arrangements of the stage are matters of controversy.

Some of the discussions of the physical construction of the stage sound as if the authors thought all stages were identical and underwent no changes until the Restoration. Perhaps we have allowed the Swan drawing to dominate too much of our thinking about stage construction. Perhaps we ought to realize that the Elizabethans were an ingenious and inventive people and that Elizabethan theatrical managers had some of the capacity for adaptation to special situations characteristic of all theatrical folk. Because Burbage and company used timbers from The Theatre in the erection of the first Globe, that is no proof that they made no changes and improvements. To assume that the owners of the Globe had learned nothing and merely duplicated the old Globe after the unfortunate fire of 1613 is to deny Elizabethan theatrical people much intelligence. To believe that people ingenious enough to arrange the elaborate machinery and spectacles of court shows and masques never carried over any of their ideas into plays performed in the public theatres is to believe that they lacked both imagination and professional aptitude. But we should not go to the other extreme and argue that because Shakespeare's company may have put on a play in some great hall 'in the round', they carried over that method to the Globe or Blackfriars. If students of the theatre depended less upon ruminations in their studies and more upon a knowledge of what actually takes place in staging a play and the way theatrical people work, they would then come up with wiser solutions of some of the problems of Elizabethan staging.

Until new documents turn up, we cannot be absolutely positive about many details of Shakespeare's Globe or Blackfriars, or or other Elizabethan playhouses. We could profitably use a fresh assessment of the scholarship of the past thirty years, one that would indicate the areas of firm agreement, the areas of probable correctness, and those conjectures that seem to go beyond plausibility and common sense.

It is now thirty-one years since the publication of Sir Edmund Chambers' *William Shakespeare: A Study of Facts and Problems*, a work that will remain a monument of learning and good sense, two qualities that are not invariably joined. Every Shakespearian must wish that Sir Edmund, like King Arthur or Frederick Barbarossa, might return in our hour of need. We need him frequently to resolve some point of controversy.

For the past three or four years I have been trying to assay Shakespearian scholarship because we have been engaged in the preparation of a popular paperback edition of Shakespeare. This edition does not pretend to be a scholarly contribution but merely seeks to provide an accurate and modern text plus such explanations as the average reader will need. We have wanted to incorporate in the text the best readings that modern scholarship can provide and to include any new interpretations that seem valid. But time after time, when we have sifted through quantities of essays, notes and monographs, we have come back to Chambers to discover that his observations carry more weight than anything written since 1930. He had the capacity to winnow the chaff from the wheat and utilize the good grain of scholarship. Please do not misunderstand me. This is not to say that we have made no advances: we have many distinguished and useful contributions. It is to insist that we need at regular intervals someone like Chambers, indeed several minds like Chambers', that can appraise all of the work that the industry of Shakespearians has piled up, and give the rest of us guidance through a maze that threatens to become a jungle. We have had enough partisanship for this or that method of approach. Shakespearian studies would benefit from a cool and detached scepticism that would seek to evaluate every instrument of learning and utilize each for what it is worth. More than all else we need discriminating wisdom.

NOTES

1. Allardyce Nicoll, *Co-operation in Shakespearian Scholarship*. Annual Shakespeare Lecture of the British Academy (London, 1952).

2. Patrick Cruttwell in the *Manchester Guardian* for 5 January 1961.

3. Muriel C. Bradbrook, 'Fifty Years of the Criticism of Shakespeare's Style: A Retrospect', *Shakespeare Survey* 7 (1954), 1–11.

4. Sidney Warhaft, 'Hamlet's Solid Flesh Resolved', *English Literary History*, XXVIII (1961), 21–30.

OUR CLOSENESS TO SHAKESPEARE

BY

R. M. SAMARIN

'We all sprang out of Gogol's Шинель [*The Overcoat*]', said Dostoevsky, referring to his contemporaries, the Russian realist-authors. This is true; but it is equally true to say that the whole of European and American literature in the nineteenth and twentieth centuries may be regarded as having sprung out of the heritage-bequeathed by Shakespeare. There is a genetic relationship between modern art and the great discoveries which were made by him in the world of poetry and theatre.

It is he who first and foremost stands as the source of that new perception and portrayal of reality which, ever changing and enriching itself, has since developed in an inexhaustible wealth in different national forms and under different names. In fact, the seventeenth century was incapable of comprehending Shakespeare's greatness fully, for, out of the specifically English conditions of his age, he wrought something which went far beyond the borders of his epoch.

It is significant that Goethe and Schiller, Hugo and Keats, Balzac and Scott, Pushkin and the Russian realists of the nineteenth century all turned to Shakespeare for guidance. Even more significant is it that in the literature of the nineteenth century the Shakespearian principle in art was acclaimed by such different writers as Rolland and Hauptmann, Shaw and Gorky. Even Tolstoy's attacks upon Shakespeare sprang from the singular urgency of Shakespeare's art for Tolstoy.

It was not the early Renaissance, still bubbling with naïve and beautiful hopes for the approach of the Golden Age, during which his mature artistry developed. The turn of the sixteenth century was a stern and hard time, the time when the humanistic ideals were being shattered, the time of the crisis of European humanism. His freedom-loving spirit soared beyond that of the crowned patrons and merchant princes of his age. Shakespeare's genius is most fully demonstrated by the fact that in this calamitous time he remained true to the basic ideals of humanism, that he overcame the breakdown of the humanistic illusions and instead of these illusions developed in himself that courageous, stern and life-loving outlook which permeated his works after 1600. In this respect Shakespeare's way contrasts markedly with the way of John Donne; Donne dealt with many of the subjects treated by Shakespeare; but his poetical world gives expression to that very crisis of humanistic illusions which was successfully overcome by Shakespeare. Donne was troubled by the same questions that tortured Shakespeare: but he gave answers that differed entirely from the thoughts originated in Shakespeare's characters by the very way the questions are put. And the chief question of all was the question of the place of man in the world and of his right to an independent and fearless decision concerning his fate.

That is why it is impossible to agree with T. S. Eliot, who asserts that for him Donne is a mighty creative individuality, always original, while Shakespeare is only a brilliant plagiarist who has himself forgotten the sources of his borrowings. To my mind, Shakespeare's art absorbs the great heritage of the Renaissance and, as it were, sums up its quest, remaining at the same time profoundly original due both to the poetical genius of Shakespeare, the artist, and to his arduously gained philosophical conception so different from Donne's poignant contradictions. The difference between them is revealed in their divergent uses of a single poetic image, that of the tempest. Shakespeare's tempest, as well as other forces of nature, is subject to Prospero. Donne's tempest, which shatters the British ships off the Azores, turns into a gigantic symbol of chaos ruling a world in which man is pitiable and helpless when confronted with the demoniacal forces of nature; he seeks salvation in God, whom Shakespeare's characters certainly call upon, but seldom in the most anxious or the most joyous moments of their lives.

Another great writer of the seventeenth century, deeply shaken by the cruel truth of reality, proclaimed that '*la vida es sueño*'. A lover of life, Shakespeare dauntlessly and unflinchingly states by the whole of his works that life is life. Shakespeare's manly and objective philosophical conception, directed at the real material actuality surrounding man and convincing by virtue of its Baconian empiricism, is dear to us.

Even in our days *Hamlet* shakes the audience of all the theatres in the world, and the editions of Shakespeare's sonnets are sold out in a few days in whatever language they appear. To be sure, there is something greater in our closeness to Shakespeare than to any other great artist of such a remote past. I, as a Soviet scholar, wish first of all to speak of the special popularity that Shakespeare has in the Soviet Union.

One of the reasons for our closeness to Shakespeare—and maybe it is one of the most important reasons—is, I believe, that fresh conception, and consequently that fresh portrayal, of man which was Shakespeare's greatest discovery.

In Shakespeare's drama man realizes himself as an individual. He discovers himself, the surrounding society and his place in it, nature and his unbreakable ties with it. In comparison with what was known before Shakespeare these discoveries appear absolutely novel. They are no less significant than the new ideas and notions of the earth and of the sky, of man's body and of the Universe that were worked out by the great travellers, scholars and artists who were Shakespeare's contemporaries and inspirers.

Maxim Gorky called literature 'the study of man'. There is no doubt that Shakespeare was one of the greatest 'students of man' of all times.

The newest and most essential elements in Shakespeare's conception and portrayal of man consisted, in my opinion, in his idea that every man is a never-to-be-repeated, unique wealth and complexity of qualities, thoughts and feelings, often extremely contradictory. The many-sidedness of Shakespeare's characters, which was always conditioned by their experience, was the first revelation in world literature of the unmatched, unique character of an individual personality, the vivid wealth and complexity of a human soul, be it the soul of prince Hamlet, the poet and philosopher, or the soul of the clown who digs Ophelia's grave; even the clown has his own philosophy, his own way of thinking and his own manner of feeling, although he says only a few words and his part might at first glance appear to be absolutely insignificant.

Chernyshevsky, an eminent Russian critic of the nineteenth century, said that Leo Tolstoy was a great master at revealing the dialectics of a human soul. Can this not be said of Shakespeare too? His characters are dearer to us than the romantic Titans of Marlowe or the 'humours' of the 'rare Ben Jonson' because 'the dialectics of the soul' provide that quality of Shakespeare's characters that excites and charms us.

Man, as an actor in the great drama of life in Shakespeare's plays, appears as a lyrical generalization in his sonnets. From all other lyrical generalizations of a similar kind, of which there are not a few in Renaissance poetry, Shakespeare's lyrical hero is distinguished by his deep individuality. The 'I' of Shakespeare's sonnets is a typical image of the man of the Renaissance period complete with his world outlook, his habits and passions—and a unique personality: he is a poet proud of his poems immortalizing his beloved; an actor serving his craft with dignity and bitterness; a rider giving way to meditation on his habitual way from London to Stratford; a lover whose eyes follow the hands of his mistress as she touches the keys; a thinker capable of giving within the strict limits of a sonnet an exhaustively full characteristic of his epoch.

Individuality in the sonnets of Du Bellay was an autobiographical feature connected with that author's journey to Italy and his scholarly leanings; Ronsard's sonnets are inspired by his passion for those to whom he gave resounding antique names; Petrarch's sonnets depend upon his somewhat abstract cult of the feeling of love. Neither in their sonnets nor in the sonnets of Surrey, Spenser or Sidney do we find the generalizing force and profound individual content which excites us in each and every sonnet of Shakespeare and which makes them one great poem about the poet and his time. If we can say that Shakespeare's universal dramatic art proclaimed the beginning of a new drama, then his sonnets are the beginning of a new era in the development of lyric poetry. It has already been said that one of the important features of Shakespeare's innovation which is especially dear to us is the revelation of man's nature in its change and development. The thinker and poet Hamlet exchanges his 'style' for a sword; the valiant soldier Macbeth, so nobly ambitious, is transformed into Macbeth the tyrant abhorred not only by his retinue but by himself. We call that the dynamics of Shakespeare's characters.

The changes which take place in Shakespeare's hero nearly always come as the result of a struggle which he wages with his adversaries and sometimes—simultaneously—with his own self; often, like Hamlet, he realizes the necessity of change and strives to accelerate it. But here likewise Shakespeare is infinitely rich and versatile, so that, for example, while the Prince of Denmark excels in introspection, it takes Othello a long time to notice the tragic changes within his soul.

Macbeth's agonizing doubts before the murder of Duncan are likewise a struggle with his own self, as are the doubts of Prospero towards the end of *The Tempest*. The dramatic mechanism by means of which all this is expressed—the Shakespearian soliloquy, directed by the protagonist not only at the other actors in the play but also at himself—brings us infinitely close to Shakespeare's characters, reveals their souls to us in a way that no other master of the world prior to Shakespeare could achieve, and it gave inspiration to other writers of the nineteenth and twentieth centuries who sought to depict the inner world of man. Any play by Shakespeare is a play of many men and their relationship, but it is also a play of one man who is its centre. That is why Shakespeare's mastery already contained the seeds of those great psychological discoveries which were to be made by the later romantic and realist authors. People in Shakespeare's plays change and act according to their individual peculiarities. But the development of man, the changes that take place in him are determined by factors of social life and are closely linked with the participation of the hero in its events. Never had man been shown as an Aristotelian πολιτικὸν ζῷον to such an extent as in Shakespeare.

Shakespeare's characters are proud of their participation in the events that give birth and strength to England, even when they take part in political gambles. Even if some of his characters anathematize society and forsake it as Timon did, they are not independent of it and thrive on their hatred for it. They defend their inner world from the encroachment of inhuman and ugly social forces as, for example, in *Hamlet* or *Othello*. For Shakespeare man is an active participant in the life of society and not a pitiable creature of God, a worm grovelling in the earthly dust, as he was for John Donne. As we see from *Hamlet* and *Julius Caesar*, Shakespeare's man realizes not only his bond with society but also his responsibility for the state of society. We are inspired by the pathos of history that permeates the plays of the great English writer, we cherish his desire to understand the historical essence of his time and to reveal it in its relationship with the past and the future.

That is why we value so highly the wide range and scope of social phenomena in Shakespeare's plays. The elaborate, mobile, changeful social structure of his plays where the passing social phenomena come into collision with the new, where in the dramatis personae there are kings and beggars, where indeed a king may become a beggar—this structure is a reflection and a realization of the complex new world that replaces the decaying principles of the Middle Ages.

And does not many a writer of the nineteenth and twentieth centuries in the attempt to show the life of social organisms as a whole and of singular human fates repeat this structure? The situation where the new struggles against the old is one of the most typical in his tragedies, comedies or chronicles; and in these the new principle triumphs. We see it in the character of the brave and self-confident merchant-adventurer Antonio or in Beatrice with her humanistic education, or in Prince Hal meditating over the corpse of Hotspur, or in the love of Othello and Desdemona that triumphs over the prejudices of the Venetian nobility. This new element changes also the essence of the characters that were moulded under old conditions; Falstaff, the embodiment of merry old medieval England, differs from Hotspur in that he has already relinquished the world of chivalry in which Hotspur still lives and for which he dies. It is this victory of the new over the old that is revealed in the general dynamics of the character of Hamlet, the humanist prince who asks himself the boldest questions that might trouble a man of his time and is not afraid of direct answers.

Shakespeare is all the nearer to us for not regarding the victory of the new over the old as an easy matter dependent upon the ethical superiority of those who believe in the new principles over the defenders of the old feudal world. It is in the tragic struggle of the new with the old, in the courageous acceptance of the necessity of distressing sacrifices which pave the way to victory that the pathos of Shakespeare's creative work—and particularly the work of his mature years—is revealed. He would have renounced truth if he had made the humanist Hamlet a prosperous enlightened king of Denmark. Instead, the crown will go to the practical politician Fortinbras. Shakespeare would have also deviated from the truth of life had his King Lear, grown wise with experience in the lowest walks of life, come back to the throne as a fabulous kind monarch to make Britain a land flowing with milk and honey. The fact that the age-old discord of two families is conquered at the price of their death makes the story of Romeo and Juliet all the more poignant. Shakespeare left 'happy endings' to other dramatists of his time—poets who were talented, sometimes even more erudite than he, but nevertheless far below him in stature.

Slow is the motion of history, innumerable are the victims that perish in its battles, waged in the fields of England—as at Bosworth—and in the halls of kings' palaces—as in Elsinore and in that Cyprian castle where Iago spreads his net. History moves—this Shakespeare knew—and it moves not in a closed circle, not according to the gloomy and sorrowful wisdom of Ecclesiastes, but in accordance with its own laws the action of which Shakespeare clearly perceived and revealed. Shakespeare realized that these laws are strict. He rose to the understanding of the fact that the birth of the new world, whose poet he was, was difficult and had to be paid for in blood and suffering. At the price of the loss of his illusions Shakespeare was convinced that the new world was not an ideal society of which the learned old man Gonzalo babbled, rather it was like Athens, cursed for its venality and indifference by Timon, when he was forsaking the city where money ruled so obviously and brazenly. There appears in Shakespeare's dramas a profoundly poetical feeling of the dynamics of history, a vision that opens before mankind in the process of its development. For the sake of these new horizons the idylls and Utopias which distinguished early humanism and which were characteristic of the young Shakespeare could be abandoned.

Our closeness to Shakespeare finds, naturally, different expression in different countries of the world. The Soviet people received the Shakespearian tradition together with what was best in the cultural heritage of Russia, a heritage in which Shakespeare occupied a prominent place from the eighteenth century onwards.

Shakespeare's creative experience was widely used by Russian criticism in its struggle to form and develop realism. For Pushkin and Belinsky Shakespeare was primarily a pattern of truthful art. Belinsky, placing him alongside Cervantes, saw in him the beginning of the new European literature. And at the same time, the study of Shakespeare was closely linked in our country with the interpretation of his plays on the Russian stage, that is to say with the cultural life of the country. Belinsky's essay on Hamlet, presenting a bold new treatment of the tragedy's social content, was written under the impress of the acting of the remarkable Russian actor Mochalov.

At all periods in the development of the Russian theatre Shakespeare's plays formed an important part of the repertory. The numerous Russian translations of his works developed in close connection with this. Many of the critical-historical studies of Nikolai Storozhenko, Russia's greatest nineteenth-century Shakespeare specialist, were connected with the staging of Shakespeare's plays in Moscow theatres.

Since 1917 the study and mastery of Shakespeare in our country has reached an unprecedented scale. I shall not give here figures concerning the number of Shakespeare productions and publications in the U.S.S.R., although these figures are indeed amazing. Suffice it to say that of all the classical foreign authors in the Soviet repertoire Shakespeare is still the most popular dramatist. It is truly extraordinary that a writer born four hundred years ago has for forty years remained the favourite dramatist of the Soviet people. The names of more or less talented modern playwrights appear and are forgotten, the plays of Molière and Lope de Vega, Lessing and Schiller, Hugo and Ibsen, Hauptmann and Shaw return to the stage and leave it again—but new productions of Shakespeare's plays appear in different parts of our country every year. Shakespeare's characters speak to the Soviet people in Russian and in Ukrainian, in Armenian and in Georgian, in Tatar and in Ossetic, in Estonian and in Lithuanian—in all the numerous languages of our Union. Yet they remain Shakespearian characters and speak primarily in the language of Shakespeare's feelings and ideas. Thus every large Soviet theatre, whether it works in the capital or in some remote region of the country, is confronted with the practical problems of Shakespearian study, from interpretation down to the smallest productional details.

It is understandable, therefore, that the Shakespeare conferences which take place in our country from time to time bring together all concerned in this study—the critics and the philologists, the directors and the actors, the scene-designers and the musical composers. It is understandable also that new editions of Shakespeare's works are sold out very quickly with us, as was the new eight-volume edition of the Complete Works issued under the editorship of A. Smirnov and A. Anikst in 1961.

Thus Shakespeare continually exerts his influence on our audiences and readers, enriches their minds, opens before them the boundless wealth of the realm of his thoughts and images. The fruitfulness of this influence can be seen not only from the fact that a part in a play by Shakespeare is a red-letter date in the biography of any Soviet actor, but also from the appearance of such works of Soviet art as Prokofiev's ballet 'Romeo and Juliet', famous not only for its music but also for Ulanova's achievement in the part of Juliet.

The great Russian poet Alexander Blok was right when, during the first months of the existence of our State, he foretold a great future for Shakespeare in it. The world of Shakespeare's heroes proved to be clear and dear to the people who created the Soviet society and its culture. For this Gorky found forceful and direct words: 'an active man, the builder of a new world, is the one to be the hero of modern drama. And to depict this hero with due force and brilliance one must learn the art of writing plays from the old unmatched masters of this literary form—and most of all from Shakespeare.'

The perception of Shakespeare is a twofold process with us. Many important productions of Shakespeare in our theatres mean also new interpretations which bring the stage history of Shakespeare something unique and original. Soviet actors have given many wonderful impersonations of Shakespeare's characters. During the past few years we have had Samoylov in the part of Hamlet and Mordvinov in the part of Othello; the wonderful Georgian actor Khorava in the same part created probably the best Moor of Venice we have ever had; the Estonian actress Aino Talvi successfully coped with the difficult role of Cleopatra. The Georgian theatre and the Estonian theatre, following their own traditions, have found their own solutions for the staging of Shakespeare's plays, just as the productions of *Hamlet* in Moscow and Leningrad have been realized in the spirit of the traditions of the Russian theatre. In each we get a new transformation of Shakespeare, who extends his influence and helps new generations of actors to expand their talents within the framework of Shakespearian character-roles. I realize that to an English audience many things on our stage would seem strange, just as we find strangeness in witnessing an English production of a Chekhov play. But it is clear that in both instances we are dealing not only with the introduction of a work of art to the audience, but also with a new interpretation peculiar to the theatre of the country and to the personality of the actors. Thus Chekhov becomes an English author and Shakespeare is assimilated by the country whose language his heroes speak when impersonated on the stage by the actors of our country.

There is something that our productions—with all their dissimilarity—share, and that is a common conception of Shakespeare's realism, his spirit of heroism and his joy of living. We can give Shakespeare away neither to the Middle Ages nor to those interpretations of his works where—following fashionable aesthetic and psychological theories—his men and women are viewed in the light of the prejudices, 'complexes' and vices of the nineteenth and twentieth centuries. In contradistinction to those who consider Shakespeare's realism purely spontaneous and unconscious I believe that the aesthetic system to which the great dramatist adhered was deliberately planned. I am persuaded of this not only by his use of imagery and the systematic nature of his creative method, but also by his own statements—the reference to 'method' in *Hamlet* and the repeated statements on 'style' in his sonnets.

Shakespeare's concepts of 'method' and 'style' differ from those in modern philology and aesthetics. This does not mean that Shakespeare's aesthetic terminology should be rejected or considered naïve: Shakespeare undoubtedly knew well what he meant when he raised his voice against the learned style or against the affected and artificial representation of man on the stage, against 'overstepping the modesty of nature'.

Shakespeare's realism is a definite stage in the development of the world's realistic art. It is distinguishable from that of Fielding and Smollett, of Dickens and Thackeray, of Hardy and Shaw. In the realistic art of these men there are qualities and achievements which cannot be found in the realism of Shakespeare. But, in its turn, Shakespeare's realism is in many respects richer and more vivid than the art of the later times. His unmatched and everlasting charm lies in the remarkable combination of the titanic and the human elements in his characters, in the fierceness of their passion, in the depth and audacity of their aspirations, in the fruitfulness of their doubts, in the author's unprecedented, vast comprehension of life, expressed in vital language which boldly breaks through all the stylistic forms of the time.

Giordano Bruno, Shakespeare's contemporary, gave to one of his dialogues, written in England, the title of 'A Dialogue About Heroic Enthusiasm'. In it Bruno raises an appeal for a courageous and persistent march forward, for the mastering of nature's mysteries, for the untiring toil in the name of knowledge.

'Heroic enthusiasm'. There is no better word to describe the atmosphere that fascinates us in Shakespeare's works. It is Shakespeare's heroic enthusiasm that is especially dear to our hearts because it is the heroic enthusiasm of perceiving life in all its dramatic contradictions, with all its sorrows and joys.

The mighty scale and the feeling of perspective that distinguish Shakespeare's realism, his pathos, were fathered, to my mind, by the revolutionary epoch in which he lived. It is this revolutionary epoch that gave him the boldness of an innovator; together with it he created the new world of his heroes. The road that a poet takes is inseparable from the road covered by his people, by his country. England, that was being born in the tempests and the drastic changes of the sixteenth century, found its tongue in his imaginative works. As always happens, the extensive picture of national life at this one concrete period of time imparted to Shakespeare's work an international character. In the national English form he presented the most typical features of the whole European society. Shakespeare's realism reflected the most typical features of the entire realistic art of Renaissance. And one of its most important features was the quality that we call народность. This word is difficult to translate into English: it means the closeness of a writer to the people—народ, a profound understanding of the interests of the people.

Народность, the popular character of Shakespeare's works, lies not only and not so much in the famous Shakespearian clowns and fools—although one can hardly imagine Shakespeare's world without their audacious and harsh irony, without their wrathful and sad wisdom set in the frame of a folklore saying or a song. Nor does the popular character of Shakespeare's works spring from those scenes in his plays where the infuriated mobs make history, not by understanding the sense of their actions but by demonstrating their strength. The popular character of Shakespeare's works primarily consists in that general estimation of the events which is seen in the fates of his heroes and in the results of their actions. Shakespeare's grandeur rests on his constant anxiety for the future of his people, for the future of mankind. This future fills him with uneasiness, and with a great desire to see people happy, and to punish those in whom he saw the active evil that stood in the way of mankind's happiness.

In sonnet 66 we read of 'captain ill', and this expresses the evil which he exposed and condemned, that which defies the joyous, man-loving, freedom-loving genius of Shakespeare.

Like our own Pushkin, Shakespeare believed that time was powerless against his art, and that the people of the future would understand the music and the meaning of his verses. Our meeting in Stratford today confirms the justice of the poet's prophecies. Our closeness to Shakespeare brings us closer to each other. For this feeling of unity in the name of the great values of universal culture we have Shakespeare to thank.

THE POPULARITY OF SHAKESPEARE: AN EXAMINATION OF THE ROYAL SHAKESPEARE THEATRE'S REPERTORY

BY

NORMAN SANDERS

I

Shakespeare's dominance of the English stage between 1945 and 1960 has been so marked that one of the more distinguished contemporary playwrights has recently bracketed his works and pantomimes as the two menaces of the modern English theatre. Every year since 1946 at least fifty professional and amateur productions of the plays are presented in the United Kingdom.[1] In Europe during the same period the level of interest has been equally high. Germany not only managed to keep Shakespeare in the theatre repertories during the war, but within four years of its termination could register thirty-three new productions in a single year, including plays like *Timon of Athens* and *The Two Gentlemen of Verona*. Even in 1958, the Schiller bi-centenary year, Shakespeare remained the most popular dramatist on the German stage, with his plays receiving six hundred performances more than those of the German dramatist, in spite of the numerous Schiller Festivals.[2] As early as 1947, Poland was able to stage an astonishing ten-play Shakespeare Festival in Warsaw[3] and, since then, it has witnessed thousands of performances of his works. In the post-war Russian theatre the Shakespeare activity has been prodigious with many productions in Moscow and Leningrad, most of the individual Republics mounting the popular plays at their 'national' theatres, and producers more and more keen to stage works, such as *Cymbeline*, *A Winter's Tale* and *Richard II*, which were previously less well known in these countries. In fact, most European and many Asian and African nations have experienced a rapid growth of interest and can produce a yearly account of native Shakespeare productions. Also, running parallel to this theatrical activity or specifically to serve it, there have been innumerable translations ranging from single plays to ambitious double-text editions of the complete works.[4]

In the United States and Canada, the rise of theatrical interest in the plays has been nothing short of spectacular. Stratford, Ontario, has seen the establishment of an annual festival, the building of a uniquely constructed permanent theatre and the development of an interesting style of acting and staging, which, due to the mobility of producers like Sir Tyrone Guthrie and Michael Langham and of actors like Paul Scofield and Christopher Plummer, may influence— perhaps already has influenced—its English namesake. A third Stratford festival has been running at Connecticut since 1955 and now draws on Broadway and Hollywood stars, and other festivals have either grown up or come to maturity during the same period: Oregon (1940), San Diego (1949), Antioch (1951), Phoenix, Arizona (1956), New York (1957) and Boulder, Colorado (1958).

The enormous popular interest is incontrovertible, but to account for it is rather more difficult. No ready explanation comes immediately to mind. If producers had had little new material with which to work, the temptation to turn to the classics would obviously be strong and we could explain Shakespeare's popularity by a dearth in current playwriting. But in both Europe and America this has not been the case. Broadway has managed to fill its theatres with a characteristic mixture of new plays and lavish musicals, and has thrown up at least two play-wrights, Tennessee Williams and Arthur Miller, who have become influential forces in world drama. France has experienced no shortage of plays by writers of the stature of Sartre, Ionesco, Anouilh and Beckett, and in England Shakespeare has had to keep his head above the 'New Wave' playwrights such as Osborne, Pinter and Wesker, as well as the older-established authors of farce, thriller and musical comedy. It is also difficult to believe that some of the academic enthusiasm for Shakespeare has seeped through to the public to account for the rising interest. When one attends a Stratford production in July or August, sees the long last-minute queues and hears the interval conversations, it is obvious that the audiences are not there because they have been told Shakespeare is a 'universal genius' but because they are genuinely interested in and stimulated by the plays as drama. And this leads to the basic questions—what, in fact, do they find appealing in Shakespeare's plays, and will they accept any play just because it is Shakespeare's no matter in what guise it is presented? One wonders not why the spectators are so many, but what they look for in a Shakespeare production; what standards they apply to what they see, and how much influence the newspaper reviews have over them; whether all the plays are equally acceptable to them; whether they demand and enjoy the fashionable elaboration of *décor* and costume; and whether they appreciate the difference between good and bad verse speaking.

II

As the fortunes of the Royal Shakespeare Theatre since the war may be seen as a concentrated reflection of this general growth of interest, its experiences in giving longer and longer seasons of selected Shakespeare plays may help to suggest some of the answers.[5] Before the war, this theatre was a place of pilgrimage for a loyal core of bardolators who came annually to visit the town and its monuments, and, during a two weeks' holiday, to attend vigorous, lively, though under-rehearsed productions of some eight or nine plays. With the appointment of Sir Barry Jackson as director in 1946, however, a new approach was taken. Given far greater power and freedom than was granted to any of his predecessors, Sir Barry instigated far-reaching changes of policy in the company's structure and in the repertory. These changes, together with the deliberate prestige-building by Anthony Quayle and Glen Byam Shaw, have raised the annual Shakespeare season to the status of an international event comparable in its drawing power, if not always in its standard, with Salzburg and Bayreuth. One of the chief ways by which this has been achieved was the adoption of the 'star policy'—the luring to Stratford of outstanding performers by offering them, not salaries equal to those of the West End, but the opportunity of working with the best directors and designers and giving them some say in the parts they were to play. Quayle has, of course, denied that such a policy ever existed. He wrote in 1951

The last point...on which it may be pertinent to touch is the question of the so-called Star System. I say 'so-called' because I have never discovered, either at Stratford or in the London theatre, any system in the matter of engaging stars. Certainly a star 'name' is apt to be good 'box-office'....But an actor is seldom, if ever, engaged because he is a star unless he is also considered by the manager to be the best actor for the part. Neither manager nor actor can be held culpable if, in the process of becoming a fine artist, the actor has also acquired popularity. The leading parts in Shakespeare demand the highest qualities coupled with great experience; it has nothing to do with a star-*system* if those qualities and that experience are most frequently found in actors and actresses who, for that very reason, have become stars.[6]

This is clever quibbling, the inaccuracy of which may be demonstrated by the fact that it took Diana Wynyard two years to adapt her formidable talent to the acting of Shakespeare—as she herself graciously admitted. Yet Quayle is right in his implication that star names do not of themselves draw the large audiences. The presence of Sir John Gielgud, Sir Laurence Olivier, Dame Edith Evans and Dame Peggy Ashcroft could not alone ensure that 'at least three hundred thousand English people took very great pains to book theatre tickets in advance....And for every one who managed to secure a seat there were four who had to be refused because there was no room in the theatre for them'.[7] Some percentage of these audiences may well have come to see Sir Laurence or Dame Peggy, but the great majority came primarily to see Shakespeare, and it was but an additional attraction that these players were in the leading roles.

It must be emphasized that, although Stratford is a tourist centre yielding first place only to London in the British Isles, the Theatre in the main is patronized by an English public. Some sixty per cent of the total audience each season is derived from what might be called the greater midland area—say from Bristol to Manchester. The remaining forty per cent is accounted for by British and foreign tourists mainly concentrated in the high summer months. In recent years there has been an increase in the one-visit groups and individuals—the coach parties from Coventry or London, the touring American groups, and the two-day stops of English and foreign motorists. One result of this has been a change in the selection of plays each season. Because the Theatre has not a substantial core of regular, all-the-year-round patrons, such as most provincial repertory companies have, its scope for experiment is limited. It could not, for example, put on a season consisting of 'unpopular' plays. Sometimes we tend to assume that the Stratford theatre could be filled during July and August probably for anything, and certainly for anything written by Shakespeare; but this is simply not true. The last non-Shakespearian play to be performed at Stratford in a summer season was *Volpone* in 1952. This is generally considered one of Jonson's best works, and the production was in many respects the best of the season, with Sir Ralph Richardson in the main part, and Anthony Quayle as a brilliant Mosca. Nevertheless, not only was it poorly attended, but the box-office and theatre management received both vocal and written vituperation from some of the public because they did not like the spirit of the play in the first place, and because it was not by Shakespeare in the second. An even more remarkable example was the production of *Titus Andronicus* in 1955; it had all the apparent advantages: celebrated director, world-famous stars and the flavour of novelty. Yet the very unfamiliarity of the play was the deciding factor; the audiences were small and even in August the piece was not playing to full houses.

III

A breakdown of the list of plays performed between 1945 and 1960 suggests that the overruling factor in attracting audiences has been the long established familiarity of individual plays. During these fifteen years all the plays in the canon have been produced, with the exception of the *Comedy of Errors*, *Timon of Athens*, and the three parts of *Henry VI*. *The Merchant of Venice*, *The Tempest* and *Othello* have had five productions each; *The Taming of the Shrew*, *Twelfth Night*, *Macbeth* and *Measure for Measure*, four; *Love's Labour's Lost*, *A Midsummer Night's Dream*, *Much Ado About Nothing*, *As You Like It*, *Troilus and Cressida*, *Cymbeline*, *Romeo and Juliet*, *Hamlet* and *King Lear*, three; *All's Well That Ends Well*, *Pericles*, *Coriolanus*, *A Winter's Tale*, *Julius Caesar*, *Richard II*, *King John*, *Henry V* and *Henry VIII*, two; and one each of *The Two Gentlemen of Verona*, *The Merry Wives of Windsor*, *Titus Andronicus*, *Antony and Cleopatra*, *Richard III*, and the two parts of *Henry IV*. In general the Theatre's policy has been to select for each season three well-known plays, one less well-known and one obscure, although, as will readily be appreciated, from time to time this basic scheme has had to be modified for various reasons, such as the availability of actors or the preferences of individual directors. Nevertheless, with some exceptions, the list is a fair reflection of the drawing power of the different plays.

The plays in the top two groups appear to owe their position either to their familiarity or to their obvious theatrical effectiveness. It is noteworthy that *The Merchant of Venice*, *Twelfth Night*, and *Macbeth* are all plays much used in schools as English literature texts for pupils between the impressionable and formative ages of thirteen to sixteen. The fact that the Theatre considers these plays sure-fire box-office would seem a flat contradiction of the common assumption that the utilization of Shakespeare for textbook and examination purposes effectively kills the plays' entertainment value. Of the three, *The Merchant of Venice* is most popular with audiences. One can see that the play has features which are automatically attractive—the character of Shylock, the power of the scenes in which he appears, and the impossible-to-wreck trial scene—but one would have thought that the casket-scenes held their longueurs for the modern theatregoer. An indication that this is so is perhaps to be found in recent productions; while the method of playing both the trial scene and the character of Shylock has not materially changed since Irving's time, the fashion has now developed for making the roles of Aragon and Morocco, together with the scenes in which they appear, set pieces of virtuoso comedy. The popularity of *Macbeth* is due probably to a combination of a school-derived familiarity, the striking theatrical and poetic power of the classic murder plot, the awful influence exercised by the two protagonists and the highly wrought tension of the central scenes. Yet when one remembers the similarity between this play and *Richard III*, which is the best received of the history plays, it is perhaps likely that the spectacle of an evil energy unchecked exercises a special fascination in the theatre. The difference between the positions of *Twelfth Night* and *As You Like It* requires some comment. Both are used as school texts and are frequently compared in academic criticism; but audiences obviously see a distinction between the theatrical qualities of each. Nor does this seem to me difficult to understand: *As You Like It* may be seen as essentially an extended conversation on romantic love in dramatic terms, whereas the miraculous balance and counterpointing of romance, high comic action and vigorous 'low' comic elements in *Twelfth Night* evidently exercise a far wider appeal.

It is unlikely that many playgoers would have become acquainted with *The Tempest*, *Othello*, *The Taming of the Shrew*, or *Measure for Measure* at school. The reasons for the attraction of *Othello* are obvious: the theme of jealousy, the peculiar fascination of Iago, the domestic atmosphere and the extreme concentration of the writing. *The Tempest's* position is rather more difficult to understand, neither the themes nor the characters having an immediately apparent appeal for the public; but perhaps the mixture of profundity and clowning, of air and earth, reminiscent of the pantomime, exercises a fascination through which some of the autumnal wholeness of the play's vision is experienced. Whatever the reason, it is one of the few plays that can—and did in the Peter Brook production of 1957—fill a theatre like Drury Lane in the 'dead' week before Christmas. The audience's knowledge of *The Taming of the Shrew* is gained from the theatre alone, yet its popularity rivals that of *The Merchant of Venice*. This is due undoubtedly to its palpable theatrical vitality. There are, however, indications that the public come to the play with certain preconceptions. If one can judge from the reception accorded to the revivals at Stratford, it seems clear that audiences see the play not as the 'classical-type' comedy of the critics, but rather as a piece full of humanity, and as romantic in its own way as *Twelfth Night* or *As You Like It*. The 1960 production, for example, with Dame Peggy Ashcroft and Peter O'Toole, owed its success in no small measure to the fact that both players wrung from their lines every ounce of warmth and humanity. By gesture, glance and action they effectively conveyed, and even stressed, a strong current of romantic love running beneath the inherent cruelty of the big scenes and the basically economic view of matrimony. The production in 1953 with Yvonne Mitchell and Marius Goring had many of the same features and was likewise popular. Both of these may be contrasted with Michael Benthall's display of virtuosity in 1948, in which imagination, wardrobe and property basket were ransacked to prove that the play is an out-and-out farce, and which significantly had its last performance on 10 September, even though the season, originally planned to end on 2 October, was extended to 30 October.

Measure for Measure is also not a favoured school text but has been produced fairly regularly at Stratford since the war. Like *The Merchant of Venice* it is a team play with a high proportion of speaking parts and therefore finds favour with the theatre. But some part of the credit for its place in the Stratford repertory probably goes to the excellence of Peter Brook's production in 1950 with sterling performances by Sir John Gielgud, George Rose and Barbara Jefford. One does, however, wonder whether we are not also witnessing the coming into public favour of a play whose mood of dark questioning and atmosphere of bitterness (as long defined by academic critics) are felt instinctively to be in tune with the disturbed conditions of our times.

IV

Most people working in the theatre would subscribe to the view that, in general, the tragedies have a stronger box-office appeal than the comedies. An example of how this can show itself is provided by the Royal Shakespeare Theatre's tour of the provinces with *Much Ado About Nothing* and *King Lear* in 1955. The *Much Ado About Nothing*, with Dame Peggy Ashcroft and Sir John Gielgud in the leading roles, had long been recognized as a classic production of the play, and the piece itself might reasonably be supposed to be capable of tapping some of the same sources of appeal as *The Taming of the Shrew*. The *King Lear* was what is usually referred to as the 'Noguchi' version; it was experimental in conception, distinctly outlandish in costume, and showed us a Gielgud strangely ill at ease in the role. Nevertheless, it was *King Lear* that drew packed audiences on foggy days in Manchester and *Much Ado About Nothing* that played to houses of just over eighty per cent.

Yet even with the tragedies there appears to be an invisible boundary beyond which experiment and unfamiliarity are unacceptable to most audiences. The fate of three recent productions of tragedies perhaps illustrates the different ways in which an audience's expectations can be outraged. The 1961 production of *Othello* had all the initial apparent advantages: Gielgud at his peak, acting in this major Shakespearian role for the first time in his career, Franco Zeffirelli producing, fresh from his Old Vic success with *Romeo and Juliet*, and a strong and experienced company including Dame Peggy Ashcroft and Dorothy Tutin. Yet, owing to either a conscious disregard or a complete ignorance of the change of pace which has been fairly well established in England since the early years of this century, the production failed, and the press notices were as kind as they were only out of an understandable respect for Gielgud's talents. The great scenic riches of the production in no way compensated the audiences for the long waits between elaborate scene changes. The stretching out of playing time with its resultant slackening of dramatic tension was rejected by audiences who expected a style of presentation based on a reaction to the 'Lyceum-His Majesty's' methods and not on a continuation of them. It is possible that the complaints about length were the easily voiced manifestations of what was really a protest against elaboration made at the expense of a play which requires no such aids to make its impact.

Of the recent productions of *Hamlet* at Stratford since the war two have been by popular standards failures, namely Alan Badel's in 1956 and Ian Bannen's in 1961. This is at first surprising because the play is certainly the best known and has long been considered the 'central' play in the canon. Yet when one recalls certain features the two interpretations had in common, it is probable that their lack of success was not primarily due to weak direction or inadequate acting but rather to the fact that they, like the Zeffirelli *Othello*, violated long-cherished preconceptions about the play which audiences bring to the theatre. The two productions, in different ways, imposed upon the play a reading which was obtrusively rooted in the cynical negations of much contemporary art and philosophy. Badel's prince has been accurately described as a

lonely existentialist hero—a desperate individual wandering in a disconnected universe, a universe with no meaning or continuity of its own. He moved on a free open platform with only a black velvet background. One isolated dark piece of cloth hung from an undefined point in mid-air....Here was no Denmark, no Middle Age, no tangible world at all, but only the lost modern soul standing exposed under a strong spotlight.[8]

And Bannen brought a somewhat similar, though less specific, quality to the role, and added for good measure a half-crazed Freudian neuroticism. Both actors effectively banished from the part much of the 'noble mind' and all trace of the princely 'glass of fashion and the mould of form', which have been basic to stage Hamlets from Forbes Robertson to Gielgud. In their place they offered to audiences an Osborneomorphic youth 'blasted with ecstasy' and he was not acceptable. Perhaps in the future audiences *may* be led to accept a new interpretation of the play similar to Badel's, but there is as yet no sign that they will.

V

For plays less well-known and, consequently, less securely fixed in the public's affection than *Hamlet* or *Othello*, rather more latitude to experiment seems to be allowed the producer. The reasons for the unpopularity of *Love's Labour's Lost*, for example, are inherent in the play, and in a large part are due to the historical distance between our age and Shakespeare's. Peter Brook clearly saw this to be the basic problem facing him when he produced the play at Stratford in 1946. He believed the text to be 'obscured by a mass of false traditions, by archaisms, by meaningless references, by outmoded conventions, by the thousand technical differences that the different theatre building of Shakespeare's day dictated',[9] and felt that his task as a producer lay in being able 'to discriminate between these externals and the essential living heart of the play—the poet's inner dream—' for which he must find 'theatrical correlatives'.[9] He introduced, therefore, certain innovations and used all the resources of the modern theatre to convey the mood, atmosphere and meaning of the play as it appeared to him. These included an anachronistic Watteauesque costuming, a forlorn drooping symbol of the sweet-sad mood of the play in the person of a 'chalk-faced white-clothed' zany for whom there is no excuse in the text, and a Dull who was the eternal comic policeman—'Toy Town, Victorian London, Harlequinade or Navarre'—duly equipped with bright-blue uniform, conventional truncheon, and a string of sausages. These and other aspects of the production scandalized the pundits, but undoubtedly pleased the public and were accepted by them, as the revival the following year suggests.

Yet even with such unfamiliar plays a 'modern' as opposed to a new or fanciful treatment is suspect. When Sir Tyrone Guthrie produced *All's Well That Ends Well* in 1959, he was obviously endeavouring, like Peter Brook, to give a theatrical facelift to an intermittently inspired play. But he tried to do this by restating the play's themes in contemporary terms, though it is debatable as to how far his desert-rat comic soldiery, Chekhovian country setting, and socially overcompensating Parolles succeeded. The audience may have been aware that the production was a serious attempt at a creative modern reading of an unsatisfactory play and not merely wantonly experimental, but the reception accorded it was suspicious, if respectful.

However, it is not mandatory for the less popular plays to have some kind of novel revamping before they are acceptable to audiences. When *The Two Gentlemen of Verona* was produced by Peter Hall in 1960 as part of his season of comedies, it was necessary, if the chronological scheme he envisaged was to be followed, that it should be the first play of the season. It opened, therefore, on 5 April, and, because of its known unpopularity, was quickly followed by *The Merchant of Venice* on 12 April and by *Twelfth Night* on 17 May. Nevertheless, although Hall's production was marked by an almost pedestrian plainness and minimum of elaboration its drawing power increased noticeably as the season progressed.

Titus Andronicus (together with the *Henry VI* plays and *Timon of Athens*) is probably the most infrequently produced play in the canon, and the circumstances surrounding its production in 1955 seem to suggest that for Shakespeare's 'unknown' plays something more than serious intention, accomplished direction and expert performances is necessary. For despite the novelty of production in its favour, and with Peter Brook producing, Sir Laurence Olivier and Vivien Leigh heading the cast, and superlative performances by Maxine Audley (Tamora) and

Anthony Quayle (Aaron), the theatre at Stratford was only about two-thirds full in August. However, once one of the popular daily newspapers had written of the horrors of the play and sensationally reported that there were faintings each night in all parts of the house, the audiences began to flock in. Presumably if we are ever to see a successful production of *Timon of Athens* at Stratford a similar combination of producer, stars and extraneous publicity fillip will be necessary.

While the absence of *Timon of Athens* and the *Henry VI* plays from the Theatre's post-war repertory may indicate a certain lack of enterprise, one can see the reasons for it. But the non-production of *The Comedy of Errors* is more difficult to understand. This, one would think, is the one Shakespeare play on which the talented producer can lavish his inventions with impunity, particularly when we recall the glowing reports of the reception accorded to Komisarjevski's production at Stratford in 1938–9. The chief problem in its presentation, however, appears to be a purely administrative one, namely its short running-time. Remembering the audience's reaction to the 1961 *Othello* on the first night, we may perhaps suppose that there is an unacknowledged ideal length for an evening at the English theatre, which the producer flouts at his peril, and which George Bernard Shaw characteristically detected.[10]

VI

Looking at the plays from the point of view of their grouping in the First Folio, there appears to be a noteworthy lack of interest in most of the history plays. A single history play can certainly be made into a popular success, when handled with the virtuosity of Tyrone Guthrie, as the acclaim given to the production of *Henry VIII* in 1949 and its revival the following year proved. But the Theatre, and perhaps the audience too, see the central historical cycle as a theatrical unit. When *Richard II*, the two parts of *Henry IV*, and *Henry V* were presented as such for a special reason (the Festival of Britain 1951), the enthusiasm and appreciation developed only as the season progressed. The event is remembered now as the best example of ensemble playing at Stratford since the war; the actors seemed to play themselves into the atmosphere of Shakespeare's historical world and to take the audiences with them.

Of the other history plays, *King John* is received without marked enthusiasm, though it is a play which can create a special atmosphere in an audience, which is, as Sir Barry Jackson wryly remarked, usually reflected in the poor interval takings in the Theatre's refreshment rooms. *Richard III*, despite its single production at Stratford (although it was staged again in 1961), is the outstanding favourite, with *Richard II* a close second. The former undoubtedly exercises an appeal due to its broad melodramatic effects, the clear-cut dramatic conflicts it contains, and probably also to the cathartic effect in the spectacle of an evil energy exercised untrammelled. It is possible too that the concentration of dramatic interest on a dominant central figure inclines audiences to class it subconsciously with the tragedies rather than with the other history plays. This may also be true of *Richard II*, though one suspects that both the intrinsic beauty and the familiarity of the poetry in the play, as well as the complex response elicited by the central figure, exert a special fascination.

VII

Stratford's addiction to elaborate scenery and costumes at first suggests that these make a popular appeal, but the spectacular nature of the scenic effects in this theatre may be the result of other forces. Due to Sir Barry Jackson's initial reforms and the development of the theatre workshops under Anthony Quayle and Glen Byam Shaw, the Theatre now has at its disposal some of the best facilities in the world to offer its designers, as well as a strong permanent team of scenic and costume experts. The permanence of this team contrasts sharply with the yearly gathering together of the acting company, and has possibly been influential in the development of Stratford's characteristic splendour in mounting plays, which in its turn has served to show up the absence of any well-defined style of acting or standard of verse speaking.[11]

It is important to observe, however, that although Stratford audiences like, or at least are willing to accept, scenic delights, they find no consolation in visual pleasure for its own sake, when other more important qualities are lacking. One cannot measure an audience's reaction to *décor* alone, but one can detect on occasion that the presence of unfunctional sets brings out instinctive standards of dramatic propriety. An obvious example of this was the *Othello* of 1961 mentioned above, and the response to Douglas Seale's accomplished production of *Much Ado About Nothing* in 1958 set purposelessly in a frenchified nineteenth-century Messina is another. Even more outstanding was the production of *A Midsummer Night's Dream* in 1949; James Bailey's sets for this were exquisitely lighted and visually as enchanting as any we are ever likely to see. Yet the standard of speaking was so poor that the intrinsically beautiful set was seen for what it really was—a pretty shell ready to receive a ravishing production if one had happened to be at hand. In short, an audience seems to be willing to accept the *décor* it is given, whether it be eccentric (*King Lear*, 1955), or bizarre (*All's Well That Ends Well*, 1959), when it is part of a genuine attempt to give a new reading of the play. But it is equally quick to see when the *décor* is offered in place of the play (*A Midsummer Night's Dream*, 1949), or destructive of its fundamental excellence (*Othello*, 1961), or merely used as a means to smother what are seen to be the weaknesses of a particular piece (*Pericles*, 1958). These observations, if true, may suggest that, while audiences can be, and have been at Stratford, lulled into accepting visual treats, they could also be educated to take their absence as normal.

Sir Tyrone Guthrie, the acknowledged master of stage spectacle and pageantry, can say after his experiences at Stratford, Ontario:

the plays can be done as they are written, as intimate and not bombastic, and the speaking does not demand the extraordinary virtuosity which is required to make Shakespeare come to life in a great operatic house. Secondly, there is no possibility of scenery at all. Any scenery is created in the imagination of the audience by the words. And that is the right way.[12]

These ideas are, of course, a direct result of his working with a stage specifically designed by Tanya Moisewitsch and himself, but they are in keeping with the recent unanimity among leading actors and producers that a movement from eye to ear, from spectacle to verse is vitally necessary in the presentation of Shakespeare's plays. From Sir John Gielgud, as one would expect, Guthrie's view receives a support founded on vast experience and successful practice:

It would be helpful if one company under the same director were to do four productions in succession at Stratford-on-Avon, trying to do the thing as simply as possible. Not seducing the audience by scenery and movement, but straight and classic.... So many directors and actors go to extremes without fully baring the meaning of the text.[13]

Michael Benthall, in his early career often guilty of perpetrating Guthrie's faults without his virtues, can now talk of his company at the Old Vic as if he were a chorus master:

It takes two to three months of working together to catch a consistent delivery. There should be two basses at least, a lot of baritones, some tenors, and of the girls quite a lot of sopranos and at least two contraltos. You cannot have a baritone actor playing Romeo, it must be a tenor.[14]

And the Royal Shakespeare Theatre's present Director, Peter Hall, is both explicit and critical:

Speaking has lagged behind other aspects of present-day production.... Shakespearian actors need a great deal of practice.... They do not get it.... More often than not the director is in the position of a choreographer asked to stage a ballet with people who haven't had a lesson.[15]

Such agreement among theatre people is immediately suspect in view of much current practice. It may well be that they sense among the public a dissatisfaction with the scenic lumber beneath which they have too often buried the living poetry. Shakespeare's plays have made their appeal through their language and it is to this that the audience wishes the emphasis to return. The evidence of such a wish among the public is to be found in the correspondence columns of newspapers, in some of the questions posed at the Forums run for the Theatre's own Summer School, in the packed houses at the poetry recitals run by the Birthplace Trust, in the long-running success of the Theatre's *Hollow Crown* entertainment, and in the large discriminating audiences that have flocked to Sir John Gielgud's recital, *The Ages of Man*, a miraculous combination of voice, presence, poetry and bare stage.

It is possible that such various pointers mean that the English audience is about to see the foundations laid for a self-perpetuating tradition in the speaking of Shakespeare, instead of having to rest content with a handful of itinerant practitioners of excellence like Gielgud, Olivier, Ashcroft, Wolfit and Evans.

VIII

Finally, how much influence have the opinions of the corps of press critics had in forming the audience's tastes, in encouraging them to go or to stay away from productions of Shakespeare's plays? And how strong is their influence within the Theatre itself? As actors, like authors, read avidly every word that is written about them, the press opinions obviously have some influence, even although that influence may be indirect. When there is a rare accord among critics, adjustments in production are almost always made. Instances of this are the exception taken to Richard Johnson's wig when playing Romeo in 1958, and the removal of the notorious trunk from which Ian Bannen spoke one of Hamlet's soliloquies in 1961. In general, however, the Theatre would probably take notice in any real sense only of *The Times*, the *Guardian*, the *Telegraph*, the *Sunday Times*, the *Observer*, the *Sunday Telegraph* and one or two of the more influential provincial papers, and would expect their audiences to do likewise. Undoubtedly, total disapproval would affect a play's bookings to some extent, although, of course, the fate of Sir Alec Guinness's *Hamlet* would not be likely to befall any 'Festival' production.

One suspects that by far the greatest influence on a given production's drawing power is the word-of-mouth recommendation. The audience knows what it wants and what it likes; and the average playgoer probably responds most positively to a respected friend's advice to go and see a play, though bad notices from, let us say, Tynan and Hobson might be able to stop his making the effort in the absence of such. Frequently, at Stratford, plays which have received mixed notices obviously possessed an enormous audience appeal. The initial reviews of the 1961 *As You Like It*, for example, were not wholly favourable, yet it was probably the best received play of the season, has had a successful run at the Aldwych Theatre, and has not in the theatre's opinion exhausted its attraction. One might conclude that so far as the Theatre is concerned the press is a useful yardstick, but not by any means totally representative of or greatly influencing its audience's views.

IX

If any general conclusion can be drawn from these observations it is that the crowds who regularly attend performances of Shakespeare's plays have fairly well-defined tastes which are often at variance with those of both the academic and theatrical experts. The foundations are undoubtedly laid at school for the likes and dislikes which in subsequent years of playgoing are enlarged to include those plays possessing an immediately striking theatricality. The audiences also almost certainly hold certain literary and theatrical preconceptions, which occasionally obscure the interest and inherent possibilities of untraditional or experimental productions; but they also possess a basic good sense and an intuitive feeling for dramatic propriety which enables them to detect gimmickry and elaboration which destroy a play's excellence. It is true that they can be lulled into accepting fashionable effects, often for a period of years, but their sense of what is essential in Shakespearian drama ultimately asserts itself.

The players may well be able to modify the prejudices or even refine the sensibilities of their many-headed monster, but in the last resort its power is absolute. In the basic relationship, by which all drama exists, between those who deceive and those who are content to be deceived, it is the latter that call the tune, and it is a tune which is ignored by the former at their peril.

NOTES

1. S. Ullmann, *Shakespeare Survey 3* (1950), 117.

2. *Shakespeare Survey 14* (1961), 119.

3. *Shakespeare Survey 1* (1948), 113.

4. In the post-war period there have been numerous single play translations in many languages, adaptations by Matej Bor in Yugoslavia and Hans Rothe in Germany, and translations of the complete works published or projected in Italy, Portugal, Hungary, Russia, Austria, Israel, France and Poland.

5. I wish to record my thanks for the help given by the Royal Shakespeare Theatre's General Manager, Mr Patrick Donnell, and the Theatre Librarian, Miss Eileen Robinson, neither of whom are, however, in any way responsible for or associated with the opinions expressed.

6. 'The theatre from within' in *Shakespeare Memorial Theatre 1948–50, A Photographic Record* (1951), p. 14.

7. *Ibid.* p. 9.

8. George R. Kernodle, 'Open Stage: Elizabethan or Existentialist?', *Shakespeare Survey 12* (1959), 2.

9. Peter Brook, 'Style in Shakespeare Production', *The Penguin New Writing*, no. 36 (1949), 144.

10. Preface to *St Joan*, Standard Edition (1932), p. 52.

11. This applies only to the period 1945–59. Since becoming Director, Peter Hall has established a semi-permanent company to serve Stratford and the Aldwych Theatre in London, and is aware of the importance of improving the overall standard of Shakespearian acting.

12. In an interview in *The Times*, 20 April 1959, and reprinted in Laurence Kitchen's *Mid-Century Drama* (1961), p. 197.

13. In an interview in *The Times*, 31 July 1959, and reprinted in *Mid-Century Drama*, p. 213.

14. In an interview in *The Times*, 7 January 1959, and reprinted in *Mid-Century Drama*, p. 170.

15. In an interview in *The Times*, 22 December 1958, and reprinted in *Mid-Century Drama*, p. 164.

SHAKESPEARE AND THE FASHION
OF THESE TIMES

BY

J. P. BROCKBANK

In the course of a very useful review of Elizabethan theatre studies over the past sixty years, Arthur Brown tells us that 'we are still in a period of stock-taking' and that we must 'continue to apply ourselves to fundamental material, to minutiae if necessary, until we are perfectly certain that the foundations for broader and more general studies are secure'.[1] Some will feel that this is the scientific spirit manifesting itself as the heroic caution of modern scholarship (as Brown says of the reception given to Hotson's views of the round theatre, 'Most scholars are prepared to be non-committal'). But others may recognize in our own period some of the signs of imaginative exhaustion. It is like the end of *Uncle Vanya*, where a routine of work is to keep us going somehow, so that future generations will profit and may even be grateful: 'First, Uncle Vanya, let us write up the accounts. They are in a dreadful state. Come, begin. You take one and I will take the other.'

Our continuing eagerness to come to rest in objectively secured positions is a sign that our age is of a piece with that which, under the distant presidency of Auguste Comte, inaugurated the New Variorum Shakespeare. But the New Variorum, particularly in its earlier volumes,[2] has been concerned less with fundamental material than with the ample and comprehensive recording of opinion; and it may be thought to have done less to consolidate objectively valid knowledge and understanding than to exemplify and testify to the fascinating relativity of critical judgement. It reminds us that understanding is a complex of knowledge and insight, and that each generation has (for all the swelling of windpipes) contrived to add something to the stock of relevant facts and to the current of relevant perceptions.

Each age—it would seem in retrospect—enjoys a privilege of available insights; but where the insights seem to us to be valid we are apt to believe them timeless, and it is only when we can watch them retreating into the more exclusively mannered shades of a period that we can recognize their essentially historical character. The point might be demonstrated by glancing at some of the comments made (and for the most part recorded in the 1907 New Variorum) on Cleopatra's suicide speech opening Act v, sc. ii:

> My desolation does begin to make
> A better life: Tis paltry to be Caesar:
> Not being Fortune, hee's but Fortunes knaue,
> A minister of her will: and it is great
> To do that thing that ends all other deeds,
> Which shackles accedents, and bolts up change;
> Which sleepes, and neuer pallates more the dung,
> The beggers Nurse, and *Caesars*.

Johnson offers a brisk paraphrase of 'Fortunes knaue'—'the servant of fortune'. But it is Johnson's strength that he expects a word to do only one job at a time. It was left to the twentieth century to speculate on a pun.[3] Caesar may be the nave of Fortune's wheel too, with Antony and Cleopatra at its periphery. The notion would lend precision to the braking metaphors, 'shackles accedents' and 'bolts up change'; but it also diffuses the sense and invites us to enjoy a grotesquely suggestive eloquence rather than a telling clarity of statement. Were we to pursue the point we should be promptly committed to a discussion of the history of poetry, and of Johnson's as well as Shakespeare's place in it. And we could not for long defer discussion of the poetry that has shaped our own kind of awareness in our own time.

A more direct demonstration of the connection between criticism and current poetic taste, however, is afforded by Warburton's meddlings with the second half of the passage. To restore 'sense and propriety' he postulates the loss of a line after 'change', and an emendation of 'dung': '[Lulls wearied nature to a sound repose] Which sleeps and never palates more the dugg: The beggar's nurse and Caesar's.' The insinuated line declares the age of Young's *Night Thoughts*. Warburton's paraphrase has Cleopatra die a victim of Augustan melancholia: 'It is great to do that which frees us from all the accidents of humanity, lulls our over-wearied nature to repose (which now sleeps and has no more appetite for worldly enjoyments), and is equally the nurse of Caesar and the beggar.'

Seward, in the same period, offers an excellent vindication of the Folio reading which sharply challenges Cleopatra's claims to transcendent vision:

When we speak in contempt of anything, we generally resolve it into its first principles: Thus, man is dust and ashes, and the food we eat, the dung, by which first our vegetable, and from thence our animal, food is nourished. Thus Cleopatra finds she can no longer riot in the pleasures of life, with the usual workings of a disappointed pride, pretends a disgust to them and speaks in praise of suicide.... Nothing can be clearer than this passage, 'both the beggar and Caesar are fed and nursed by the dung of the earth'. Of this sense there is a demonstration in 'Our dungie earth alike feeds beast and man'.

The Augustan Roman refuses to be taken in.

Dr Johnson, as we might expect, is yet more revealing—about the play, about himself and about his age:

The difficulty of the passage, if any difficulty there be, arises only from this, that the act of suicide, and the state which is the effect of suicide, are confounded. Voluntary death, says she, is an act *which bolts up change*; it produces a state, 'Which sleeps and never palates more the dung, the Beggar's nurse and Caesar's'. Which has no longer need of the gross and terrene sustenance, in the use of which Caesar and the Beggar are on a level. The speech is abrupt, but perturbation in such a state is surely natural.

It is a nice insight into the syntax that discovers the elliptical transition from the act of suicide to the state which is its effect. But Johnson finds virtue in the ellipsis only by explaining it as an appeal to decorum of manners. He shows the same resource when confronted by Hotspur's similarly romantic nihilism ('pluck bright honour from the pale-fac'd moon'), which can be 'soberly and rationally vindicated' as 'the hasty motion of turbulent desire' and 'the dark expression of indetermined thoughts'. It is a humane and civilized placing of extravagant rhetoric (compare Worcester on Hotspur and Dolabella on Cleopatra). Nevertheless, we have only to notice the decorous tautology 'gross and terrene sustenance' which mediates between Johnson's endorsement of the sentiment and his reluctance to let it strike his senses, to be returned to the eighteenth century and to the boundaries of its values. Within those boundaries, too, Johnson's own Irene meets death in a state of perturbation which licenses abrupt syntax and extravagant sentiment:

> O, name not death! Distraction and amazement,
> Horrour and agony are in that sound!

A complete account would clearly require us to dwell on Augustan attitudes to death, and on the representative quality of Johnson's private fears.

The nineteenth-century editors divide their allegiances fairly equally between 'dug' and 'dung'. Boswell and Knight take the 'nurse' to be 'death', not 'dung', but they retain 'dung' in the text. Collier and Dyce appeal to palaeography and bibliography with an alleged compositor's misreading of MS. 'dugge', but the argument is merely permissive and it settled nothing. It would be premature to generalize about the changing tenor of critical judgements through the nineteenth century (although the New Variorum gives many unhappy instances of its individualism); but it is noticeable that several commentators in the period concur in recognizing a wilful contempt in Cleopatra's words where the Augustans had found moral weakness, exhaustion or distress. In 1860 the American R. G. White says, 'As I am unable to discern what is the dug which is 'the beggar's nurse and Caesar's', and as the word in the text is expressive of the speaker's bitter disgust of life, I make no change'. Hudson, writing in about 1880, puts the point in the accents of his time: 'Cleopatra is speaking contemptuously of this life, as if anything which depends upon such coarse, vulgar feeding were not worth keeping'; and F. A. Marshall finds 'dung' to be 'simply a periphrasis for the fruits of the fertilizing earth, used, certainly, in a spirit of bitter mockery and supreme contempt'. It is apt enough that Dowden and Swinburne have in the meantime assimilated Shakespeare's Cleopatra into their mythologies of fatal women, and Funivall has recalled us to Shakespeare's own fickle and serpentine mistress, the Dark Lady.

Thiselton, writing at the turn of the century, may be taken to illustrate one of the ultimate fantasies of character criticism. Noting the poetry's glance back to Antony's words about the dungy earth, he finds in it one of several reminiscences that 'suggest the integrity of Cleopatra's attachment to Antony'; by this subtlety of technique 'Shakespeare meant us to leave Cleopatra, notwithstanding her failings, with feelings of sympathy and admiration, and that our last thoughts should be of 'the glory of her womanhood'.

Furness allows himself the privilege of a last word, commending 'dung' for its 'elemental vigour...wholly lacking in Warburton's substitution'. The controversy was revived in the *Times Literary Supplement* of 1926, but the correspondence was eclectic—hardly any of its proposals had not been made before, including the conjectures 'tongue' and 'wrong'. But to exemplify the insight of our own age at its most commanding, it may be possible to single out for some future Variorum, Wilson Knight's remarks on the passage in *The Imperial Theme*:[4]

So far we have noted death's effect from the side of life: now we pass to its own essential sovereignty. First, it is like sleep; second, it tastes no longer that 'dungy earth' which is unworthy of its child; finally, it is nurse alike to Caesar in his glory and the beggar in his penury—a kindly presence, dear nurse to life, eternity calling back the child of time to its bosom. Thus we pass from noting its aesthetic appeal to a quick and tight analysis of its apparent effects, and finally contemplate its more personal, moral attitude to man: that of a nurse to a child. Is this 'death'? What is the 'death' of *Antony and Cleopatra*? Not that the word itself is elsewhere absent: but it is continually welcomed as something of positive worth and sweet nourishing delight, like love:

> Where art thou, death?
> Come hither, come! come, come, and take a queen
> Worth many babes and beggars!

Knight's appeal is to the secret organization of the metaphor, which he mimics in the course of his description (contriving to suggest 'dug' even as he takes the reading 'dung'). Images of breeding and death are quietly assimilated into each other until the two kinds are almost identical: from Antony's teasing of Lepidus:

> as it ebbes, the Seedsman
> Upon the slime and ooze scatters his graine
> And shortly comes to Harvest

to the closing scene when the asp is a baby that sucks the nurse asleep. When the play is read with this kind of responsiveness it is easy to see how the squabble about 'dug' and 'dung' arose; had the Folio read 'dugge' some watchful editor would have emended to 'dung', and his successors may all have changed their mounts.

Is Wilson Knight among the first to recognize this tragic equation between death and nourishment in *Antony and Cleopatra*? Is he representative of a generation better placed to understand this aspect of the play, or have others in other times enjoyed the same insights but abstained from flaunting them? Both the stage history and the critical history suggest that Knight is healing a long sustained insensibility. Although it is just possible that the play was given at Blackfriars before 1642, the Theatre Royal under the Restoration seems not to have exercised performance rights, and it may be that an authentic version was first mounted by Phelps at Sadler's Wells in 1849. The stage had in the interim been dominated by *All for Love* and by a number of Shakespeare Dryden travesties; and it is characteristic of them that they etiolate the Shakespearian metaphors. Dryden, perhaps mimicking the soothingly erotic 'languishingly sweet' manner of Fletcher in *The False One*, was to win Scott's applause for his Cydnus speech because it was 'flowery without diffuseness and rapturous without hyperbole'. Judging from descriptions of late nineteenth-century performances, even the rediscovered Shakespearian version was not allowed too close a contact with Nilus slime.

Large critical comment on the play (as distinct from glosses on detail) again testifies to a prolonged failure to receive its elemental insights. Johnson is particularly ungracious about the poetry (in spite of his skill at disentangling it). He enjoys the tumult of events and the moral fable, but that endeavour of art by which visionary hyperbole seeks to foil death is alien to him: conceit, hyperbole and wit have no place in his Augustan charnel house.

Coleridge was the first Englishman to approach the play primarily through its 'happy valiancy of style' which he called 'but the representative and result of all the material excellencies so expressed'. Yet his resolutely general tribute is defective in insight where it might have been triumphant. Cleopatra's passion, he says, 'is supported and reinforced by voluntary stimulus and sought-for associations, instead of blossoming out of spontaneous emotions'. Like many a witness from Johnson to L. C. Knights, Coleridge is echoing Dolabella's cool, sympathetic, civilized disclaimer, 'Gentle madam, no'. But Coleridge not only disowns the extravagance, he detects the culpable moral energies that promote it—sensation seeking and self-dramatization. And yet he can marvel at the 'angelic strength' and 'fiery force' of the language. Does he believe that Shakespeare collaborated with the sensational appetites of his heroes in order simply to 'astonish us'?

Oddly enough, modern criticism has been sensitized by Coleridge at precisely the point where Cleopatra answers Dolabella:

> yet t'imagine
> An Antony were Natures peece 'gainst Fancie,
> Condemning shadowes quite.

Shakespeare's distinction between fancy and imagination requires that the Antony of Cleopatra's final vision should be made neither by nature alone nor by fantasy alone, but by an eternalizing imaginative transfiguration of nature—a feat of the poet's art and the lover's. The vision is hard-won by both Cleopatra and by Shakespeare (and by the audience) from a full experience of the play.

Antony and Cleopatra offers to vindicate the imagination in a fashion that the Romantics should have found highly congenial ('The gates of the senses open upon eternity'). But it had to wait for a new romanticism before it could be fittingly acclaimed by hyperbole; a romanticism whose critical postulates owe much to Nietzsche's *The Birth of Tragedy from the Spirit of Music*.[5]

Modern romanticism (a fugitive and provisional category scarcely fit for so confident a label) knows the value of extreme commitments and seeks to excite ranges of thought and feeling hostile to decorous moral and intellectual conformities. It is an intensifying rather than a directing temper of mind, and it has energized many rival and irreconcilable kinds of art and criticism (Yeats, Lawrence, Pound, Joyce). T. E. Hulme exemplified it even as he undertook to denounce it; Wyndham Lewis presented Shakespeare to readers of *Blast*; and Frank Harris, who saw himself as the prophet of a long overdue emancipation from puritanism, betrays the lines of continuity that might be traced between Nietzsche and the novelette.[6]

We have now, perhaps, reached a last phase with the work of Samuel Beckett which, with its trick of sanctifying boredom, recalls Schopenhauer rather than Nietzsche. *End Game*, for example, is a Schopenhauerean parable, and it may be read as one sign among many of a romantic nihilism infecting (or reinfecting) an area of contemporary sensibility. Ionesco's *Rhinoceros* is in comparison a cynic parable, inviting social man (an absurd creature and unhappy) to revert to the condition of a beast (still absurd but less unhappy). It is likely that these moods too will bring their privileges of insight, and it may be that the time is ripe for a study of Shakespeare's pessimism, for some inquiry into what lies behind that disturbing cluster of paradoxes in *Timon of Athens*:

> My long sicknesse
> Of Health, and Liuing, now begins to mend
> And nothing brings me all things,

34

and behind the radical renunciations of rhetoric and life in 'Lippes, let soure words go by and Language end'. Renaissance pessimism might well serve to qualify and refine our own, with Shakespeare supplying the most instant points of contact; some pessimisms are more vital than others.

We would take a false impression, however, from a history of critical sensibility which confined itself to responsiveness to the *poetry* of Shakespeare's plays. The expressiveness of a play is more than the language alone affords; it is won from the playwright's deployment of a complex range of theatre conventions—the treaties controlling our interpretation of speech, character, action and spectacle. It is in this area, perhaps, that we may most immediately recognize an opportunity to sharpen our reactions to the subtleties and indeed the simplicities of Renaissance drama. The ironic self-consciousness of modern playwrights from Chekhov and Pirandello, together with their readiness to play upon the nerves of the audience by dislocating the established conventional relationships, should (quite properly) make us more watchful for this kind of thing in the past.

The convention particularly affected is the soliloquy. What we make of the soliloquy convention depends largely upon what we assume and believe about 'the self', about human identity. One reason why nineteenth-century criticism differs so strikingly from our own is that it could use words like 'character', 'individual' and 'soul' much more confidently than we can (see, for example, Carlyle on The Hero as Poet, talking of Shakespeare). We are more apt to brood upon the question first pursued in a characteristically modern way by David Hume; what do we mean by human identity, what is it that makes a man unique? Or, to focus the question on stage situations, what is it that sets a man apart? M. C. Bradbrook some years ago remarked that 'the graduation between the frank appeal *ad spectatores* and the subtlest nuances of Shakespearian dramaturgy make the dead level of modern dialogue seem a very primitive affair'.[7] It is in this respect (in the plays of Beckett at least) less primitive than it was; but the range of possibilities in Renaissance drama remains insufficiently recognized. In talking of soliloquy and aside in Shakespeare we need to keep in mind the multiple kinds of 'apartness' that 'characters' are made to cultivate or suffer. The Elizabethans did their best thinking (I believe) in the theatre, and by and through the conventions of theatre. Appeals to 'the soliloquy convention' can be premature and ingenuous without an awareness of the swift and intricate changes that occur minute by minute, or line by line, in the course of its more sophisticated developments.[8]

One such development may be traced in the second scene of *The Winter's Tale*, taking as starting-point Leontes's aside:

> I am angling now,
> Though you perceive not how I give line. (I, ii, 180)

This may not be technically soliloquy since at least two other characters are on the stage, and the last words 'How now boy?', if not the whole speech, are addressed to Mamillius. Within the context, however, the technical question is an idle one. Leontes has not long uttered that notoriously obscure speech with the apostrophe: 'Affection! Thy intention stabs the centre.' He is supposed to be talking at the time to Mamillius, but the boy can be taken to make no more of it than Polixenes who 'overhears' and then asks of Hermione, 'what means Sicilia?'; she, nonplussed (like most of the commentators) can only say, 'He something seems unsettled'; and a moment later we learn from the dialogue that Leontes 'held a brow of distraction'—a precise direction for the playing of the episode. The obscurity is a calculated effect. We are made witnesses to the recession of Leontes' character into private, obsessed monologue, addressed to himself. It would not do for the words 'Affection! Thy intention stabs the centre' to be instantly lucid; for them to be a means of direct communication with other people; the obscurity collaborates with the 'aside' to quicken the drift into isolation. But the words are not inconsequential raving either. They are haunted by several possible meanings which have to be teased out in the light of what we recognize of Leontes' obsession. We might paraphrase: 'Love indeed! Your disloyalty is manifest to me and it cuts to the heart'; but the point is that the language at this moment is not public—it is pre-articulate, imperfectly formed, like most *private* thought.

So it happens that when we reach the soliloquy 'I am angling now' we are sufficiently aware of its perversely private nature. Having accepted the intricate terms of our treaty with the playwright we feel that we are listening to self-communing mutterings. Whether Camillo and Mamillius are also listening is a minor question asking 'are they, like us, witnesses to this betrayal of a private obsession?' There is a disturbing discord in this scene between the social and the private self; at a high moment of hospitable ceremony the ego turns in upon its own fragmented being. And this effect is attained in spite of the more routine soliloquy convention which allows a man to appear to talk to himself without seeming mad. Leonte, in brief, 'talks to himself' in a more naturalistic as well as in a theatrical sense. Our reaction is not, 'we must by convention allow these words to disclose the facts about Leontes'_state of mind'. It is rather, 'he's talking to himself, he must be off his head'. The interjection, 'Go, play, boy, play' is addressed to a Mamillius who is encroaching on his father's vocal self-torturings, trying to treat them as if they were what the earlier 'distracted' speeches half struggled to be—conversation, straight dialogue. We watch the breakdown of communications; the severing of a human bond.

So far the Leontes soliloquy is a piece of quasi-naturalism; this figure soliloquizes on the stage because he is representing a character talking to himself in court. But there is a momentous *peripeteia* to come. The obsessive nature of the speech has made it intimate to the point of exclusiveness and the audience is sufficiently insulated from Leontes to treat him as a maniacal self-styled cuckold, totally out of touch with normal values. But Shakespeare does not allow the audience to keep its watchful Olympian security for long:

> thy Mother playes, and I
> Play too; but so disgrac'd a part, whose issue
> Will hiss me to my Grave. Contempt and Clamor
> Will be my Knell.

The pun on 'plays' announces an astonishing excursion into the soliloquy of direct address. Leontes ceases to appear to be the King of Sicilia, playing cuckold to a playful wife, and reverts to being an actor playing the part of Leontes before an audience which brings to the theatre its own anxieties about adultery:

> There have been
> (Or I am much deceiv'd) Cuckolds ere now,
> And many a man there is (even at this present,
> Now while I speake this) holds his wife by th Arme
> That little thinkes she has been sluyc'd in's absence,
> And his Pond fish'd by his next Neighbor (by
> Sir Smile, his Neighbor:).

It may be that a pause after 'by his next Neighbor' can catch the audience grinning and turn the next words 'Sir Smile, his Neighbor' into an allusion to 'the man next to you in the theatre'. Gielgud once played the speech this way, Sprague tells us, with electrifying effect.

The obsession which, a moment before, was by use of one soliloquy convention attached exclusively to the self-deluded cuckold figure on the stage, is now, by the use of another convention, excited communally. But the terms of the treaty are daring and hazard the very play convention itself—yet deftly so, and almost unobtrusively.

These enterprising uses of convention have grown out of, or been adapted from, a number of more commonplace, more conventional, conventions. And conventional conventions are used often enough in *The Winter's Tale*; the second scene, for example, ends with a disarmingly transparent use of soliloquy when Camillo explains to the audience his intention to quit the court. The association of soliloquy with 'talking to oneself', with madness, paranoia or obsession, haunts a number of plays in the Elizabethan repertory, starting perhaps with Kyd's *Spanish Tragedy*. A history of the convention might begin with Seneca, *Hercules Furens* and *Hercules Oetaeus*, and reach a climax with *Lear* and *Macbeth*. Lear's storm and heath speeches are not strictly soliloquies but they are utterances of the isolated self, and the presence of other figures on the stage intensifies the isolation. But the simplest precedent to the Leontes speech is the cuckold soliloquy. The isolation of the paranoiac cuckold is a clear opportunity for soliloquy; there is no one he can trust, and no one in whom he can confide without shame. Kitely talks to himself in *Every Man in his Humour* and fears that he has been overheard. Shakespeare's Ford is a soliloquizing cuckold and there is a hint of the convention operating (among other more complex soliloquy conventions) in *Othello*.[9] The convention permitting the actor *as actor* to address the audience directly is usually confined to prologues and epilogues, and it is hard to find a close parallel to Leontes on adultery.

Probings into convention conducted in this spirit—at the instigation, as it were, of the modern playmaker—would reveal a highly accomplished resourcefulness in the control of the distance between the players and their auditors. Each kind of play tends to use soliloquy to express its own characteristic modes of isolation; in the comedies they are often the isolations of the unrequited or the jealous lover, in the histories the isolations of power or of weakness, and in the tragedies the isolations of malice, madness and suffering. But one would not wish to promote categories of this kind. It is enough that we keep our eyes open to the possibilities. To trace for example, the nuances of self-observation, self-dramatization and self-analysis through *Hamlet* would reveal an astonishing suppleness of changing relationships between soliloquizer and audience. Soliloquy in this play is closely expressive of sense of guilt—the king is most guilty but the prince has (diminishingly) the keener consciousness of guilt; hence the impression of Hamlet taking into his consciousness the sins of the realm, and fitting himself (in the eyes of the audience) for a tragic death. Most of the *Hamlet* soliloquies, including the tardy prayer of Claudius, are by their impulsive syntax and complex shifts of thought designed to be *overheard*. The possible exceptions are, ''Tis now the very witching hour of night', and 'Now might I do it pat'. But these have the histrionic quality which we associate with Hamlet the good actor—he is playing the part of revenge killer, imitating the Lucianus of the mouse-trap play; and it is a part that neither his sensibility nor circumstance allow him to play for long.[10]

As these last remarks are intended to hint, there is much more to be said about the dialogue between our own preoccupations and those of the Renaissance. It could touch all that Sir James Frazer might have found particularly interesting in English Seneca, *Titus Andronicus* and *King Lear*.[11] Or it could pursue, in an idiom that Pirandello and Yeats would have found congenial, the Renaissance fascination with masks, assumed parts and the playing of roles.

It would be misleading, however, to leave the impression that modern sensitivities and insensitivities to Shakespeare must be exclusively controlled by our experience of modern literature and thought. The plays keep alive many modes of understanding and delight that are alien to current life and belief, and the miracle is that the art can stay quick when our understanding of it is virtually dead. In such cases it is better to consult more thoroughly the fashion of Shakespeare's times and let our own go momentarily unregarded.

I take, for an instance, the trial scene of *The Merchant of Venice*. In the course of one of his sensitive accounts of the play J. R. Brown draws attention to a pervasive difference of opinion between those who have written on the trial scene in recent years; some, like Coghill, idealize and allegorize, seeing Portia against Shylock as Mercy opposed to Justice, the Old Law and the New; and there are those who find it 'most ingenious satire'.[12]

I think it characteristic of the play that from the beginning we watch it with, as it were, one auspicious and one dropping eye, or changing the implication slightly, an innocent eye and a sceptical. With an effacing tact Shakespeare reminds us that Belmont is doubly golden—vibrant with rare harmonies and richly endowed with money. And Venice offers both an image of youthful inconsequence and an image of the acquisitive society. In the same way the legal masquerade of the fourth act can appear in two lights. To the more sceptical eye it appears a magnificent exercise in lawcourt virtuosity. Shylock is most skilfully outplayed, for this is another game, another 'merry sport' turned to earnest. Even the famous mercy speech is an adroit piece of tactics, for it disables Shylock from a mercy plea and nevertheless puts him at the mercy of Antonio and the Duke's court. Sceptically received, the episode is what Gratiano takes it to be in his wrestling image, 'Now, infidel, I have you on the hip'; it is a consummate piece of jew-baiting. But if we take it only sceptically we find ourselves sentimentalizing Shylock and brutalizing Portia.

There is an equal and opposite response which greatly enriches the play's allegory. Portia comes to the Venetian court from Belmont and brings with her a sum of money, her wit, and a principle. The money is refused, and the wit succeeds only because it serves the principle. And to illuminate that principle we must consult, not the *Gesta Romanorum* or the Record Office, but the Renaissance philosophers of law. If we ask why the play is memorable alike for the music of Belmont and the trial scene, we find an answer in (for example) Hooker's *Laws of Ecclesiastical Polity* and Bodin's *The Six Bookes of a Commonweale*. Music both symbolized and effected those higher harmonies that contingent laws tried to promote in civil societies.

Before insisting on the analogues, however, we do well to remember that the play keeps constantly in touch with its comedy traditions of romance and intrigue. Belmont transforms hard-up courtiers and scheming runaway couples into dedicated lovers by the agency of music:

> Since nought so stockish, hard and full of rage,
> But music for the time doth change his nature.   (v, i, 81–2)

'For the time' is a realistic, if not a sceptical touch, just as it is realistic if not sceptical to place those memorable evocations of the music of the spheres in a space of idyllic leisure enjoyed by young lovers. The pythagorean vision:

> Such harmony is in immortal souls,
> But whilst this muddy vesture of decay
> Doth grossly close it in, we cannot hear it
>
> (v, i, 63–5)

owes as much to one of the rarer moods of courtship as to Lorenzo's education at Padua.

It is nevertheless relevant to glance at Hooker's handling of the same range of ideas:[13]

Touching musical harmony whether by instrument or by voice, it being but of high and low in sounds a due proportionable disposition, such notwithstanding is the force thereof, and so pleasing effects it hath in that very part of man which is most divine, that some have been thereby induced to think that the soul itself by nature is or hath in it harmony.

In harmony the very image and character even of virtue and vice is perceived, the mind delighted with their resemblances, and brought by having them often iterated into a love of the things themselves. For which cause there is nothing more contagious and pestilent than some kinds of harmony; than some nothing more strong and potent unto good.

They must have hearts very dry and tough, from whom the melody of the psalms doth not sometime draw that wherein a mind religiously affected delighteth.

Ideally, by Hooker's account, the harmonies that are intimated in music ought to pervade the total hierarchical structure of laws from the Divine, through the Natural to the Civil. But the more contingent laws—touching directly the fallen and mutable world—cannot be relied on to operate harmoniously. Hence it sometimes happens that Equity must redress the false balance of the Law:

We see in contracts and other dealings which daily pass between man and man, that, to the utter un-doing of some, many things by strictness of law may be done, which equity and honest meaning forbiddeth. Not that the law is unjust, but unperfect; nor equity against, but above, the law, binding men's consciences in things which law cannot reach unto. (Bk. v, ch. ix, sec. 3.)

Hooker establishes for us some of the proper perspectives for the play. The situation in Venice is the sort that he postulates: by contract and by strictness of law, something is about to be done 'which equity and honest meaning forbiddeth'.

It might loosely be said that Portia brings from Belmont the principle of Equity 'above the law' but not against it. But this of course understates the wit of the intervention—Equity is vindicated in Venice by an attention to the letter of the law which is yet more strict than Shy-lock's. Hooker recognized that the 'literal practice' of law might sometimes prejudice equity, and Shylock would seem to prove his point; but Shylock, in refusing the mercy plea, refuses to allow Equity its most humane opening; the words of the bond are squeezed harder, and an ultimate loyalty to the letter of the law is found, after all, to vindicate its spirit. Lawcourt virtuosity is therefore indispensable to render the letter of the law equitable and so keep it consonant with the high intimations of divine harmony touched so lightly and finely in the music of Belmont.

But what of the ring trickery that ends the play? It is a hint that the comedy of intrigue and romance might go in other directions too; that a clever plot can sound a discord and contrive a concord in the harmonies of marriage. Bodin's translator, Richard Knolles, offers us these marginalia: 'Harmonicall Justice of all others the best'; 'Harmonicall proportion good to be in marriage observed, and so likewise in the government of a whole Commonweale'; 'The judge bound unto the verie words of the law, is not yet therby embarred to use the equitie of the law or yet the reasonable exposition therof'.[14] All come within a page or two of each other, as guides to a sustained and highly technical discussion of music, marriage, and the duty of the magistrate on certain occasions to admit equity into law. It is unlikely that Bodin was among the volumes that Shakespeare imagined Nerissa carrying from Belmont; but we can be confident that had Richard Knolles seen the play he would not have supposed that 'Shakespeare planned a *Merchant of Venice* to let the Jew dog have it, and thereby to gratify his own patriotic pride of race'.[15]

The *Merchant of Venice* is not a profound play. It touches profound issues but with a becoming lightness, within the decorum of comedy. Portia is made sufficiently human; her rare gifts remain this side the magical and divine. And Shylock is sufficiently stereotyped; the sources of his obsessions are distinctly traced to the flaws in Venetian society, a broken family and a wounded psyche, but they are not tragically explored. And Shakespeare, like Spenser, carries on tip-toe his burden of Renaissance thought.

There is a Japanese test for colour-blindness, by which defective vision recognizes one configuration in a pattern of coloured dots and true vision recognizes another. So it is, perhaps, with changing phases of judgement and sensibility. The metaphor need not deter us from 'the common pursuit of true judgement' but it might make us more wary. For it may even happen that where true vision finds mere medley the colour-blind discover a most dainty design.

NOTES

1. *Shakespeare Survey 14* (1961), 14.

2. *Romeo and Juliet* (1873) carried the general preface to the series. It is Positivist in temper, but the principal debt acknowledged in that volume is to Mommsen's edition of *Romeo and Juliet*.

3. Helge Kökeritz, *Shakespeare's Pronunciation* (1953). In discussing the sounding of 'k' in 'knave' he touches the possibility of a pun very lightly.

4. *The Imperial Theme* (1931, 1951), p. 312. For Knight's earlier view, preferring 'dug' and citing *2 Henry VI*, III, ii, 392, see *The Sovereign Flower* (1962; article reprinted from *The New Adelphi*, September 1927).

5. A full account of the English assimilation of Nietzsche would probably begin with Pater, who showed a similar awareness of the significance of the Dionysiac strain in ancient literature and modern thought. See 'A Study of Dionysus' [1876], 'The Bacchanals' [1878], *Greek Studies* (1895): 'Denys L'Auxerrois', *Imaginary Portraits* (1887); 'Apollo in Picardy' [1893], *Miscellaneous Studies* (1904). Arthur Symons wrote about Nietzsche and Tragedy in 1903 (*Plays, Acting and Music*, 1907) in a critical rhetoric much fitter for *Antony and Cleopatra* than that which he used in his early essay on the play (reprinted in *Studies in the Elizabethan Drama* 1920). Wilson Knight discusses his own immediate obligations to Bradley, Murry, Colin Still and others in his preface to the 1951 edition of *The Imperial Theme*.

6. '...when we English have finally left that dark prison of Puritanism and lived for some time in the sunlight where the wayside crosses are hidden under climbing roses, we shall probably couple "Antony and Cleopatra" with "Hamlet" in our iove as Shakespeare's supremest works' (*The Man: Shakespeare*, 1909).

7. *Themes and Conventions of Elizabethan Tragedy* (1935, 1952), p. 112.

8. The second scene of *King Lear* is a rich example.

9. Othello enjoys the isolation of the Tamburlaine-like hero (alone fit to voice his own virtue) and suffers the isolation of the Jonsonian cuckold; he is trapped by the deployment of the soliloquy convention which isolates Iago, Morality-fashion, as devil and intriguer. Like Edmund, Iago is made a self-consciously theatrical figure.

10. I owe this point to Roy Walker, *The Time is out of Joint* (1948).

11. See Robert Hapgood, 'Shakespeare and the Ritualists', *Shakespeare Survey 15* (1962), for a review of criticism pursued under the shadow of Frazer. John Holloway, *The Story of the Night* (1961), writes in the Gilbert Murray tradition, and has a chapter dealing with the Idea of Human Sacrifice. *Titus Andronicus* takes a human sacrifice as a starting-point, and its imagery often reminds us that blood must be shed to fertilize the earth.

12. H. Sinsheimer, quoted J. R. Brown (ed.), *The Merchant of Venice* (1955), p. li.

13. *Laws of Ecclesiastical Polity*, Bk. v, ch. xxxviii, 1. Quotations are from Keble's edition (1874).

14. Jean Bodin, *The six bookes of a commonweale*, trans. R. Knolles, 1606 (*STC* 3193), Bk. 6, ch. 6. Bodin also writes: 'And this is it for which the auntient Greekes aptly fained, Love to have bene begotten of *Porus* and *Penia*, that is to say, of *Plentie* and *Povertie*, love growing betwixt them two; so as in song the Meane betwixt the Base and the Treble, maketh a sweet and melodious consent and harmonie.'

15. H. B. Charlton, *Shakespearian Comedy* (1938), p. 127.

AN APPROACH TO
SHAKESPEARIAN TRAGEDY:
THE 'ACTOR' IMAGE IN 'MACBETH'

BY

V. Y. KANTAK

I

If Shakespeare continues to appeal in the modern world it is because of his peculiar 'independence', independence of any intellectual creed, moral or other, which might gain acceptance in one age and lose its plausibility in another. In an important sense, Shakespeare is independent of his time: he does, indeed, express his age perfectly; 'but he expresses it a little too perfectly to be its child'. And the time he expressed was marked by the intense vitality of the Elizabethans, by their confident and adventurous participation in a world of expanding horizons. It was a time of deep and rapid change, and Shakespeare asserts the significant human values during a period which produced a kind of fusion of Renaissance action with medieval thought. We are still moved by the momentum then generated. Even the Orient, lately awakened and still rubbing her eyes after a night of bad dreams, now feels its pressure. We are again living in a time of deep and rapid change, torn between man's self-sufficiency and the need to have faith in a power beyond him. In such a time as ours Shakespeare's steadily human values make special appeal, the more so because the confidence of the earlier day has been replaced by uncertainty, challenge and peril.

The integrity of Shakespeare's vision is, of course, something which cannot be expressed within any single, simple formula; on the other hand we may say with assurance that, whatever its complexity and depth, it owes its strength to a complete response to the wholeness of creation. His is a 'round' vision which sees all sides at once and as one—a quality which is painfully bewildering to rigid minds. He knows all men with that sympathy which each feels for himself. His art is organic through and through; we get little feeling of artifice or mechanical contrivance; it seems to be art strangely congruent with Nature. And again and again when he treats of essential tragic evil no less than when he treats of the humour of a Falstaff or the sunshine fun and 'the deep marriage-consciousness' of his ladies, he confronts us with a peerless wisdom.

Generations of critics have tried, often vainly, to explain and expound this integrity that is Shakespeare's. The effort to interpret it must necessarily go on; but one thing has to be stressed— any interpretation that loses sight of the essential element in his appeal does more harm than good. And, remembering this truth, we are bound to believe that certain currents in the ever-increasing stream of modern Shakespearian criticism are inclined to bear us away from the essential core of his appeal. The recent concentration upon the nature and function of poetic imagery has, it is true, made us aware of a new dimension—the power exerted by these images in weaving a fabric full of imaginative significance. At the same time, we are forced to recognize that, in the excessive zeal with which these explorations have been pursued, there is developing a dangerous separation between the poetry and the drama, with the result that the uniqueness of Shakespeare's works is being obscured.

In view of this, two propositions may be submitted: (1) The 'character' approach, obviously erroneous in the form it took during the nineteenth century, is still a legitimate approach basically related to the dramatic form. In attending to the imagery we should not overlook its importance. (2) The poetry that a character speaks, in an important sense, 'belongs' to and is revelatory of that character. It cannot simply be regarded as though it 'belonged' only to Shakespeare in the way lyric poetry belongs to an author.

The recent emphasis on imagery and the symbolic element started as a reaction to the excesses of the nineteenth-century concentration upon Shakespeare's characters. It was indeed proper that the cruder and more naïve manifestations of that vogue should have been held up to ridicule. The treatment of Shakespearian characters as if they were living human beings who had some-how made their escape from their literary situations could lead only to curious, and sometimes comic, biographical probings which, although sometimes innocuous (as in the question, 'How did the boy in *Henry V* learn to speak French?'), were often of a kind fully deserving L. C Knights' slashing judgement: 'The habit of regarding Shakespeare's persons as "friends for life" or may be "deceased acquaintances" is responsible for most of the vagaries that serve as criticism.'[1] Naturally, the attack on this 'character' approach centred upon Bradley, whose monumental work represents the best in that earlier tradition which Coleridge may be said to have initiated. For Knights, Bradley's attitude seems more that of a detective than of a critic, and he takes exception to the pronouncement which provides the basis for all Bradley's investigations: 'The centre of the tragedy may be said with equal truth to lie in action issuing from character, or in character issuing in action…what we feel strongly, as a tragedy advances to its close, is that the calamities and catastrophe follow inevitably from the deeds of men, and that the main source of these deeds is character.'[2]

It may, of course, readily be admitted that Bradley tends to treat Shakespearian characters as living human beings, seeking to interpret their words, their motives, their activities in terms we normally assume to be true of the world of living persons, whereas these characters exist only within the carefully determined shadow-world which is the drama in which they make their appearances. They have no reality other than that which is fixed by the words given to them by Shakespeare. Bradley himself was aware of the dangers involved in straying too far from the play's words, but he insisted that the response in the mind of reader or spectator was funda-mentally important: 'Any answer to the question proposed ought to correspond with, or to represent in terms of the understanding, our imaginative and emotional experience in reading the tragedies. We have, of course, to do our best by study and effort to make this experience true to Shakespeare; but that done, the experience is the matter to be interpreted.'[3] In other words, how else can we interpret the characters and what they feel and how they act except by using our understanding of people's motives and behaviour in our ordinary lives? The ability to read the clues provided in the dialogue of the dramas is basically the same as the ability we bring to bear upon our understanding of living persons around us. 'Action issuing from character or character issuing in action' is the basic element in drama; it is what initially determines the kind of total response we make to it as a work of art.

Exploring character in action, Bradley came to the conclusion that the ultimate power in

Shakespeare's tragic world cannot be adequately described as a law or an order which is just or benevolent, nor can it be described as a fate whether malicious or merely indifferent to human happiness or goodness; there is in it an equal emphasis, a sort of a tension, between the destiny within and the destiny without. 'Shakespeare', said Bradley, 'was not attempting to justify the ways of God to men. He was writing tragedy, and tragedy would not be tragedy if it were not a painful mystery.'[4] What is central in that view is that Shakespeare maintains a kind of even balance of vision, holding in check our natural desire to embrace some religious or philosophical conception that would explain all. This view is now being assailed with the shift of attention to the symbolic force of imagery. Critics are now trying to show, for instance, that in the total poetical design of *Macbeth* there is an assertion of a moral order and a complete acceptance of the Christian ethic. It is argued that Shakespeare is closer to medieval traditions than was hitherto supposed, and *Macbeth* is now being read simply as a 'Morality' in which the characters figure as symbols of moral entities all diagrammatically disposed to illustrate the Christian code. Macbeth, the evil man who makes the fatal choice, is poised between Lady Macbeth and Banquo, the bad and the good angels respectively.

Irving Ribner thus believes that 'as Shakespeare became more and more absorbed in the religious and ethical dimensions of tragedy he concentrated more and more on the development of the symbol with *a corollary unconcern for character consistency*'.[5] He would thus explain Bradley's failure to see a moral order in Shakespeare's tragedies: 'stage characters analysed as though they were human beings could reflect only the mystery and seeming indirection of human life. Bradley could lead his readers only to a Shakespeare without positive belief, to a conception of tragedy merely as a posing of unanswerable questions, and to a moral system in the plays which is upon close analysis not moral at all'.[6] Such an approach, however, seems to ignore the fact that 'the posing of unanswerable questions' is, in the end, the very foundation of tragedy. The peculiar tension in a tragedy arises from our difficulty in accepting, not from our reluctance to accept the moral order. The moral order is there, but something has to run counter to it to produce that tension. Bradley found that force centred in the character itself, for instance, in Macbeth as he lives through the ravages of evil. It would seem that the symbolic pattern and all the thematic imagery of the play have to be brought into contact with that element to produce the tragic effect peculiar to the Shakespearian conception. Even the witches have significance only as an opportunity for evil without to respond to evil within.

There is surely something wrong in the approach that considers Shakespeare's realism of character as a sort of technical proficiency valuable in its way but not at all very essential to his tragic vision. It is true that the characters are not 'real', but part of Shakespeare's artistry lies in convincing us that they are and in getting us emotionally involved with them. The symbolic function they seem to perform in the over-all pattern of the play does not exist independently. We have to create it in our minds by entering fully into the real lifelike situation of character and action. It is only thus that the tragedy has the effect of creating 'a kind of tension beween feeling and action, between our emotional involvement in a specific situation and our rational contempla-tion of its meaning'. It is precisely this kind of tension that is centred in the character of Macbeth. The 'over-all intellectual concerns of the play' require Macbeth to be an unredeemable sinner but his poetic ability, his power to grasp fully and concretely what is happening to himself, sets up disturbance in our minds and makes his thematically ordained damnation so painful to accept.

This effect Bradley would put down simply to the fact that Macbeth happens to have the poet's imagination; but the new critics find it difficult to accept that statement, because they feel that such a reading of Macbeth's character implies confusion between life and art. Kenneth Muir, commenting on Macbeth's soliloquy in I, vii, says, 'The imagery of the speech shows that Macbeth is haunted by the horror of the deed, and impresses that horror on the audience. But if we go further and pretend that this poetic imagery is a proof that Macbeth had a powerful imagination, that he was, in fact, a poet, we are confusing real life with drama.'[7] In other words, the poetry that a character speaks is not to be considered in relation to and as revelatory of his nature, but only as part of the general poetic design of the play. What we must ask is whether this is not confusing drama with what it is not. Surely a closer approach to the truth rests in H. S. Wilson's judgement:

We may think that the 'confusion' of Macbeth's poetry with Shakespeare's is precisely the effect Shakespeare aimed at in the theatre. As we listen to Macbeth's eloquence, we forget about Shakespeare the poet, we forget that we are listening to a poem, we think only of the figure imaginatively evoked for us and embodied upon the stage....If this is to confuse drama with real life, it is also the 'Willing suspension of disbelief that constitutes poetic faith'....We feel that Macbeth is a poetic person and we value him for the poetry of his utterance.[8]

Macbeth's poetry has, in fact, the effect of confounding those who seek to read in the play the most perfect illustration of the Christian theme of sin and damnation; it is no less an inconvenience to those others who arrive at the same conclusion from an exclusive attention to the poetic pattern created by the imagery regardless of who uses the images and at what point of the action. By giving Macbeth poetic power Shakespeare has achieved for us most poignantly the ambivalence of the tragic effect that Aristotle described. That ambivalent response is inescapable if we honestly confront the 'principle of morality' which is present in Macbeth's imaginative fears and which enables him to grasp fully the moral implications of his action, to participate in the full horror of it and to report the havoc caused by the evil within him. Any criticism that fails to see the impressiveness of Macbeth in his final self-portrayal of his soliloquy, 'To-morrow and to-morrow...' seems surely to miss whatever tragic purpose Shakespeare had in mind. Logically it should be the last stage of the corruption caused by evil; and yet somehow, as Santayana said, 'Macbeth is divinely human here!' Abercrombie is right in asserting that the final harmony of good and evil is achieved in the character of Macbeth which creates and endures evil. Macbeth has staked everything and lost and for nothing—a bleak imbecile futility: 'But he seizes on the appalling moment and masters even this; he masters it by knowing it absolutely and completely by forcing even this quintessence of all evil to live before him with the zest and terrible splendour of his own unquenchable mind.'[9]

Kenneth Muir comments on this, 'The fallacy here is simply that Abercrombie is confusing the powers of expression possessed by Macbeth with the poetic powers of Shakespeare himself. Once again it must be emphasized that because Shakespeare makes Macbeth talk as only a great poet could talk, we are not to assume that Macbeth is a great poet: he is merely part of a great poem.'[10] One might have great difficulty in understanding what, according to Kenneth Muir, belongs to Macbeth as a component of the play and what to Shakespeare. Of course, all, in one sense, is Shakespeare's poetry, but within that larger ambit there is the simulated life of a man who is given his *own speech* and his *own activity*.

It is easy to see how far this kind of criticism wrests the poetry from its dramatic moorings. For Muir, 'Every character in a poetic play may speak poetry; but this poetry does not necessarily reflect their poetic dispositions—it is merely a medium. The bloody Sergeant utters bombastic language, not because he is himself bombastic, but because such language was considered appropriate to epic narration....So too with Macbeth, we may say his imagery expresses his unconscious mind...but we must not say he is therefore a poet.'[11] The important point missed here is that Macbeth's words are distinct in kind from those of the bombastic Sergeant; Macbeth's speech alone has the power of suggesting the subconscious—and, after all, whose subconscious does his lines express if not that of himself?

II

It looks as though we are still far from arriving at a balanced approach to the functioning of the images of a Shakespeare play despite the numerous studies accomplished in this field. Few, indeed, are inquiries of the kind suggested in Clemen's *The Development of Shakespeare's Imagery* and Morozov's *The Individualization of Shakespeare's Characters through Imagery*, in which attempts are made to relate the function of imagery to the development of character. A statement such as 'Every character in a poetic play may speak poetry but that does not necessarily reflect their poetic dispositions' leaves unexplained how it is that, though all speak poetry, the poetic speech of one has a distinct quality setting it off from that of another. There is consistency in the speech of a character; each is given a sort of personal idiom which is maintained throughout. When there is a pronounced change or growth in the character it is reflected in a corresponding change of tone and imagery and in the rhythm of the poetic speech. Thus, for example, there is such a change in Romeo when he learns to face the dangers of his situation and emerges into maturity. When we see him in Mantua at the beginning of Act v we at once perceive by his first words that he is a new man entirely.

Imagery, too, is used to intensify some peculiar aspect of the developing action as in the celebrated case of the commerce between Iago and Othello in which Othello is found using Iago's imagery unconsciously as Iago's plan has begun to succeed. If we neglect the principle of character individualization implicit in the imagery of Shakespeare's poetic medium we should be obscuring the effect of a potent dramatic device he uses again and again. The variety that he rings on that medium is disposed in relation to character and developing action. It is necessary to assume that the imagery does two things at once;. it illustrates the theme and expresses character. Often the speaker may be unconscious of the full force of his words, as Banquo is unconscious of the deeper significance of his references to 'the temple-haunting martlet' and the genial quality of the air at Inverness castle. His words advance the theme of the grace of bounteous Nature and are heavy with the anticipatory irony of the hospitable castle presently turning into a charnel-house. But at the same time they embody his own character as that of one who, though not far above common humanity, can yet say truthfully, 'In the great hand of God I stand'. But whether conscious or unconscious, the personal reference is never entirely lost and the poetry is never reduced to a purely *choral* comment on the character or the action. The image is at once a reflection of the speaker's state of mind and a poetic vehicle for developing and enriching the play's thematic content.

It is necessary to stress this double value, since the increasing study of imagery has induced many critics to view the images from one point of view merely; and this has led to a regarding of the characters, not as having the consistency and functional unity of living beings, but only as more or less abstract counters which serve as vehicles for Shakespeare's poetry. Charlton's complaint against those critics who treat Shakespeare's characters as 'plastic symbols in an arabesque of esoteric imagery' seems to be justified. The result is that character, event, action and the motives behind the action, all lose the normal sense we attach to them, leaving with us a continuous dramatic poem—in reality, more like a lyric—which only because of certain extraneous features we call drama. This argues a fundamental misconception about the category 'drama'. Is it possible to talk about that category without assuming that a simulation of the kind of unity of motive and behaviour that characterize the actions of living human beings is essential to it? What may be called 'the fundamental realism' of drama, not the stylistic development called 'realistic' drama, requires that everything in a play, even a poetic play, be cast in the shape of human activity making it an image of men in action. The poetic pattern aids the plausibility of that image. It is itself made up of the words uttered by characters and its logic is the logic of men expressing themselves in free activity. That is what makes the distinction between 'dramatic poem' and 'poetic drama' not merely fanciful but real.

Drama is an art which eventuates in words but which in its essence 'is at once more primitive, more subtle and more direct than either word or concept'—that is the irreducible idea of drama, says Francis Fergusson, and in the following words he merely reiterates what has always been a fundamental premise of dramatic criticism:

But a drama, as distinguished from the lyric is not primarily a composition in the verbal medium; the words result, as one might put it, from the underlying structure of incident and character.... *The process of becoming acquainted with a play is like that of becoming acquainted with a person*; it is an empirical and inductive process.... We seek to grasp the quality of a man's life, by an imaginative effort, through his appearances, his words, and his deeds.... We grasp the stage-life of a play through the plot, characters and the words which manifest it.[12]

Criticism in which this element of simulated human activity becomes something merely adventitious misses the force of the poetry as well. What distinguishes tragedy is its 'activist' character, making man 'the arbiter of his own values'. In Shakespearian drama the springs of action are volitional and arise directly out of the Elizabethan pre-occupation with the problem of moral responsibility, 'which is seen at its simplest in *Doctor Faustus*, and its most complex in *Hamlet* and at its most naïve in, say, *The White Devil*'.[13]

Wilson Knight has exhorted us to take a Shakespeare play as an *expanding* metaphor. 'Though the original vision has been projected into forms roughly correspondent with actuality', he said, 'the persons ultimately, are not human at all, but purely symbols of a poetic vision'.[14] 'To analyse the sequence of events, the "cause" linking dramatic motive to action and of action to result in time, is a blunder instinctive to the human intellect.'[15] L. C. Knights has maintained that in a poetic play our 'apprehension of the whole can be obtained by a lively attention to the parts whether they have an immediate bearing on the main action or "illustrate" character or not'.[16] And more recently, D. A. Traversi has declared that Shakespeare's use of symbolism from *Macbeth* onwards implies a new conception of plot, without giving us an indication as to what that new conception is. All these pronouncements have a bearing on the progression within a play. The normal way of understanding that progression as the linking of dramatic motive to action and of action to result in time, far from being a blunder, is what distinguishes a poetic drama like *Macbeth* from a dramatic poem like *The Waste Land*. The images in *Macbeth* have their peculiar force because of the situation they are uttered in, the person who utters them and the stage of his dramatic mental history at which he utters them. The images of *The Waste Land* follow a different kind of progression, and not being linked with the line of development that drama requires, can look back and forward more freely, all drawn, as it were, by a centripetal force to the dominant mood and vision of the poem. All the 'dramatic matter' of the poem whether ritualistic, situational or of character (Madam Sosostris and the Tarot pack, Tiresias, the typist girl and the carbuncular young man, Cleopatra-Elizabeth on the barge, Heironymo, Phlebas the Phoenician, Mr Eugenides the Smyrna merchant, Stetson or the more shrouded figures like those of the Fisher King, Buddha-St Augustine or Christ), is held together by another logic than the progression implied in drama and responds to the over-all control of an impulse which is primarily lyrical. Whereas all that happens in a Shakespeare play is subjected to the gradual unfolding of a vision through the imaging of a volitional activity of characters issuing in action. The images aid and illuminate that process; they strengthen the total pattern, making the relation between character and action more intense.

By concentrating attention on poetic imagery in isolation from this progression, numerous modern critics, on the one hand, over-simplify and blur the actual complexity of a poetic play and, on the other, encourage an extremely subjective approach which is indefensible. T. R. Henn pertinently asks: 'Does the plot now become merely a frame-work for the dramatic poetry, or rather for a particular aspect of that "poetic content"? Are the ethical problems, the roots of will and choice in character, merged in a larger unity to which we are given no clue save our total "poetic response" to the play? And if that is so, are we committed to a new subjective aestheticism in which the image becomes paramount; even though it is, in essence as in fact, a device for communicating intense passion in speech?'[17] Even T. S. Eliot had only asked that we read character and plot in the understanding of the 'subterrene music' of the play. But the latter-day critics have gone farther; they have brought that music above ground, one fears, by simultaneously depressing the foreground of character and action out of sight, reversing the normal approach. The effect is not perhaps unlike judging a photographic portrait by looking at the negative.

III

Perhaps it is possible to show how an image can simultaneously reinforce both theme and character-in-action by examining a notable passage like Macbeth's last major soliloquy:

> Tomorrow, and to-morrow, and to-morrow,
> Creeps in this petty pace from day to day
> To the last syllable of recorded time,
> And all our yesterdays have lighted fools
> The way to dusty death. Out, out, brief candle!

> Life's but a walking shadow, a poor player
> That struts and frets his hour upon the stage
> And then is heard no more: it is a tale
> Told by an idiot, full of sound and fury,
> Signifying nothing.

It has been remarked how several lines of imagery previously apprehended seem to converge and reach here a kind of summation—the mechanical procession of Time infructuous, contrasted with all the earlier emphasis on child images; the opposition of darkness and light, muffled sunlight and starlight, the fire below the Witches' cauldron and the light of the domestic candle lighting the way· to bed (a fling back to the weird shadows made by Lady Macbeth's sleepwalking); the empty posturing of the stage-actor and finally the reverberation of sound echoing. But the image that powerfully stands out in the whole series is that of the 'poor player'. A little pondering reveals its peculiar appositeness to what happens in the play as a whole as well as to Macbeth's character and destiny. It is in fact the dominant master-conception 'underlying this varied but inter-locked imagery of desire and act, outward appearance and inward purpose, the clothes that fit another and thus cannot be borrowed, time and the moment of timelessness, the pattern we would impose on time and time's freedom from our contriving'.[18]

What is its implication for Macbeth's character? The closing phrase of 'the statement of evil' presents something like the transformation and the cutting adrift of man from the firm nexus that binds him to Nature into the world of things and manoeuvrable illusions. Perhaps the marionette is the closest objectification of that effect. He ceases to be a free agent and becomes completely determined. Time no longer confers freedom, but binds, is barren. Macbeth has lost Time the renewer and has come into the grip of Time who binds him to his past. Nature combines, fosters mutuality and breaks through into the future with the possibility of further freedom, holding the door open. In its place there is now the mere mechanical joinery of the puppet which mocks the unity implicit in Nature.

This is connected with Macbeth's isolation which, signalled by Lady Macbeth's anxious query, 'How now, my lord, why do you keep alone?', grows into an enormous exclusion from all that is natural. Insensibility to natural feeling ('She should have died here-after!') becomes an impenetrable wall separating him from his kind. There is only one thing that remains before Macbeth is utterly simplified and placed for ever in past time, and that is the power of the actor to see himself as performing. Before *his* light is finally extinguished this 'stage-light' must afford him one glimpse of himself in the stage posture of the walking shadow whose empty sound and fury is presently going to be no more. Thenceforward, it is the mask that animates the person with the animation peculiar to stage-types. The sounding of alarums and Macbeth's hollow, nervous brag herald the end. It is in the world of melodrama that Macbeth dies and the melodramatic necessity of 'Behold, where stands the usurper's cursed head' must be satisfied. But we know better and refrain from judgement.

It is easy to see how this image of the stage-actor gives unity to all the various strands of meaning conveyed by the play's imagery. L. C. Knights emphasized the numerous images that signify the great bond of Nature which makes the whole world kin and which Macbeth tears to pieces. All these images are made to stand in sharp contrast with the automation of the stage-actor into which Macbeth is propelled irresistibly as he cuts himself off from the vital connection.

Cleanth Brooks, brilliantly analysing the garment imagery, brings out the symbolic force of the 'naked babe and the manly cloak'.[19] Borrowed robes that are ill-fitting, painted faces, daggers 'unmannerly breeched with gore' have all a reference, however dim, to the mechanics of theatrical action. Similarly, as Kenneth Muir notices, the meaningful opposition between the hand and the eye or the heart, between the eye and the other senses, has a relation to the business of the stage. Macbeth's great concern is to divorce the hand from the heart. He observes the functioning of his own organs with a strange objectivity, much as does the actor upon the stage. In the same way, reiteration of images emphasizing time free and time controlled, living light and light smothered, desire and act, inward purpose and outward appearance has a scarce-hidden reference to the movement from life to the illusion of the stage.

The different stages of Macbeth's entire career seem to reflect that movement. Before the evil has gained firm lodgment his references to this element are marked by questioning, not acceptance: 'Why do you dress me in borrow'd robes?' When he is busy in Nature's mischief his one wish is to 'disconnect': 'Let the eye wink at the hand,' and the heart not recognize what the hand is doing. Macbeth's wish seems to be to do the act as if it is a stage affair, for to engage his heart would mean disaster. In the subsequent scenes his prayer is ironically fulfilled; the illusion is confirmed into the only reality for him. The things in his head can be acted before they are 'scanned' till 'the very firstlings' of his heart become the firstlings of his hand. He is no more conscious of the opposition between the hand and the heart; what he had been 'acting' has now become confirmed in nature. His last sin against humanity, the murder of Lady Macduff and her children, is undertaken with a perfect spontaneity indicating the progress in the 'disconnection'.

Macbeth's very first full encounter with the idea of the murder that would lead him to the 'golden round' is cast in theatrical terms:

> Two truths are told,
> As happy prologues to the swelling act
> Of the imperial theme.

'This is the birth of evil in Macbeth. He might have had ambitious thoughts before, may even have intended the murder but now for the first time he feels its oncoming reality' (Wilson Knight). Macbeth's words at this critical moment echo the 'wooden O' passage in *Henry V*:

> A kingdom for a stage, princes to act,
> And monarchs to behold the swelling scene.

'Prologue', 'swelling', 'act' and 'the imperial theme' are all there. The Chorus in *Henry V* is calling attention to the deficiencies of the theatre, 'prologue-like' begging the audience to eke out those deficiencies with their own imagination—a strictly theatrical business, word and thing. And Macbeth himself at the first onset begins to enact his role in his imagination though the horrid image unfixes his hair and makes his seated heart knock at his ribs against the use of nature. In fact the whole passage is strangely filled with suggestions of the stage:

> My thought, whose murder yet is but fantastical,
> Shakes so my single state of man that function
> Is smother'd in surmise, and nothing is
> But what is not.

Macbeth is rapt and saying to himself, 'Of things now about me I have no perception, being intent wholly on that which has no existence' (Johnson). Nor does it seem an accident that stage imagery should come to the fore again when Lady Macbeth dwells upon the same event in her apostrophe to the 'murth'ring ministers':

> Come, thick night,
> And pall thee in the dunnest smoke of hell,
> That my keen knife see not the wound it makes,
> Nor heaven peep through the blanket of the dark,
> To cry, 'Hold, hold!'

'Hell', 'pall', 'knife', 'dark'—'The peculiar and appropriate dress for Tragedy is a *pall* and a *knife*. When Tragedies were represented, the stage was hung with black' (Clarendon), and it has been suggested that the 'heaven' or canopy over the stage likewise underwent some gloomy transformation. Even 'the blanket of the dark' might have some relation to the sable hangings.

When the act is performing, just before and after it, images contrasting appearance with reality multiply, and suggestions of theatrical illusion keep seeping through with varying nuances of significance. Macbeth sees 'the dagger of the mind, a false creation' and rubs his eyes with 'Mine eyes are made the fools o'th'other senses'. Lady Macbeth attempts to allay his fears after the deed with ''Tis the eye of childhood that fears the painted devil', and puns horribly about gilding the grooms' faces to make it seem their guilt. There is the grim play-acting of the Hell-gate Porter. There is Macduff's wild adjuration, 'Shake off this downy sleep, death's counterfeit...and see the great doom's image!' And through all the tumult we hear the agonized native voice of Macbeth attempting, as it were, a disconnection between his natural self and his 'stage' self who has performed the deed. 'To know my deed, 'twere best not to know myself.' And there is at least one appalling instance of play-acting on the part of Macbeth in which the hypocrite, the deceiver, merges into the 'hypocrite', the actor. When the murder is discovered Macbeth utters words which are meant to deceive but which curiously at the same time express his deepest feelings:

> Had I but died an hour before this chance,
> I had liv'd a blessed time; for, from this instant,
> There's nothing serious in mortality;
> All is but toys: renown and grace is dead;
> The wine of life is drawn, and the mere lees
> Is left this vault to brag of.

'Macbeth intends', says Murry, 'the monstrous hypocrisy of a conventional lament for Duncan; but as the words leave his lips they change their nature and become a doom upon himself.'[20] (These lines recall his 'real' lament in the later soliloquies—'I have lived long enough; my way of life has fall'n into the sere, the yellow leaf...'. It is a curious effect for which there is no parallel, and with it Macbeth seems to have entered fully into the theatrical image of himself. Here the face and mask are one.)

It is thus that in his last moment of deep sentience the image of the stage actor comes to his mind as the fitting symbol of what he has become. It not merely illustrates the theme but expresses character, for it arises from Macbeth's poetic power and his radiant self-knowledge to the last. What is more, it gives a certain direction to our response to the whole tragic spectacle. The governing master-conception has the effect of keeping the play's meaning and whatever ethic it implied well within the confines of the naturalistic ethic of Shakespearian tragedy. It is important that Macbeth's growth should be symbolized by the image of the actor, but what is still more important is that he should be able to see himself as one. The final verdict on him is not what is conveyed by the word 'damnation' nor by the word 'redemption'. *Macbeth* is placed in an ethic which is 'open' not closed. 'While we must recognize the firm orientation of "good" and "evil" we do not identify with one and contemplate the other either openly or secretly. Macbeth's nature unfolds itself, and is unfolded for us. This enactment is entirely self-supporting; it requires no moral props, no philosophical buttressing.'[21]

NOTES

1. L. C. Knights, *Explorations* (1946), p. 16.
2. A. C. Bradley, *Shakespearian Tragedy*.
3. *Ibid.*
4. *Ibid.*
5. Irving Ribner, *Patterns in Shakespearian Tragedy* (1960), p. 3. [Italics mine.]
6. *Ibid.*
7. Kenneth Muir, *Macbeth* (Arden Shakespeare), 1951, p. lix.
8. Harold S. Wilson, *On the Design of Shakespearian Tragedy* (1957), p. 69.
9. L. Abercrombie, *The Idea of Great Poetry* (1925), p. 176.
10. Muir, *op. cit.* p. ix.
11. *Ibid.* p. lix.
12. Francis Fergusson, *The Idea of a Theatre* (1949), pp. 24-5. [Italics mine.]
13. T. R. Henn, *The Harvest of Tragedy* (1956), p. 152.
14. G. Wilson Knight, *The Wheel of Fire* (1930).
15. G. Wilson Knight, *The Imperial Theme* (1931)
16. Knights, *op. cit.* p. 18.
17. Henn, *op. cit.* p. 153.
18. John Lawlor, *The Tragic Sense in Shakespeare* (1960), p. 130.
19. Cleanth Brooks, *The Well Wrought Urn* (1947), *passim.*
20. J. Middleton Murry, *Shakespeare* (1936), p. 332.
21. Graham Martin, *Interpretations*, edited by John Wain (1955), p. 30.

SHAKESPEARE'S IMPACT TODAY
IN FRANCE

BY

A. JOSÉ AXELRAD

Impact—this, to me, suggests a missile hitting its target. And indeed, there was a time when the term was quite appropriate. The English actors who gave *Othello* in Paris soon after the battle of Waterloo were soundly booed, for reasons which were not altogether artistic or literary. The attempt was obviously premature. Yet the name of Shakespeare was already well known in France, even if his works had been sadly defaced and misunderstood during the eighteenth century. On our own classical age he seems to have had little influence. It is true that we sometimes seem to hear echoes of his thought and of his poetry in the plays of such writers as Mont-fleury or Tristan L'Hermite, the latter of whom had visited England twice and whose *Folie du Sage* is so strangely reminiscent both of *Hamlet* and of *Romeo and Juliet*. Those baroque playwrights have not so far received their due from the critics. As Léon Chancerel recently pointed out in a series of broadcasts very properly entitled *Shakespeare et nous*, all Tristan's plays have a Shakespearian manner: the general outlook, the sense of, and taste for, action, the feeling for humanity and the truth, as well as the outspoken vigour of the dialogue are features which do not surprise us nowadays, but of which seventeenth-century audiences were taught to disapprove. The rigid discipline of classical art could not accept the vigorous liberty of Elizabethan dramatists. And yet it would not be true to say that even during the seventeenth century Shakespeare's name and works were totally unknown in France: there was one copy of his works in the library of Louis XIV, and another in Fouquet's.[1] And Nicolas Clément, librarian to the king, who must have read at least some of the plays in the original text, is quoted as having written: 'This English poet is gifted with a handsome imagination, his thoughts are natural, his expression delicate, but all his fair qualities are spoilt by the scurrilities he scatters into his comedies.'[2]

The eighteenth century saw the beginning of Shakespeare's fame in France, though not without difficulties. Voltaire, who had been instrumental in introducing the poet to his country, soon regretted his move and became one of his bitterest enemies. But he could not undo what he had done: such men as the Abbé Prévost, Louis Racine, Le Franc de Pompignan and Marmontel had discovered that there once lived a man of genius named Shakespeare. La Place and Le Tourneur were the first to try their hands at translating his plays into French, though the first-named of these pioneers seems to have understood that translating Shakespeare was a well-nigh impossible task. As for the notorious Abbé Ducis, who wrote the first versions of Shakespeare's plays ever to have been acted in France, suffice it to say that he first of all aimed at granting *Hamlet* and *Macbeth* their naturalization papers, turning them into five-act classical tragedies with all the usual features, stating in his preface with characteristic nerve and, perhaps, modesty, that he did not know any English![3]

Our poet was first really introduced to this country by the French romantics. It was a long and difficult struggle, in which the young men who fought the so-called battle of *Hernani* used

Shakespeare more as a weapon to achieve their aims—to free the French stage from the shackles of the now defunct classical standards—than as a poet whose work had to be vindicated and appreciated. When we read Stendhal's *Racine et Shakespeare*, for instance, we may well wonder whether the writer understood at all what Shakespeare stands for and the reasons for his enduring fame: the form of art Stendhal seems to have been aiming at has, in our opinion, little in common with what he found in the English poet. Their contribution should however not be underestimated, for romantics such as Vigny and Victor Hugo did pave the way for what was to come.

It is indeed striking that the first French translation of Shakespeare which may still be used today should have come from François Victor-Hugo. With him there began a period of genuine understanding and appreciation. He was the first of a long line of scholars, some of them genuine poets, who strove to understand not only the written works of our poet but also his time, his people, his mind and his art.

The popularity of Shakespeare in France is at the present time as firmly established as that of any of our classics. Publishers' catalogues demonstrate that there is an excellent market for translations of the Complete Works, preferably with extensive introductions and notes by competent Renaissance specialists: there are at least four reputable firms in Paris issuing such editions to date, all selling very well. The success on the stage is probably even more striking. During the present season, I have already noted a production of *The Merry Wives* and *The Merchant of Venice* in Paris, of *Timon of Athens* by the Comédie de Bourges, while the Centre Dramatique National du Nord is touring the north and east of France with *Hamlet*, to be shown in some thirty-seven cities; and it should be pointed out that *Othello* was given on television at the beginning of February, a performance about which the critics seem to have been divided.[4] It is true to say that a Shakespearian production always arouses a keen interest and attracts a wide audience. Why the French public, so long conditioned to like some forms of art, should have now developed such a taste for Shakespeare is interesting to investigate. For the past fifty or sixty years, we have witnessed in this country a co-operation between the scholars, that is to say the professors of English, and the men of the theatre, actors, producers, designers. Names such as those of Gémier, Antoine, Copeau, the Pitoeffs, Dullin, Vilar, Barrault, Planchon, Reybas illustrate this extraordinary revival. At the same time, the universities discovered English literature in general and Shakespeare in particular. It may surprise an Englishman to know that English literature did not become one of the major subjects in French universities until the very last years of the nineteenth century. The men of my generation had the singular good fortune to be taught by such scholars as Emile Legouis, André Koszul and Floris Delattre. These men did not work directly with the professionals of the theatre; but their patient labours with difficult texts, their habit of grappling with many translation problems, must have helped, to a considerable extent, those writers who supplied the acting versions needed by the stage. Some of us, like our colleague Henri Fluchère, academics with a strong interest for the theatre, have often with great success carried out the necessary liaison work. We might ask: to what effect?

What the French public of today discover, often to their amazement, is the extent to which Shakespeare is civilized. True, his sense of dramatic action, his ability to contrive situations and to create characters attract playgoers. But what strikes most people is his awareness of the dignity of man, his knowledge of that dignity, and the way he has of remembering it time and again even when he is dealing with a criminal. Man in Shakespeare acquires a dimension none of his contemporaries ever succeeded in giving him. To his enemies, Macbeth may well be 'that dead butcher'; but not to us. Great as his crimes may have been, the author has managed to get us interested in his way of thinking and feeling. Shakespeare's stroke of genius here was to endow this man with imagination and lend him all the resources of his language, his verbal and musical mastery. So that, at the end, the 'dead butcher' has become a kind of poet whose death brings us neither joy nor relief, as he was so strikingly able to express the anguish, the fears or the insane hopes which are the lot of the murderer trying to escape retribution. Shakespeare was no lawyer, his business was not to try and save a murderer from the gallows; but his understanding of the man, of the worthy and faithful soldier turned regicide and tyrant, his poetic rendering of such understanding, have earned him from the pen of one of our eminent colleagues the magnificent title of 'poet for the defence'. To deserve such a title is to be highly civilized.

Hamlet is probably the most popular and the best known of Shakespeare's plays in France. One might wonder why. The melancholy prince had a special appeal to the romantics, and most people in this country still see him as the contemporaries of Delacroix did one hundred years ago. Our mission of late years has been to try and rid his character of all the romantic mists and hazes, and get, if not a vision of the *real* Hamlet (for each of us has his own Hamlet), at least a plausible image of the character as conceived by the Elizabethans. To destroy the conventional, sickly image of Hamlet in the minds of an audience is indeed a stimulating task. It may be a very good illustration of the way some of Shakespeare's characters have of becoming greater under the storm as they resist it. Their attitude in the midst of their misfortunes, their behaviour under adverse circumstances, the strange faculty they have to increase in stature and to face their tormentors as darkness closes in all around them, all motivate the kind of admiration we feel for them, and enable us to look up to them, not because they are better men than we are, not because they are right where we are wrong, but because they are men, very much like ourselves; the playwright who chose to describe them, to show us their feelings in action, did not mean to offer them as examples, as patterns of behaviour; but merely to tell us: 'Hear and see: this is a man—and what a piece of work it is! See how imperfect, how weak, how small he is—just like you. But see, also, that this thing who loves and suffers, and thinks, and dies, has in him something which is of a divine nature, which nobody has the power to destroy—his human quality, his soul, if you like, which you also share with him.' And the playwright might well ask his spectator the question: 'Do you believe that, given the circumstances, you would or could behave otherwise, and are you not proud of all that greatness, that valour, that beauty you have in common with Hamlet, with Othello, with Lear?' In such a way, Shakespeare has a great deal to teach us, even when he deals with a character he cannot be expected highly to respect. Richard III he turns into a fascinating creature whom we must fear and hate, but whose intellect and grim humour together with his physical courage extort from us a kind of grudging admiration; and after the horrors we have lived through for the past thirty years, Shylock's question 'Hath not a Jew eyes?' and all it implies strikes a human note which has a special ringing in our tormented, ghost-ridden country.

I do not want to raise political issues; it is however impossible not to mention here the case of *Coriolanus*, that most admirable tragedy whose hatred of mob-democracy has always had a special appeal to the partisans of authoritarian regimes. As one will perhaps remember, a certain performance of that tragedy in February 1934 by the Comédie Française was used as a signal for the abortive fascist coup, the consequences of which were to be so serious for the ensuing years.

It thus becomes clear that Shakespeare has become part and parcel of our culture. It is unfortunate that, when we act him in translation, most of the poetry has to be lost, just like the puns often referred to under the heading: 'Intraduisible en français.' This is a kind of heartache which those of us who have worked for the theatre and for Shakespeare know only too well. All we can do is to preserve the spirit; and, when reading the press-cuttings the day after a performance, we sometimes think that we have succeeded in serving our poet faithfully. For he is now our poet. We have at last learnt that he is not to be tampered with, that he must not be forcibly frenchified. We may see in him things and thoughts that might not strike his country-men as important; or, on the other hand, plays such as *Antony and Cleopatra* which might have been deemed to have a special appeal for the French may fail to move a Parisian audience. Let us not be indignant: what is really important and should raise our admiration, in the words of Jean Jacquot, is that we should feel him closer to our experience and that, even as we see the very foundations of our civilization shattered, we should turn to *Richard III*, to *Hamlet*, to *Lear* for situations similar to ours, for an answer to those problems that torment us.[5]

For England's Shakespeare is now also France's Shakespeare. We have travelled a long way since the days of M. de Voltaire.

NOTES

1. Valued 'Un sol' in 1684!

2. 'Ce poète anglois a l'imagination assez belle, il pense naturellement, il s'exprime avec finesse, mais ses belles qualités sont obscurcies par les ordures qu'il mêle a ses comédies.'

3. 'Je n'entends point l'Anglois, & j'ai osé faire paroître Hamlet sur le Scène Françoise.' Abbé Ducis, 1769.

4. The 'Comédie de L'Ouest' is also giving *Henry V*, the 'Grenier de Toulouse', *Twelfth Night*. Shakespeare's contemporaries are represented in this list by Marlowe's *Edward II* (Roger Planchon, Lyons) and Jonson's *Alchemist* (Théâtre de Bourgogne).

5. 'Ce qui est beau et grave, c'est que nous le sentions plus proche de notre expérience, et qu'alors que nous voyons ébranlés les fondements de notre civilisation nous nous tournions vers *Richard III*, vers *Hamlet* vers *Lear* pour y chercher l'équivalent de situations qui sont les nôtres, une réponse aux questions qui nous tourmentent.' Jean Jacquot, in *Mises en scène de Shakespeare et des Elisabéthains en France d'Antoine à nos jours* (Paris, 1960).

SHAKESPEARE AND THE MODERN WORLD

BY

WOLFGANG CLEMEN

Today it would be a commonplace to say that the greatest poets may be read and understood anew by each age and each generation, that new aspects of their work are continually being discovered and that they appeal to each generation in a new and different manner. This statement, however, provokes the question whether the understanding and interpretation of Shakespeare in each new generation is rather a reflection of the preoccupations and contemporary problems of that generation or whether it represents a genuine advance of scholarly insight—a better, because fuller and more objective comprehension. The truth may perhaps lie between these two alternatives: for our present knowledge and appreciation of Shakespeare, besides incorporating some of our own concerns and predilections, is also cumulative; much of what was discovered in Shakespeare during the eighteenth century, the Romantic period and the later nineteenth century has been taken over by present-day criticism and has been included in and integrated into our reading of his plays. Thus an analysis of Shakespeare's impact on the modern world would have to point out the connection existing between new and characteristic responses on the part of a modern audience to Shakespeare's plays and the chief trend of modern Shakespeare criticism, both seen in relation to the typical problems and preoccupations of our own generation.

There appear to be three main questions at issue when we follow up this inquiry. The first is to discover how far the aspects of Shakespeare, which contemporary critics have singled out for particular attention, have been dictated to them by the kind of problems which they find themselves faced with in the modern world. Would they have noted or emphasized these aspects unless they had been already powerfully present in their minds? The second question concerns the new critical methods or approaches applied to Shakespeare. How far may they be understood as a result of our changed sensibility, reflecting a new stage of consciousness and awareness? Thirdly, we would have to ask ourselves which elements in the plays may today be seen in an altogether different light. Often these three questions will be interrelated.

A good example is the understanding of character in Shakespearian drama. Even if we grant that a character in a play is by no means the same as a living person and must not therefore be subjected to the procedures of psychology, the interpretation of dramatic characters is nevertheless bound to depend, to a large extent, on the views or theories which are held by each generation about the nature of human character. The nineteenth century aimed at a clear-cut picture of character which was thought to consist of certain unmistakable qualities, qualities which would reveal themselves in a man's actions and would change little during his life. This rationalized concept of a fixed character composed of definable qualities, from which a man's actions could be logically derived, appears to underly the approach to Shakespeare's characters in the nineteenth century and later, though allowance must be made for the oversimplified formula used here to indicate a more complicated issue. But a perusal of nineteenth-century Shakespeare criticism discloses that the critic's business was often to establish a consistent picture of the hero's qualities. The critics appear to have been employed in supplying the characters with coherent motives for all their actions, rationalizing their conduct and supplying any logical links which seemed to them to be missing from the structure of the plays. They tried to bridge the gap between what appeared to be the psychological core of the character and his behaviour. This rationalizing and psychologizing analysis of Shakespeare's characters necessarily led to the discovery of inconsistencies in his portrayals of character and called forth complaints about insufficient motivation. Any discrepancy between the hero's character and his deeds was detected and stamped as 'unpsychological'. And if the critics, by their standards, were unable to find sufficient motivation for a character's actions, they were apt to blame the primitive stage conventions which Shakespeare was using. What, however, the critics often did not take into account was the fact that these so-called 'inconsistencies' and incompatibilities in Shakespeare's portrayals of character entirely escape the unbiased playgoer in the theatre and are noticed only through the spectacles of scholars who scrutinize the play line by line. In the two decades after Bradley's *Shakespearean Tragedy* it was more and more recognized that the criteria of psychology and of realism could not be applied to Shakespeare's characters and that characters in a play moved in a sphere different from that of reality. But this did not stop the search for motivation and the effort at character-analysis went on. Certain features in Shakespeare's characters were still therefore either misunderstood or not grasped at all.

However, the situation has changed greatly within the last thirty years, for in our own days much more complex ideas of human character have been developed. These make it possible for us to accept those very features in Shakespeare's characters which were formerly either misunderstood or rejected. Moreover, certain traits of Shakespeare's characters and problems connected with them which thus have become intelligible can appeal to us today more strongly because they are the very problems which modern experience has brought home to us. We now believe that there is no such thing as a fixed and thoroughly consistent character, and we also know that man is full of surprises and contradictions, full of paradox and unpredictableness, inscrutable and elusive. Consequently, we not only sympathize with Shakespeare's presentation of these very features but we feel that we are watching a phenomenon which we recognize around us daily. And we invariably discover even in ourselves such potentialities.

A few of those character problems may be tentatively mentioned here which in this sense appeal to us as being akin to our modern consciousness of man. Recent critics have observed that many of Shakespeare's main characters display a clash of opposites and reveal contrarieties. They do this not only in the moral sense that 'the web of our life is of a mingled yarn, good and ill together' (*All's Well*, IV, iii, 81–2), but also in the more complex sense of contradictory attitudes, qualities and states of mind. It also looks as if the situation of frustration, of disillusionment, and of inner dilemma, so often occurring in Shakespeare's plays, is not only more acutely noted and analysed by present-day critics, but also meets with a more intense response on the part of modern readers and audiences. We are strongly impressed by the fact that Shakespeare's characters look at themselves as at something strange and unknown, wondering what they themselves actually are, searching for causes or motives and not finding any, or failing to find the right ones—a situation well known from Hamlet, Macbeth and Angelo. We are willing to accept these persons as they are, we are willing to accept the mystery, the uncertainty of human character; and we are accordingly ready to give up the vain effort to supply logical causes or missing links in the chain. The changed attitude in the criticism of Hamlet's character is a case in point: 'Shakespeare's triumph is to make the hero fail to understand himself. Hamlet gives us reasons enough for delay, causes none; for the cause remains unknown to him, and to us.' Thus we read in Lawlor's recent book *The Tragic Sense in Shakespeare*.[1] A similar warning is expressed by L. C. Knights: 'Hamlet's state of mind, the Hamlet consciousness, is revealed not only at the level of formulable motive, but in its obscure depths; and it is revealed through the poetry.'[2]

Thus the modern reader and student is ready to elicit the meaning of a character and of a whole play not from explicitly formulated utterances and passages only; he seeks to apprehend it also through other media which need not be enumerated here. This readiness, towards which we have been trained by modern poetry and modern criticism, has considerably helped us to get closer to the truth. And it is ultimately not only an 'advance of scholarship', or more refined and complex methods of interpretation, but the changed consciousness of modern man which has produced this change in critical attitude. There also appears to be more readiness to see the interrelation, indeed the fusion, of thinking and feeling, of abstract thought and emotion in Shakespeare's characters. We no longer so easily separate reflection from emotion, for we know that this division of man's faculties into reasoning, abstracting, concluding, feeling, perceiving, and so on is artificial. Coleridge's warning 'to keep alive the heart in the head'[3] has been fully accepted by our own generation, even without reference to the findings of modern psycho-analysis.

The situation is similar with regard to the modern reader's attitude towards Shakespeare's dramatic method of presenting fundamental problems, of raising and answering questions in his plays. Not infrequently critics of the nineteenth century tried to find out what Shakespeare himself may have thought about the theme or the problem which he appears to make the central issue of a particular play. The effort has been made to define Shakespeare's 'Weltanschauung' and to deduce what we may call Shakespeare's 'beliefs and attitudes' from certain passages in his plays. The fallacy of such an undertaking was discovered in due course; for the passages quoted to illustrate Shakespeare's beliefs proved—when looked at more closely and within their context—to be utterances made by certain dramatic characters at certain moments in the course of the action. Often enough these utterances were prompted by private intentions of these characters and could therefore not be taken as revealing their inner convictions. Thus the endeavour to get at the core of Shakespeare's beliefs, to establish his scale of 'values', has again and again eluded critics and scholars. This desire to discover Shakespeare's own 'philosophy of life' will probably never die out, but there appears to be, in our present world, more readiness to accept the impenetrability of Shakespeare's own 'Weltanschauung'. In fact we even see a mark of greatness in the dramatist's ability to hide himself behind the multifarious world of his characters and to give shape and dramatic reality to their views and principles rather than to his own unknown convictions. Shakespeare's capacity to enter the minds of his characters, to identify himself wholly with their attitudes and opinions and to present even a villain's set of beliefs with extraordinary objectivity and impartiality has long been recognized as one of his greatest achievements. But only in our century has it been fully realized that this 'negative capability' precludes to some extent the dramatic presentation of a consistent and definable 'philosophy of life' which could with some assurance be described as Shakespeare's own. This is not to say that there are not, within the total volume of Shakespeare's plays, recurrent features, ideas and principles which strike us as unmistakably Shakespearian and which may—with due reserve and caution—serve as pointers and clues to what we may call Shakespeare's world picture. But the ultimate mystery of what Shakespeare himself may have believed will remain and is indeed more readily admitted by the modern reader than by the one of the nineteenth century. We have come to realize that this mystery is intimately bound up with Shakespeare's growing impact on our present-day generation.

Almost the same holds true if we consider, not Shakespeare's 'Weltanschauung' in general, but the 'Weltanschauung' of a single play. Earlier critics were more optimistic and self-assured in defining not only the problem put by a play, but also the answer given to it, as it was expressed by the whole action and by scattered pronouncements of the leading characters. It has indeed been one of the major concerns of Shakespeare criticism to elucidate and analyse the main themes, issues and problems of the individual plays, especially the tragedies. But the more work that has been done in this field, the clearer it becomes that even this limited critical endeavour to find out the 'Weltanschauung' of a single play has its fallacies.

A case in point is *King Lear*. Here, again and again, the problem of the justice of the gods is put before us and we are led to inquire into the 'ultimate power' that moves this world and directs the actions of men. These questions emerge not only from the total effect of the play and from the course of the action; the characters themselves ponder over it. However, the answer they give to this fundamental question and the references they make to it contradict each other to a considerable degree.[4] It appears then that these statements are conditioned by the temperament of the individual character, by the moment at which he speaks and by the hidden intention he may have in mind. Again, it would be misleading to take any one of these single passages as revealing the tragedy's underlying idea. But the effect of these pronouncements on the audience is nevertheless great, for they stir up the same questions in the spectator's or reader's mind: they produce that mood of inner restlessness, of questioning perturbation which is, on the part of the audience, a major factor of the whole play's profound impression. Generations of theatregoers may have felt this in the eighteenth and nineteenth centuries, too. But critics, in search of a definable answer to the problems posed by the play, were unwilling to recognize this peculiar effect as belonging to Shakespeare's greatness as a dramatist. It appears, however, that this art of Shakespeare's of raising questions but not answering them, of making us think intensely about a problem of which the solution may elude us or be grasped only with difficulty, finds a better response in the modern reader and theatregoer and is more readily accepted and in fact admired than in the nineteenth century. Shakespeare's way of leaving it to the audience to draw its conclusions and to form its views both presupposes and demands a more active co-operation on the part of his readers and spectators. It strikes us as being in some measure akin to what modern poetry or modern art do with their readers or spectators. The open question, the unsolved problem, the unanswered issue and the never wholly disclosed and unveiled idea are powerful incentives and elements in the wide realm of modern art.

King Lear yields another example of Shakespeare's dramatic presentation of fundamental issues which may be said to appeal strongly to a modern audience, for in *Lear* Shakespeare does not take over any of the traditional moral or religious tenets which could serve, either positively or negatively, as underlying principles for the action and for what the characters say. On the contrary, he calls all these habitual values in question; during the great scenes on the heath we feel that the foundations of our human existence are shattered and that the very essence of man's nature is weighed and exposed. Nevertheless, the play moves forward towards positives which dimly emerge on the horizon when we come to the fourth and fifth acts. But these positives, taken by L. C. Knights as 'fundamentally Christian values', are reached, as Knights aptly says, 'by an act of profound individual exploration: the play does not take them for granted; it takes nothing for granted but Nature and natural energies and passions'.5 Our own generation will share the doubts raised by *King Lear* about traditional values, and the 'act of profound individual exploration' will appeal to this generation as a more convincing, and better, way of reaching a new assurance or of acquiring belief. And even the immense suffering and the painful breakdown of past creeds and illusions which in *Lear* are necessarily connected with this ultimate goal may, for a modern audience, be more meaningful than for past generations. We are apt to acknowledge the validity of only those values which, in the crucible of hard and painful experience and of utter exposure, have gone through the test that can show what is to survive and what is to perish.

The problems of life, the aspects of man's nature and the vicissitudes to which he is subject in the world as presented in Shakespeare's plays are numerous and cover a very wide field of human experience. Most of these aspects are moreover the eternal themes of life, which in each generation will evoke response. But it looks as if, even with these everlasting themes, some appeal to our present generation more strongly than to the nineteenth century. Thus the attention recently bestowed by critics on the theme of appearance and reality in Shakespeare's plays appears to reflect our own growing awareness of this discrepancy in our modern world. This is not to claim that our generation has been the first to discover that man deceives himself and is constantly deceived, that our world consists of illusions and fallacies and that we all of us wear a mask. But modern psychology and the ruthless searching eye of modern novelists may have sharpened our perception of the manifold and hidden contrasts between outward behaviour and inner intention, between the spoken word and the actual motive. And although our civilization is poisoned by false slogans and pretensions, having developed a whole system of deception and misleading presentation of 'appearances' instead of 'realities', those who care for art and literature today and belong to our 'sceptical generation', may be better trained to look 'below the surface', to seek for the naked and undisguised truth, to shun romantic illusion and find out reality. The gullibility of man, the extreme difficulty of recognizing and seeing things as they actually are, the readiness of the individual as well as of mankind to be deceived by appearances or even to be satisfied by them, all this constitutes one of the great problems for everyone who tries to find his way 'among the thorns and dangers of this world'. Thus Shakespeare's multifarious presentation of this clash between appearance and reality, leading up to many dramatic situations and subtle effects, but underlying, too, his shaping of characters and his manipulation of plot and story, will be followed up and understood with an intense sympathy by an intelligent modern audience.

In this connection the modern concern for irony and ambiguity in Shakespeare's plays should also be noted. For these effects, too, presuppose the existence of an obvious or 'outward' meaning contrasted with an inner hidden meaning, or an opposition between conscious and unconscious utterance. Ambiguity and irony are closely related to the universal and comprehensive theme of appearance and reality and should therefore be studied with a view to this wider frame of reference. But the detection of ironies and ambiguities in Shakespeare's dramas may also offer an example of how Shakespeare's 'modernity' in this respect is likely to be over-rated. For although the modern reader's faculty for understanding a text 'on several levels' and his ability to look at words and phrases with a sharpened eye for their multiple meaning has undoubtedly led to the discovery of many subtle effects which so far had been hidden, helping us for example to understand many of Shakespeare's puns, the search for irony and ambiguity in Shakespeare's texts seems frequently to have been overdone. And it may well be that after two or three generations this preoccupation of modern critics with irony and ambiguity in Shakespeare's language, justified though it be when applied to contemporary poetry, will be taken as an exaggeration and an idiosyncrasy of our own generation.

On the other hand, the emphasis on irony and ambiguity is related to the new appreciation of the poetic texture of Shakespeare's plays, including his imagery. The renewal of poetic drama in our time by T. S. Eliot, Christopher Fry and the dramatists of the 'Irish Revival' was accompanied and stimulated by the re-discovery of the dramatic impact of the poetry in Elizabethan plays, in fact by a recognition that poetic drama possesses *dramatic* effects which may reach farther and exert a more profound influence than the language and devices used by prose drama. The false notions about the superiority of prose drama over verse drama (as being less 'artificial', more 'natural' and therefore more 'acceptable') were re-examined and eventually replaced by a new evaluation of poetic drama and consequently by a new understanding of its specific elements. The recognition that 'The human soul, in intense emotion, strives to express itself in verse' and that 'if we want to get at the permanent and universal we tend to express ourselves in verse' (T. S. Eliot), strange and revolutionary though it may have sounded in 1928, has meanwhile become an inherent factor in the surprising and intense response of modern audiences to the poetry in Shakespeare's plays. The more aesthetic appreciation of this poetry as shown by the Romantic age has in our times been superseded by a new feeling for the dramatic qualities, the unsurpassed 'modern' expressiveness and force of Shakespeare's poetic language and his imagery. Thus Shakespeare's impact on the modern world includes among other elements this new spell exerted by the poetry and imagery in his plays on even an average audience. The ascendancy of poetic drama in our age has unsealed a new organ in the modern reader and theatregoer for perceiving these essential elements of Shakespearian drama; it has moreover opened up a new field of reciprocal influences and encounters between modern and Elizabethan drama and theatrical practice.

NOTES

1. John Lawlor, *The Tragic Sense in Shakespeare* (1960), p. 67.
2. L. C. Knights, *An Approach to Hamlet* (1960), p. 50.
3. Quoted by Dorothy Emmet in her paper *Coleridge—on the Growth of the Mind* (1952): see Knights *op. cit.* p. 69.
4. This was first pointed out by A. C. Bradley in *Shakespearean Tragedy* (1905 ed.), p. 271.
5. L. C. Knights, *Some Shakespearean Themes* (1959), p. 91.

MODERN 'THEATRICAL' TRANSLATIONS
OF SHAKESPEARE

BY

RUDOLF STAMM

Many historians of the theatre and drama have been attracted by the study of stage versions because they certainly are the most important relics of the performances of the past. They contain thousands of details characteristic of the taste of the artists who used them and of the audiences that enjoyed them. With the necessary tact and caution they can be interpreted as first-rate period pieces from which inferences concerning general tendencies can be drawn.

Studies of this kind have left the present writer with one very strong impression: Shakespeare's plays cannot only be considered as theatrical material to be given a new shape and stage reality by every succeeding generation. Nor are they merely a passive measuring rod by which we can recognize the stature of an age; they are mute, but strict, judges pronouncing sentence on the imaginative grasp and the sensibility of every generation of artists and spectators. Like the stage versions, the translations accepted by a considerable number of theatres can be viewed as period pieces. The German translation by Schlegel and Tieck is a supreme example of one; it is a period piece, however, which has long outlived its fashion and its age. It continues the most frequently acted version in Germany, Austria, and Switzerland in spite of its shortcomings, discussed by many a critic, only recently by Margaret Atkinson.[1] Among them we may recall the facts that these versions are based upon the limited scholarship of the eighteenth century, that they contain obsolete and old-fashioned expressions and, finally, that they are a perfect expression of the poetic mode of the Goethe-Zeit. This last-mentioned feature may be a shortcoming in the eyes of the actors trying to make themselves understood in a modern theatre, but it is at the same time a proof of the authenticity of this great work. With certain revisions it continues to be acted because it contains so many of the essential Shakespearian ingredients, more of them, it seems, than any other German version on record.[2]

Fortunately, the prestige and authority of Schlegel and Tieck have not been of the kind to deter contemporary writers from their attempts to create twentieth-century versions of the plays. From among those who have tried their hands we mention Richard Flatter, Friedrich Gundolf, Walter Josten, Hans Rothe, Rudolf Schaller, Rudolf Alexander Schröder, Hedwig Schwarz and Theodor von Zeyneck. Most of them have translated selected plays only, but Hans Rothe and Richard Flatter have both of them provided an almost complete series, and their versions have seen a considerable number of productions. Besides, they have one important trait in common. In their attempts to supersede the Schlegel-Tieck text they claim to satisfy the demands of the modern theatre. This is why it is important to examine the work of these two men, concentrating upon what they have actually done as translators rather than upon their professions.

We need therefore only glance at the theories by which Hans Rothe tries to justify the extraordinary liberties he takes with the received texts, liberties not less daring, but less naïve, than those of the well-known seventeenth- and eighteenth-century improvers of Shakespeare.[3]

When Rothe decided, in the years after the First World War, to make the translation of Shake-speare the main business of his life, he fell under the spell of such textual disintegrators as Eduard Sievers, J. M. Robertson and the young John Dover Wilson. Although not a scholar himself, he made a highly subjective and selective use of their views, and decided, with great assurance, many a ticklish question of textual criticism for himself. Today the greater part of the theories on which his texts are based have become obsolete—a fact which seems to trouble some of his readers more than Rothe himself. For him, the importance of the scholarly disintegrators had not really lain in their specific theories. Their great gift to him had been the liberation from the authority of the texts, an all-pervasive conviction that practically all of the quartos contained work by several hands and that the Folio preserved particularly unreliable texts. From this resulted certain quasi-mystical insights: the certainty, for example, that Shakespeare's works were a group achievement rather than an individual one, that an anonymous 'theaterbedingte Urkraft' was their real well-spring, and that the imperfections of the texts, far from being caused by deplorable accidents, were necessary aspects of the characteristically Shakespearian 'open form', which invites the theatres of all succeeding ages to rewrite the plays in perfect freedom so as to make them an expression of their own spirit and a joy for their own particular taste. These assumptions may seem dangerously nebulous special pleading to most of us, but this should not unduly prejudice us against Rothe's practical work: he might, after all, be a good translator with a bad theory.

His approach varies considerably from play to play. Some of the dramas he attempts to meet in the true spirit of translation. In his early *Macbeth*, for instance, he wrestles with the text honestly and without evasion, achieving good results in some passages, suffering his characteristic defeats in others. Later, when he tries to cope with *King Lear* in the same spirit, he cannot always resist the temptation of following his intuitive insight rather than the plain meaning of the original. When he comes to Lear's exclamation:

> But, for true need,
> You Heavens, give me that patience, patience I need!

he decides that Lear's true need is not patience, but lucidity. He therefore makes him say:

> Doch eins brauch ich —
> Klarheit, gebt sie mir Götter, ich brauche Klarheit![4]

This alteration betrays an attitude which impairs our trust in Rothe even where he seems to act the part of a true translator. It is an attitude he adopts quite openly when he is dealing with the plays he considers, rightly or wrongly, as less Shakespearian than the great tragedies. Thus his *Komödie der Irrungen* is an adaptation for lovers of knock-about farce and broad fun. Here his method demands extensive cuts as well as the introduction of new characters and scenes of his own making.[5] Although these interpolations seem to fall very far below the Shakespearian level, there is one thing to be said in favour of this *Komödie der Irrungen* and of a number of similar violent adaptations: the spectator is, at least, told on the playbill that he is going to see an adaptation and not a translation of the original. The question may be asked, of course, whether it is desirable at all that a modern producer—instead of starting from the most authentic text available and devising his acting version, if he finds it necessary to make one, on his own responsibility and at his own risk—should permit an adapter-translator to interfere in this way under the pretence of making things easy for him.

We come to the most objectionable part of Rothe's work when we turn to those of his versions which are declared to be translations, although, in reality, they are adaptations, too. His *Julius Caesar* is an instance of this. It is again characterized by cuts, transpositions, elimination of minor characters and additions of the adapter's own devising. They are less frequent than in the avowed adaptations, but their effect is, for this very reason, more insidious. The proportions of the play as a whole as well as its most important characters become seriously distorted. The added lines are, moreover, often shockingly platitudinous, or even vulgar.[6] The far more numerous lines translated from the original are by no means all of them bad, but many of them show the imprint of a hand alarmingly uncertain in matters of style and taste. For the sake of theatrical expediency many a subtly complicated rhetorical structure is broken up. When Rothe tries to follow Shakespeare to the heights of his passionate metaphorical language he often fumbles and stumbles, nor is he capable of doing justice to his author when Shakespeare is quite simple and direct.

Thus we cannot find that Rothe's widely and cleverly advertised attempt to replace the so-called literary and poetical text of the Romantics by a truly theatrical Shakespeare, speaking the language of our century, has been even moderately successful.

The late Richard Flatter's professed aims did not differ too much from Rothe's.[7] He, too, found Schlegel-Tieck too literary in their approach and too poetical in a fashion tending to distort certain Elizabethan characteristics. He was also fascinated by the idea of doing justice to all the theatrical values in the originals, especially by making the most of the numerous hints he discovered in the line arrangement and the punctuation of the First Folio. The trust he placed in the typographical details of this book was a little excessive, but far less so than Rothe's radical distrust. Their attitude to the First Folio is not the only difference between the two men. In every respect Flatter's methods were more scrupulous and disciplined. For one thing he knew how to distinguish between translating and adapting, and, for another, his acquaintance with modern Shakespearian scholarship was sufficiently close to permit his own interesting contributions to it. When he translated, he tried to find the best German equivalent to the best English text modern criticism could offer him.

His version is solidly grounded on the achievement of his predecessors. Where Schlegel and Tieck have coined a perfect phrase or line, Flatter adopts it. Where they have erred, he corrects them carefully, not without overshooting his mark occasionally. Who is not astonished to find the *Hamlet*-line (III, iii, 79), appearing in the first quarto as

> this is a benefit,
> And not reuenge:

and in the second quarto as

> Why, this is base and silly, not reuendge,

and in the Folio as

> Oh this is hyre and Sallery, not Reuenge,

translated as 'Meuchelmord wär' das, Hinrichtung — nicht Rache!'?[8] Where the diction of the Romantic translators appears difficult for the modern actor and spectator, Flatter does his best to remove obstacles. Obsolete and uncommon expressions are replaced by current ones, involved constructions analysed and simplified, obscurities paraphrased. This method is not without its dangers. It sacrifices the fine stylistic unity of the old translation, and, vacillating between different kinds of diction, leads to patchwork. The desire to produce an easy and fluent text seduces Flatter into removing legitimate obscurities, necessary ambiguities, syntactical and metaphorical complexities. This interpreting kind of translation does little harm to passages of prose and easy colloquial verse, but it turns the great passionate speeches into something comparatively conventional and tame. These drawbacks are partly compensated by Flatter's expertness in reproducing the metrical and rhythmical peculiarities of the original. In this important field he frequently surpasses the best of his predecessors. The author of *Shakespeare's Producing Hand* knows how to preserve the full effects of broken lines and of missing or extra syllables. Sometimes he even tends to exaggerate the dynamic qualities of a speech, so that it becomes more broken and violent than in the original. And he also overplays his hand occasionally when he reacts against the poetic diction of the Romantics. Wishing to avoid expressions which he considers too reticent and polite, he, too, though to a lesser degree than Rothe, becomes a prey to the opposite fault of crudeness and vulgarity.

This is only a sketchy survey, but it may help us to understand why the detailed and careful study of Flatter's and his most important competitors' work, recently published by Walter Jost, is entitled: 'Stilkrise der deutschen Shakespeare-Uebersetzung.'[9] The attempt to create a modern Shakespeare for the German-speaking theatres has not resulted in anything as balanced and adequate as the Schlegel-Tieck version. The main reason for this is that no poet-translator of sufficient power has yet attempted the task. It is true that Rudolf Alexander Schröder has given and is giving us a number of masterful translations, but his idiom, rich in rare and archaic forms and words, makes use of the language of several centuries. Rothe and Flatter are no poets of importance. Flatter has published some original verse and has produced some free poetic paraphrases of Shakespeare's songs; but, ironically and significantly, the poetic style of this critic of Schlegel and Tieck definitely belongs to the Romantic tradition. This is his version of the second stanza of Ariel's song in the first act of *The Tempest* (I, ii, 399 ff.):

> Dein Vater, der liegt auf dem Meeresgrund,
> So friedlich als ob er schliefe;
> Die spielenden Wogen wiegen den Fund,
> Verwandeln ihn sacht in der Tiefe.
> Nichts ist verloren, nichts wird vergehn,
> Mag alles auch zerfallen:
> Aus den Augen werden Perlen entstehn,
> Aus den Knochen werden Korallen.
> Und die Meerfraun läuten die Glocken dazu,
> Sie läuten, läuten, läuten zur Ruh':
> Ding — dong, ding-dong-dong —
> Ding — dong — dong —[10]

A competent, though verbose and highly interpretative exercise in the mode of a past period.

Rothe has fewer words here. They are also interpretative, half prose, half verse—a summary of the song without any consistent style:

> Fünf Faden tief liegt dein Urahn
> im Meer.
> Zu Korallen ward sein Gebein,
> Perlen sind in der Höhlung seiner Augen gewachsen,
> denn nichts geht verloren.
> Das unablässig schaffende Meer
> verwandelt
> veredelt
> alle Dinge
> und sie werden kostbar und selten.[11]

For a beautiful and adequate new version of these lines we must turn to the poet-translator R. A. Schröder:

> Fünf Faden tief dein Vater liegt,
> Von Korallen sein Gebein,
> Perlen in sein Aug gefügt,
> Darf nichts an ihm vergänglich sein,
> Wandelt sich am Meeresgrund
> In ein Kleinod rar und bunt.
> Das Stundenglöcklein: bim, bam, baum
> Läuten ihm die Wasserfraun.[12]

By way of conclusion I wish to point to a contribution we scholars can make in order to produce an atmosphere favourable for the work of a new great translator. We can help to eradicate the nefarious notion that there was and is a difference between Shakespeare the playwright and Shakespeare the poet and that, consequently, there is a theatrical and a literary approach to his works. According to this notion a translator can produce either a theatrical or a poetical version of the plays. It has done much harm to Rothe's and to Flatter's work—even when it serves merely as an excuse for certain weaknesses inherent in their minds as well as in those of their admirers. We should insist that anybody proposing to create either a theatrical or a poetical version of Shakespeare is certain to shirk one half of a good translator's task. For the scholar, the translator, and the producer there is only one undivided approach to the poet-playwright, whose greatness can be adumbrated by saying, with Otto Ludwig, that, for him, theatrical values were poetical and poetical values theatrical.

NOTES

1. *August Wilhelm Schlegel as a Translator of Shakespeare. A Comparison of Three Plays with the Original* (Basil Blackwell, Oxford, 1958).

2. A cheap paperback edition of some of the most important plays with the original text and the Schlegel-Tieck translation on opposite pages, both revised by L. L. Schücking, is being published by the Rowohlt Verlag. Contributors are Walter Schirmer, Wolfgang Clemen, and Ernest Th. Sehrt. It is a welcome and necessary enterprise,

and bids fair to spread among the German-speaking actors, producers and theatregoers the knowledge of the results of modern textual and aesthetic criticism.

3. Until recently the materials for the study of Rothe's theory were the introductions to his translations (of which there exists a collected edition, published by the Holle Verlag (Baden-Baden und Genf) under the extraordinary misnomer *Der elisabethanische Shakespeare*) and a booklet, entitled *Der Kampf um Shakespeare*, published in 1936 and, in a revised form, in 1956. In 1961 *Shakespeare als Provokation* (Albert Langen–Georg Müller, München) was added to the list. This bulky volume of some 500 pages has a certain journalistic charm, to which numerous busy book-reviewers, incapable of detecting its serious faults, have responded with immediate loud praise in German and Swiss newspapers. Their critical failure is hardly surprising since it is extremely difficult for the non-specialist, and unrewarding for the specialist, to disentangle knowledge, prejudice, and invective in this cleverly written apologia of Rothe's work as a translator. Some of the more obvious tricks played on the reader are the presentation of an outmoded textual theory as modern, the exploitation of that well-known gulf between the stage and the study, between the theatrical and the literary interpretation of Shakespeare which certainly existed in former periods and may still linger in some places, the wilful invention of a similar gulf between the Anglo-American and the German Shakespearian scholarship, and the suggestion that whoever dares criticize Rothe's versions must be inspired by evil intentions against the person of the translator and, which is supposed to be one and the same thing, against Shakespeare himself.

4. *Der elisabethanische Shakespeare, Konig Lear, Troilus und Cressida, Der Kaufmann von Venedig* (1955), p. 74.

5. In order to illustrate the style in which Rothe attempts to emulate Shakespeare we quote the words in which his Luciana expresses her happiness at the end of the play:

> Ich bin selig Schwester! wie schön ist es zu irren,
> weil jeder Irrtum eine Tugend zeigt:
> er ist geschaffen Nöte zu entwirren,
> bis aus dem Falschen kühn das Wahre steigt!
> Jede von uns hat einen Antipholus:
> nur durch Verwirrung dringt man zum Genuss!

(*Shakespeare in neuer Uebersetzung. Jugendwerke* (Leipzig, 1935), p. 449.)

6. We quote the scene leading up to the suicide of Rothe's Brutus:

> *Brutus.* Es ist vorbei gebraust, da hasten sie
> und wollen siegen; ich, Lucius, will nicht siegen.
> Siegen will Marc Anton, ein Mensch voll Fehler—
> wer ihn erschlägt hat eine einzige Häufung
> von Fehlern überrannt. Fehler, was sind sie?
> Alles worauf ich stolz bin, was mein Leben
> vor mir erhöht, was einst die Nachwelt rühmt:
> für Marc Anton sind es nur meine Fehler,
> vielleicht auch für die Nachwelt. Ich will nicht siegen.
> Den grossen Caesar habe ich gehindert
> dass er siegt, und er, mein Freund und mein Gewissen,
> heute hindert er mich. In seiner Grösse
> gönnt er dass ich ihm gleich bin. Ich bin es nicht.
> Du folgst mir, Lucius?
> *Lucius.* Wohin?
> *Brutus.* Ich meine, du verstehst mich?
> *Lucius.* Nein,
> doch wirst du heute Marc Anton besiegen.
> *Brutus.* Es ist mir lieb dass du mich missverstehst
> in dieser letzten Stunde, denn nur einer
> versteht mich —

Lucius. Caesar, Herr?

Brutus. Mein Junge,
ich danke dir für deine letzte Antwort.

Lucius. Meine letzte — ?

Brutus. Still. Weil ich nie wieder frage,
auch dich nicht frage. Mir ist Caesars Geist
neulich erschienen, du schliefst in meinem Zelt,
seitdem hat er sich nicht von mir getrennt.
Doch können wir nicht hoffen guter Lucius,
dass Caesar selbst den Dolch gegen mich hebt,
wie ich es einst vermochte gegen ihn,
denn das ist keiner wert der einen Caesar
getötet hat. So wenig bin ich wert,
obwohl ich so viel Grösse mitbekam.
Das ist der Dolch den ich nach Caesar stiess —
nicht halb so gern, wie ich den Dolch jetzt brauche —
leb wohl, er bleibt bei mir, und ich bei ihm.

                    (*er tötet sich*)

(*Der elisabethanische Shakespeare, Julius Caesar, Zähmung der Widerspenstigen, König Heinrich der Vierte* (1956), pp. 110 ff.)

7. His theory of translation is contained in the comments accompanying the plays in his *Shakespeare. Neu übersetzt* (Walter Krieg Verlag, Wien—Bad Bocklet—Zürich, 1952–5), 6 vols., and in the pamphlet *Das Schauspielerische in der Diktion Shakespeares* (Walter Krieg Verlag, 1954).

8. *Shakespeare. Neu übersetzt*, III, 119. Flatter's note to this passage runs: 'Die Stelle ist viel erörtert und arg missverstanden worden. Nach der Meinung des Amerikaners Kittredge zum Beispiel will Hamlet sagen, die Tötung des Königs gerade jetzt wäre so, als hätte er, Hamlet, ihn dazu bestellt, ihm den Vater zu ermorden, und als zahle er ihm nun den Lohn für den Mordvollzug. Andre Herausgeber suchen nach Emendationen. Dover Wilson zum Beispiel druckt in seiner Ausgabe "*bait and salary*". In Wirklichkeit will Hamlet sagen, die unzeitgemässe Tötung wäre nicht Rache, sondern etwas andres — und dieses andre steckt in "*hire and salary*", wobei die Zahlung an Stelle dessen steht, wofür bezahlt wird. (Solches *quid pro quo* kommt in Shakespeare häufig vor.) Man heuert ("*hire*" ist das selbe Wort) einen Meuchelmörder für einen Einzelakt und besoldet regelmässig ("*salary*") einen angestellten Scharfrichter. Den König derart um die Ecke zu bringen, wäre das Werk eines Meuchelmörders oder Scharfrichters, aber nicht das, was er selbst auf die geziemende Art durchführen will — ritterliche Rache. Daher die Uebersetzung: "Meuchelmord wär' das, Hinrichtung — nicht Rache!"' (*op. cit.* pp. 224 f.).

9. *Deutsche Vierteljahrsschrift fur Literatur und Geistesgeschichte*, Jg. 35 (1961), Heft 1.

10. *Shakespeare. Neu übersetzt*, III (1954), 412.

11. *Der elisabethanische Shakespeare, Macbeth, Was Ihr Wollt, Zweierlei Mass, Der Sturm* (1955), pp. 336 f.

12. William Shakespeare, *Sturm*. Deutsch von Rudolf Alexander Schröder, Letzte Fassung, Gesellschaft der Bibliophilen (Frankfurt am Main, 1959), p. 28.

SHAKESPEARE AS
'CORRUPTER OF WORDS'

BY

MICHEL GRIVELET

Though the fact has often been deplored, it is perhaps a good thing for us, in France, that we have had no 'classic' translation of Shakespeare, comparable, for instance, with that by Schlegel and Tieck. Shakespeare in Germany, because of the lasting success of this remarkable version, tends to remain, as L. W. Forster puts it: 'a member of the eighteenth-century classical tradition, an author of the "Goethezeit" on a par with Schiller and Goethe himself'.[1] But no French translation has been good enough to naturalize the Elizabethan dramatist as a contemporary of Voltaire, or Victor Hugo, or Gide. Neither has the use of a kind of sixteenth-century idiom enabled learned translators like Derocquigny to turn him into the contemporary of Montaigne that he actually was. Shakespeare's text does not belong to our past and we must therefore refer it to our present. With each new generation we have to conquer him anew, to render him in our own language for our own times.

At least we are challenged to do so. But we may wonder whether the task is not of special difficulty today, when French dramatic style is largely represented and influenced by writers who seem mostly intent on calling the bluff of language. Playwrights, who deal necessarily with the idiom of their day, cannot but reflect a situation in which an intemperate use of the written and the spoken word goes along with a growing sense of their untrustworthiness. Thus, in the plays of Beckett or Ionesco, language—having ceased to be of real use as a means of communication between people, or of people with themselves—proliferates like a senseless, and a threatening, object. Hence the impulse not only to denounce but also to destroy the menacing absurdity. In a way, it may seem the poet's first duty to shatter common speech—when it has hardened into lifeless phraseology—in order to make room for a new growth. Meanwhile, however, we have writers who torture and corrupt the language they use. The words themselves, as happens with Ionesco, break into mere fragments, mere sounds. Is this a language that Shakespeare could be taught to speak? Can we hope for a living translation of his plays in a literary climate dominated by such iconoclasts?

For Shakespeare is, above all, creative energy, 'sagesse pourpre', as Charles Du Bos has said, a wisdom instinct with a 'splendide pléthore de sang vital'.[2] He is the coiner of words and phrases that have become and remained current since then. And moreover his own vigour thrives on the vigour of the language itself, a language which has not had time to harden and degenerate but is still in its early youth, full of hope and vitality. The contrast, certainly, is great between this linguistic exuberance and modern destructiveness. And yet, wide as the difference may be, it is not everything; for Shakespeare's use of language has more than one aspect. Other impulses than those towards creation are at work in his verbal effervescence, impulses more in sympathy with what modern practice experiences. And in this kinship, which makes us feel in a specially persuasive way that Shakespeare is for our time also, a chance offers itself perhaps of a renewed, more perceptive interpretation, of a more congenial reading of his plays. It might be the opportunity of the present-day translator.

Asked by Viola whether he is Lady Olivia's fool, Feste, as we know, answers: 'No, indeed, sir; the Lady Olivia has no folly: she will keep no fool, sir, till she be married....I am indeed not her fool, but her corrupter of words' (III, i, 37–41). There is really no surprise for us in the phrase 'her corrupter of words' since, not much before, we have heard Feste's words to Sir Andrew: 'I did impeticos thy gratillity; for Malvolio's nose is no whipstock: my lady has a white hand, and the Myrmidons are no bottle-ale houses' (II, iii, 27–9).

This is partly the kind of nonsense every fool is expected to utter. Words here are at liberty and have little meaning apart from that which editors, at the cost of great labour, finally manage to impose upon them. However, with 'impeticos thy gratillity', Feste seems to surpass himself and to deserve both his self-given title and the enthusiastic applause elicited from Sir Andrew: 'Excellent! why, this is the best fooling, when all is done.' But what does this 'best fooling' consist of? 'Impeticos', we read in Onions' *Glossary*, 'burlesque word put into the mouth of a fool, app. as a perversion of "impocket", and perhaps intended to suggest "petticoat"'. 'Gratillity', in the same glossary, has only 'clown's humorous perversion of "gratuity"'. Could we not add—perhaps intended to suggest 'gentility', in the sense of good manners (as in *Love's Labour's Lost*, I, i, 127)? It would seem, then, that both these burlesque words are the result of contamination, the basic process of punning carried to absurdity. Though thrown in carelessly and not repeated, the trick of 'impeticos thy gratillity' is significant enough. It is a caricature which implies that all word-play is, at bottom, word-corruption.

Feste's conversation with Viola throws light on this. In his own wanton way with language, he simply does what the 'good wit' of his times is only too prone to do: 'To see this age! A sentence is but a cheveril glove to a good wit: how quickly the wrong side may be turned outward!' And Viola is compelled to agree: 'Nay, that's certain; they that dally nicely with words may quickly make them wanton.' The untrustworthiness of language is something Feste knows all about. 'Words are very rascals,' he says, though unwilling to give his reasons for saying so, for 'words are grown so false, I am loath to prove reason with them.' In this predicament, what else can he do but play the 'corrupter of words'?

Of course he does not do so in downright scepticism. For he is a wise fool, one whose 'practice' is,

As full of labour as a wise man's art. (III, i, 73)

Concerned as he is with the happiness of Olivia, his 'labour' is intended precisely to warn her against too great a confidence in words. Not the words of Orsino, since she is obviously proof against them, but those of his spokesman, the 'poor monster' Cesario-Viola, with whom she has fallen in love. And how deceived she is in this love, Viola knows only too well: 'Poor Lady, she were better love a dream' (II, ii, 27). Here, as elsewhere, the wise fool does what he can to cure his betters, the seeming wise, of their folly. But it is Feste's bias to detect this folly in the illusions of speech. Viola's beauty and her disguise, that 'wickedness', are not for nothing in Olivia's infatuation. Yet it is Viola's 'text' which makes her take fire. And when the page has left, persuading herself that 'he' is indeed a gentleman, it is the sweet words that she remembers first:

'I am a gentleman'. I'll be sworn thou art;
Thy *tongue*, thy face, thy limbs, actions, and spirit,
Do give thee five-fold blazon. (I, v, 310)

Feste must be aware of her weakness to think that treatment by word-corruption will do good to Olivia, and in this way at least it appears that he still hopes to 'prove reason'.

Such is the spirit of the comedies: nonsense makes for better sense; it is a remedy, not a poison. 'Dallying nicely' with words clears the way for a sounder belief in their essential rightness. A play like *Love's Labour's Lost*, in which there is so much verbal criticism and irony, in which not only the blunders of Dull and the coarseness of Costard, but also the high words of Armado, the inkhorn terms of Holofernes, and still more perhaps Berowne's 'taffeta phrases', are all set against one another and ridiculed, nevertheless expresses trust in 'russet yeas and honest kersey noes'. And though 'Vowes are but breath, and breath a vapour is', Berowne need not despair of being one day graced with the white hand of Rosaline. Even when carried as far as they are by Beatrice and Benedick, all the extravagances of punning end in common sense, and marriage. In the same way, Rosalind's 'idle talking' with Orlando proves a cure for the madness of love, if not for love itself. With the advent of Hymen, 'God of every town', linguistic scepticism gives way to renewed confidence in both life and language.

And yet—to return to *Twelfth Night*—though here too 'Journeys end in lovers meeting' (II, iii, 44), this can hardly be regarded as a triumph of truthfulness over illusion. No doubt Olivia's dream comes true, since there is a Sebastian, wonderfully like Viola, to fill the place of the false Cesario. But it is rather as if, undeceived to the last, she remained the prisoner of her own fancy. Neither does Malvolio, though taught a cruel lesson, desist from his own wilful error. So it is no wonder if a note of sadness is sounded at the end of the play, when Feste, left alone, concludes on a song more of disillusioned than of playful nonsense. To 'prove reason' with words was decidedly a vain hope.

Shakespeare's dramatic work has a dimension in which no comforting limits can be set to the deceptiveness of language. For words are misleading not so much because they do not correspond to things as they are—there is really no *man* that goes by the name of Cesario—but because, in spite of this, they retain their magic and lose nothing of their hold over the imagination. Their power, rather, becomes more insidious. Once let loose from reality, they run wild and proliferate in an unhealthy manner, as the repetition suggests when Troilus exclaims: 'Words, words, mere words, no matter from the heart', or Hamlet: 'Words, words, words...'. A verbal power is released in the tragedies which has something of the evil growth in the 'unweeded garden'.

There is obviously no room for a corrupter of words in such surroundings. Or rather, since Feste's alter ego is seen with King Lear, he is there in utter helplessness, a pathetic figure. In vain does he labour 'to out-jest (the king's) heart-struck injuries' (III, i, 17). Lear, who has failed to understand the 'nothing' of Cordelia, has no use either for the nothing, the nonsense, of the Fool:

Can you make no use of nothing, nuncle?
Why, no, boy; nothing can be made out of nothing. (I, iv, 142)

But it is essential here to discern the true cause of the Fool's helplessness. Wise folly is of no avail with Lear because, in his madness, he beats it at its own game. 'Having been unutterably wronged by fair but treacherous speech, Lear seeks to degrade language by steeping it in grossness and cruelty.'[3] Though at first impervious to nonsense, and still believing in the rightness of hollow words, a time comes when he seems about to see through them:

> I will be the pattern of all patience; I will say nothing. (III, ii, 38)

But too late. And though he 'would not be mad', it is only in delirious talk that he succeeds at last in mixing 'matter with impertinency' (IV, vi, 176). The exercise of nonsense is then irremediably fused into the ecstasy of tragic imagination.

Tragic utterance at its wildest is the most desperate form of word-corruption. As Lear, struggling against the terrors of lunacy, and Edgar feigning madness, and the Fool venting his wise folly, join in a litany which confounds nonsense with nonsense, violence is repeatedly inflicted upon the language. It often lapses into ejaculations which are little more than mere sounds: 'Do de, do de, do de; alow, alow, loo, loo; sessa, sessa; sa, sa, sa....'.

Though in this as in many other respects the major plays are all different from one another, all tragic speech in Shakespeare has this as a common feature that it combines meaning and meaninglessness within the single act of tense and vivid image-making. Punning was common enough with the Elizabethans, but Shakespeare's virtuosity in this domain seems to have always been exceptional, and subtle to the point of mingling with poetic creation. Now, as we have seen, Feste calls himself a corrupter of words because, for him, 'dallying nicely' with words eventually leads to 'I did impeticos thy gratillity', to the contamination of word with word, meaning with meaning. Originally, we are told, punning is based upon 'the Elizabethan faith in the rightness of words....If a word has several meanings they are shown...to bear a kind of transcendental relationship to one another.'[4] Where the belief in this rightness gives way there is no more 'transcendental relationship' but isolated and even conflicting significances. The heightened punning which gives so much effervescence to Shakespeare's imagery does not only irradiate meanings but also tends to confuse them with one another and to place darkness at the heart of bright vision.

What has been said of *Macbeth*, that it is 'a wrestling of destruction with creation', does not apply to this play only, even if the multitudinous antitheses it contains give scope and emphasis to the contrast.[5] It is true of all the tragedies and essential to Shakespeare's tragic style when— in the most memorable images—something seems to explode, multiplying and destroying signification. Even in plays with comparatively little imaginative violence, like *Antony and Cleopatra*, there are many wonderful occurrences of this kind. As when Cleopatra laments Antony's death with

> O, wither'd is the garland of the war,
> The soldier's pole is fall'n (IV, xv, 64)

where 'pole', which (perhaps) implies not only a military but also a cosmic fall, both enlarges and perplexes thought, blinds it even with the darkness that fills the heart of the queen. In such moments, with more or less violence, we experience something of the disruptive force which shakes the world of Shakespearian tempests.

In comedy then, and in tragedy, with the lover and on the confines of madness, there is occasion for the corruption of words as an effort, made in hope—or in despair and confusion—

to relieve the mind from the pressure of its own conceit. But this is the place to remember that:

> The lunatic, the lover, *and the poet*
> Are of imagination all compact.

Can we doubt that Shakespeare, who has provided Olivia with a Feste and made Lear speak more 'impertinency' than his Fool, has also taken care to be his own corrupter of words? It would be worthwhile to speculate with what success. No better than Feste's perhaps, if not in the utter torments of the wheel of fire. He never seems to have been unaware of the potential delusion inherent in his extraordinary power over words. With his zest for language, there was a time when, drawing the stuff of his plays from the energies, eccentricities and tensions of speech, the dramatist must have felt that he was clearing the way for a more genuine means of communication. But the linguistic scepticism rampant in the age was early with him also. M. M. Mahood observes that 'in the great tragedies disbelief in the truth of words is balanced by a recognition of their connotative power'.[6] The poet's insight into such an ambiguous power may well have had something of a 'cursed spite'. His tragic heroes have an extraordinary command of the language, but instead of earning them 'honour, love, obedience, troops of friends' (*Macbeth*, v, iii, 25), it drives them to deeper and deeper isolation, a solitude in which they are estranged not only from everything and everybody else but even from themselves. Who can say how far the most destructive efforts of word-play were with him reaction or surrender to a poet's loneliness?

The realization of destructiveness in Shakespeare's attitude to language is a necessary step in the approach to the problems of translation. To acquiesce in Shakespeare's nonsense may seem, in English, comparatively easy, and even so easy that it often passes unnoticed. But easy acceptance is denied to the translator. Where commonplace punning is concerned, no great harm is done if he merely attempts a lame equivalent, or gives up the attempt with the usual 'Jeu de mots intraduisible en français'. At most, it means that Shakespeare's dialogue will sound a little more tedious and aimless than it really is—not, sometimes, without a super-added touch of wry humour. But it is quite another thing when the ironies of word-contamination combine with pregnant imagery. If Cleopatra's 'knot intrinsicate of life' actually knits together, in the daring Elizabethan neologism, half a dozen or more meanings from both 'intrinsic' and 'intrinse',[7] a translation like Gide's 'le noeud embrouillé de la vie' certainly lets us down with its mere *idea* of complexity, when what is felt—as the queen winces under the 'sharp teeth' of the 'worm'— is the unspeakable and the senseless, at this one moment of cruelty in a peaceful death. If Hamlet's flesh is 'too, too solid'—as 'thaw', 'melt', 'resolve', and the prince's suicidal obsession amply bear out—and at the same time 'too, too sullied', which his reflections on his mother's marriage more than imply, the 'rub' then is not chiefly that, by dropping one or the other meaning, French versions leave out something of essential significance, it is much rather that, without the ambiguity, we suspect nothing of the blurring of ideas, the mists of uncertainty that rise into a mind already threatened with madness.

The gulf was always difficult to bridge between Shakespeare and French poetic tradition. While, as J. J. Mayoux has shown,[8] Racine brings the darkness of passion up to the light and objectivity of clear expression in order to make dialogue possible, Shakespearian tragedy leads us away from dialogue, using language to explore the depth and darkness of the flesh, the separateness and incoherence of individual passion. This is why, from the start, Shakespeare has exerted such a pressure on French poetic style—as appears in the first Frenchman who ever tried to make the author of *Hamlet* speak French. For, after rendering the 'To be or not to be' soliloquy in utterly conventional verse, Voltaire is urged, almost in spite of himself, to place before his readers' eyes a 'traduction littérale' in which, among other things, he does not fear to speak of 'prendre les armes contre une mer de troubles'.[9] It is striking also how the connection is established, in Victor Hugo's preface to *Cromwell*, between the recognition of Shakespeare as poetical summit of modern times ('Nous voici parvenus a la sommité poétique des temps Modernes. Shakespeare, c'est le drame...') and the then revolutionary idea that 'la langue française n'est point fixée et ne se fixera point'. Ever since it first entered our literary history, the work of the English dramatist has acted as a ferment, bringing about renewal through decay.

In this sense too, therefore, it might be argued that Shakespeare is a corrupter. But it is only fair to say that in England also he has sometimes been regarded as such. 'He often obscures his meaning', says Dryden, 'by *his words*, and sometimes makes it unintelligible. I will not say of so great a poet, that he distinguished not the blown puffy style from true sublimity; but I may venture to maintain, that the fury of his fancy often transported him beyond the bounds of judgment, either in coining of new words and phrases, or *racking words* which were in use, into the violence of a catachresis.' Replace the assumption of involuntary excess by that of deliberate effect and it is a judgement to which one would willingly subscribe. Was not, one wonders, something of that kind in Byron's mind when he wrote that Shakespeare was 'the worst of models, though the most extraordinary of writers'?[10] The zeal of too sensible editors and emendators may well have succeeded in concealing from us much of Shakespeare's intractable nonsense. And it is beyond doubt that far more has been done towards suppressing it altogether by the helplessness of French translators.

There should be a change for the better in the linguistic conditions of the present day. Such is at least the conviction of Yves Bonnefoy, himself a considerable poet and translator of Shakespeare. While taking the view that rendering the English dramatist into French involves no less than a conflict of the language with itself—'la lutte d'une langue avec elle-même, au plus secret de sa substance, au plus vif de son devenir'—he holds that French poetry is now more capable than in past times of this struggle.[11] If it is indeed possible to overcome the difficulty of transmitting the inner violence, the entanglement of sense with nonsense which is at the root of Shakespearian imagery, then French opinion, traditionally alive to the critical element of Shakespeare's genius, will also be able to respond to the more positive aspects of its vast and penetrating vision.

And on the other hand it will be well if imaginative interpretation, intent on tracing out the texture of meanings in the large web of interrelated imagery—and sometimes unduly prone to seek the security of doctrine in the perils of drama—is reminded of the darkness and void from which, in tragic experience, all these images proceed. Shakespeare, it has been said, appeals to us because of the meaning he gives to a chaotic experience which is very much our own. But he will only do so if we feel that he shares our apprehension of its possible meaninglessness.

NOTES

1. *Aspects of Translation* (*Studies in Communication 2*), p. 21.
2. *Approximations*, II, 66.
3. George Steiner, *The Death of Tragedy*, p. 258.
4. M. M. Mahood, *Shakespeare's Wordplay*, p. 170.
5. Kenneth Muir, introduction to the new Arden edition, p. xxxiii.
6. *Shakespeare's Wordplay*, p. 175.
7. I. A. Richards, *The Philosophy of Rhetoric*, quoted by Mahood, p. 16.
8. 'Le dialogue tragique dans Shakespeare' in *Réalisme et Poésie au théâtre* (Paris, 1960).
9. *Lettres Philosophiques*, 18

> Demeure, il faut choisir, et passer à l'instant
> De la vie à la mort, et de l'être au néant.
> Dieux justes ! s'il en est, éclairez mon courage.
> Faut-il vieillir courbé sous la main qui m'outrage,
> Supporter, ou finir mon malheur et mon sort....

Après ce morceau de poésie, les lecteurs sont priés de jeter les yeux sur la traduction littérale:

> Etre ou n'être pas, c'est là la question;
> S'il est plus noble dans l'esprit de souffrir
> Les piqûres et les flèches de l'affreuse fortune
> Ou de prendre les armes contre une mer de troubles,
> Et en s'opposant à eux, les finir. Mourir, dormir....

10. Quoted by George Steiner, *The Death of Tragedy*, p. 202.
11. 'Shakespeare et le poète français' (*Preuves*, Juin 1959).

SHAKESPEARE IN GHANA

BY

D. S. BAKER

I

When Ben Jonson wrote his eulogy on 'Master William Shakespeare and what he has left us', he may have had some idea of the temporal, but little conception of the territorial, extension of 'Master William's' fame. Jonson could not possibly have foreseen to what extent Shakespeare's 'buskin' was 'to shake a stage' in the various dim and then little-known corners of the world. He might quite easily have dismissed the idea of a Shakespearian production in the Americas as unlikely, whilst, if he had considered the matter at all, the suggestion of a performance in febrile West Africa, where, according to Hakluyt, sailors such as Job Hartop called from time to time, would have seemed to him like the ravings of a plague-struck mariner. Yet Shakespeare's 'unblotted' and Marlowe's 'mighty' lines are now frequently heard in that part of Africa which, until the comparatively recent years of anti-malarial drugs, has long been known as 'the white man's grave'. In attempting to describe some of the problems confronting the teacher and producer of Shakespeare in West Africa, I shall confine my comments to questions which arose out of my experience of lecturing on Shakespeare to training college students in Ghana, but I tentatively suggest that these are fundamental questions to any teacher who is concerned with the explanation of English literature to students whose mother-tongue is not English.

The problems facing the lecturer in English in West Africa seem to me to fall roughly into two categories: (1) the linguistic, which has certain difficulties for English students but which has more varied and wider implications in West Africa, and (2) the cultural, which is peculiar to the country in which one is working.

Language and culture are becoming much more of an identity, and nowadays are quite often defined in national, or geographically national, terms as the history of the efforts to impose a unity of national consciousness on countries composed of numerous groups of peoples, each with a distinct language which expresses a distinct culture, has tended to show. The relationship between language and culture has been pointed out by various linguists; Stephen Ullmann, for example, after recalling that students of language have always 'fully appreciated' the importance of verbal context in the consideration of meaning, remarks that 'This somewhat narrow view of context has been considerably enlarged of late; it is now increasingly realised that the non-verbal elements of the situation, and the wider influence of social setting and cultural background, are also of direct relevance to the full understanding of an utterance and its components.'[1] My belief that a lack of understanding or appreciation of European culture is a fundamental obstacle to be overcome in any approach to Shakespeare assumes that, for all practical purposes, language and culture may be considered as one, even if the two concepts are not entirely coincident. This assumption is given some support by a further remark of Ullman's: 'These contexts (the non-verbal elements of the situation) can be pictured in the form of concentric circles clustering around the concrete act of speech. "It can be described", writes Professor Firth, "as a serial contextualisation of our facts, context within context, each one being a function, an organ of the bigger context and all contexts finding a place in what may be called the context of culture.'"[2]

II

Any consideration of the practical difficulties of teaching Shakespeare in West Africa might very well begin with an outline of the cultural differences that exist between a European (in the non-geographical sense) and a Ghanaian as they are reflected in some aspects of Shakespearian study.

In Ghana, the Shakespearian romantic comedy is, at best, likely to be misunderstood, and, at worst, ridiculed mercilessly. As producer of *The Merchant of Venice* I remember awaiting the opening of Act v with a feeling of growing anxiety, knowing that the change in the play's texture from the stark realism of the Court scene to the romantic world of the moonlit bank would, perhaps, demand too great a change in attitude on the part of the audience; few people would attempt to sit on a bank, moonlit or otherwise, in Africa, and when the audience reacted with laughter as I fearfully expected it would, the whole scene no doubt demonstrated to Ghanaian students another of the strange and wondrous ways of Europeans.

If, as H. B. Charlton has claimed, 'Romantic comedy is pre-eminently the comedy of love',[3] the theme running through Act v of *The Merchant* will, on the whole, be unappreciated, since it expresses a tradition of sex relationships which is foreign to Ghanaian culture. To whatever source one may ascribe the cult of *amour courtois* and the elaborate rituals of the 'Courts of Love', their influence on English life and thought cannot be underestimated; they were the founts of inspiration for the literature of medieval romance and by the time of Shakespeare had so irrigated the cultural soil that the growth of Shakespeare's own composition was conditioned naturally by it. As Charlton puts it: 'Shakespeare and his fellows were romantic in the strict sense that they clamoured for fuller draughts of that spirit of romanticism which the Middle Ages had first discovered and revealed in their tales of chivalry and knight-errantry.'[4] Even if Shakespeare did not know the original source of his inspiration for the love of Orlando and Rosalind, Orsino and Viola, Lorenzo and Jessica and the many other romantic pairings, the conventions within which he was writing, although redirected by courtly influence, filtered in translation and at least partly Christianized, still administered a powerful fertilizing effect on his imagination.

Perhaps these conventions survive in modern Britain under the general heading of 'good manners', examples of which are opening doors and offering seats to ladies, standing when a lady enters the room and always allowing a lady to go first, all of which tend, in the true courtly love tradition, to exalt the position of the woman in society. An example of the opposite conception of womanhood which derives from an entirely different tradition came to me, when, in complete ignorance of the possible repercussions, I was discussing Leigh Hunt's poem, 'Jenny kiss'd me', with some middle-aged Ghanaian students. The poem was considered not so much amusing (a reaction which I think I would have understood) but as almost indecent in that no woman, they said, would have behaved in such a way; the woman's business was to await instructions from the man!

It is certainly true that in Ghana the attitude towards womanhood is changing, an attitude no doubt partly influenced by European traditions, but strongly urged with increasing vehemence by powerful sections of the Ghanaian female population to which the politicians cannot afford to be completely deaf. On the other hand, even now women students often refrain from entering into discussion because men are present in the class.

Shakespeare, however, does not always 'clamour for fuller draughts of the spirit of romanticism'; occasionally, having obtained 'the draught' he apparently pours it away—whether in fun or in a fit of cynicism is debatable. That *The Taming of the Shrew* is Shakespeare's tilt at romantic comedy seems a reasonable supposition, and it is in the tilting that Ghanaian audiences find delight and a certain measure of understanding. The satirical thrusts at the language of romance in Lucentio's conversation with Tranio in I, i may be lost, but the general tenor of anti-feminism in the play as a whole is thoroughly appreciated by the male members of the audience. In particular the famous scene between Petruchio and Katharine in II, is characterized by the vociferous and very partisan support given the respective protagonists by the audience.

III

In the main, the romantic comedy is not the easiest kind of Shakespearian play for Ghanaians to study; the difficulty is almost entirely due to the great difference in attitude towards the relationship of the sexes, which in Europe has, I think, partly through the conventions of *amour courtois*, become idealized, but which in Ghana, an essentially masculine society, remains largely functional and realistic.

The history play, or the tragedy which is set against a background of family or national strife, is much more readily accepted. The bonds of tribe and the ties of family which extend to the most remote relations are still extremely strong and give rise to an intense loyalty within the tribal or family group. The converse of this attitude towards tribe and family is the lack of loyalty shown towards a supra-tribal authority, or rather a failure, quite often, to understand the necessity for it in the modern world.

The situation regarding these attitudes towards various loyalties is, I believe, not unlike that which provided the raw material for many of Shakespeare's history plays. If we view these plays as a group we may at least catch hints, if not direct expression, of Shakespeare's interest in the emergence of a national consciousness in terms of geographical extent, as the recurring image of 'earth' in *Richard II* possibly suggests; the theologico-philosophical implications of this emergence may be traced in the theme running through the sequence of the 'Henry' plays, where Shakespeare seems to be exploring the effects of these implications on the structure of Elizabethan society. The violent opposition of the Lancastrians to Yorkists, the intrigues, the continual grouping and regrouping of interested parties, and the frequent ebullition into open war of the pot in which the fortunes of England were melting may all make a very direct and real impact on a West African audience, which is able to read its own problems and aspirations into the particular play.

A further aspect of the history plays, especially *Richard III*, which appeals to Ghanaians is that of the rise to power of a man who is physically strong, even if his morals, from a European point of view, are somewhat suspect. On the whole the Ghanaian tends to respect the man who is 'crafty' (using the word in its Old English sense of power employed skilfully), and the Renaissance hero is often depicted as a 'crafty' man—as Shakespeare's attempt to draw such a character in Richard III clearly shows. The qualities of skill in diplomacy and debate, in organizing the forces at his disposal, and the physical courage Richard displays are well appreciated, although the fact that Richard is deformed may tend to cloud his dubious achievements in the eyes of the audience, since physical deformity is viewed rather differently by Ghanaians. A man of good physique would, I think, in their view be much more likely to engage in the activities described in the play than a cripple '...rudely stamp'd...Deform'd, unfinish'd,...scarce half made up'.

A similar difference in outlook between Ghanaians and Europeans is encountered in *Henry IV*, where the fatness of Falstaff, an object of fun in itself to European audiences, is sometimes misconstrued, since a man of ample proportions is respected, possibly on account of the doubtful correlation between girth and financial prosperity. This point was illustrated to me when a student, whom I had not seen for a year or so, proudly pointed to my waist and respectfully commented that I was 'growing nobly'! The deformity of Richard may be greeted with laughter, which, although I am not entirely convinced about this, has often been attributed to embarrassment on the part of the audience; it seems to me more likely that an audience does not quite see the coincidence of Richard's aspirations and prowess to his twisted body. I do not for one moment suggest that these reactions to Richard and Falstaff are inevitable or universal, but I think there is always the distinct possibility of misunderstanding or misreading of their characters on account of physical appearances.

I have been indicating that in some way physique and power to govern are identified in the Ghanaian consciousness; both the physical and mental qualities involved are respected, and I think this is precisely the reason why the Roman plays are so popular. *Julius Caesar*, for example, has been performed in African costume with much success. The play contains fine oratory, which the Ghanaian thoroughly enjoys; especially is this true of III, ii in which the sympathies of the crowd are so quickly changed. The points made by the chief speakers are quickly taken, and that Antony is more subtle in his appeal than Brutus is appreciated with ease and much vociferous delight. Where oratory of an exciting and perhaps inflammatory type is inspired by a man as 'crafty' as Antony must surely appear in this play, enjoyment and understanding are almost certain. One would hesitate, however, to expect equal success with *Antony and Cleopatra* for reasons which I have outlined above, but *Coriolanus* should, on balance, be acceptable although I have not the first-hand experience of taking this play with Ghanaian students.

IV

The questions of sex relationships, loyalties and attitudes which I have been discussing, whilst not immediately apparent to a European teacher of Shakespeare, are nevertheless fundamental, since they represent differences in culture, differences which must be recognized and, as far as it is possible to do so, explained in the hope that something of the essential feeling and thought of Europeans will be caught. These questions are largely cultural. The second of the two major problems in Shakespeare teaching—the linguistic—however, remains.

On the first and purely lexical level of meaning there are words the concepts of which are not understood because they are not experienced in the African environment. There are obviously many words in this lexical group; references to particular animals and birds not indigenous to Africa, or to specific objects such as 'windmills', 'the brook' and 'chalky cliffs'. In *1 Henry VI*,

I, i, we have: 'No more shall trenching war channel her fields'; this is reasonably straightforward for Europeans, but the concept of 'field' is alien to a West African, especially in the forest areas, where fields in the sense of an open tract of grassland are unknown.

The phrase in this quotation requires a simple explanation of fact, but the second kind of answer to the linguistic question is much more complex, since it must cover the wide extension of the word's semantic range and include its linguistic overtones. Answers to the question of meaning at the semantic, as distinct from the lexical, level are much more difficult to give to those whose mother-tongue is not English. One of the most important and common group of concepts to be explained from this angle is rather more climatic than cultural, although the relationship between climate and culture may be fairly close at certain points. An illustration of this relationship is seen in the fact that much Shakespearian imagery derives from climatic conditions and the vagaries of the English weather; the inability on the part of his lady to give a correct weather forecast gave Shakespeare reason for poetical complaint on one occasion at least.

The seasons and the emotions they suggest possess a language with linguistic overtones which present very obvious difficulties. For example, the opening lines of *Richard III*—'Now is the winter of our discontent | Made glorious summer by this sun of York'—may be explained in geographical terms by pointing out quite simply that in summer the sun is warmer than it is in winter. But there is also a certain, implied judgement in the relatively pleasurable experience inspired by each season. Shakespeare, without the means of easy transport and the attractions of well-organized, twentieth-century winter sports, accepted the late sixteenth-century opinion that winter is less pleasurable than summer.

These lines of Richard can be explained factually, but if one endeavours to apply the same principles of explanation to Macbeth's self-revealing words, 'My life is fall'n into the sere, the yellow leaf', the implications that yellowing leaves indicate the approach of autumn and that autumn is associated with physical degeneration and old age are not necessarily followed by Ghanaian students. When the leaves fall in the tropics (although in some forest areas the trees are never entirely bare) one is approaching the dry season and the dry season is, on the whole, much more healthy for Africans (and Europeans) than in that time of the year when all vegetation is extravagantly green during the rains. Seasonal images and the conclusions one may draw from them must be seen in the context of very different climates, which in their turn have provided different cultures with a specialized language pregnant with implied meanings.

Images of the type which are dependent on the extension of semantic range can, I think, be explained in three stages. For example, in *1 Henry IV*, III, ii, the following lines occur: 'He was but as the cuckoo is in June, | Heard, not regarded.' Basically the image is dependent on the understanding of the nature of the habits and call of the cuckoo, which is a bird unknown in West Africa. At the first, or lexical, level of meaning these facts must be given. Secondly, by a process of extension or transference of meaning the general point may be made that 'familiarity breeds contempt', with special reference to the cuckoo's note in June. It is upon this transferred meaning, representing the middle stage in explanation, that Shakespeare bases his image of Henry's comment on the contempt in which the populace holds Richard; this is the third and final stage in the growth of the image as a whole. Thus in any explanation of the lines we cannot take any stage of the image-producing process for granted; each stage must be dealt with separately, with the fairly obvious net result that there is little or no visualization through the audio impact of the words, and the image thus loses its immediacy and effect.

V

In the foregoing discussion I have tried to indicate some of the differences in culture and language that exist between Europeans and Ghanaians as they are reflected in a study of Shakespeare: a recognition of these differences, I believe, forms a firm basis for beginning to explain the obscurities and complexities in the dramatist's work. Differences of culture there undoubtedly are, but there are also points of contact, and I have suggested earlier the kind of play which is more likely to appeal to a West African audience. I have, for example, produced *The Merchant of Venice* in African costume with the Duke in the regalia of a tribal chief (which, perhaps, is not far removed from the original idea of a 'Duke'). With the reservation that the Portia/Bassanio plot was not of great interest, the rest of the play, particularly the cunning argument against Shylock in the Court scene, was followed with very close attention and tremendous enthusiasm; one must confess, however, that Act v was somewhat bathetic. On another occasion, never-to-be-forgotten, I witnessed a performance of *Macbeth*, produced entirely by students. Macbeth's castle was furnished with armchairs and a table, with flowers in a vase standing on it, whilst around the walls various pictures were hung. This was a student's conception of life in Britain. That it was full of anachronisms did not matter, and in spite of the *naïveté* and (should it be said?) the ignorance, there was clearly a certain 'gusto' about the quality of the acting which portrayed the violence, the colour and possibly the 'rant' of the times that Shakespeare was describing and on which his theatre thrived.

Knowing something of the background against which one must teach and produce Shakespeare in Ghana, the choice of play, especially for beginners, is all important. But even if the understanding of a play is only partial or superficial, there are degrees of vitality, freshness and sheer fun in Ghanaian Shakespeare that one hopes will not be extinguished in the interests of textual criticism and purely academic study.

NOTES

1. Stephen Ullmann, *The Principles of Semantics* (2nd ed., Oxford, 1957), p. 61.
2. *Ibid.* p. 61.
3. H. B. Charlton, *Shakespearean Comedy* (3rd ed., 1945), p. 21.
4. *Ibid.* p. 20.

'TIMON OF ATHENS'

BY

DAVID COOK

As is well known, there are certain major themes which Shakespeare handles again and again throughout his plays, ideas which form the framework of his thinking as it continually develops. One such concept is, of course, that of order: the elaborate consideration of social order in the history plays leads to an investigation of emotional and moral order, in *Measure for Measure* for instance, in *Lear*, and finally, with a different emphasis, in the last romances. I find another recurrent theme in the consideration of human pride, and the difficulty of distinguishing proper pride, which is essential to human dignity and which keeps a firm hold on certain fundamental values, from presumptuous, fiercely egotistical pride, which is a denial of human contact. This duality is particularly apparent in Shylock; Iago strikes a different balance. Othello is destroyed by positive pride, and so in his death positive values are more important than the wastage of life; Macbeth, in his negative pride, destroys himself and rejects humanity. Cordelia properly asserts human dignity, and so can serve as the instrument to winnow what is destructive from what is constructive in Lear's pride. *Timon of Athens, Coriolanus, Measure for Measure* and *All's Well That Ends Well* investigate more specifically the distinction, often a fine one, between negative and positive pride: in doing so they move towards the resolution of the human dilemma which Shakespeare offers as an alternative to tragedy in the final romances. Of these plays, *Timon of Athens* analyses pride most objectively, and offers least resolution of the issues raised.

It is the magnificent scale of Timon's presumption which determines his dramatic stature. But his extreme self-assertion is made possible only by an equal self-blindness which, unlike that of Coriolanus, is irremediable even in the last resort; thus it is impossible for Timon to pass beyond the limitations set by his pride and by his ignorance of himself; he can arrive at no fundamental self-knowledge nor meet any new dispensation in death, as do the greater tragic figures.

It will already be clear that I do not share the view of *Timon of Athens* which sees its 'theme' as the depiction of 'the ruin of a frank and generous soul by ingratitude, public and private'.[1] The manner of the play is certainly homiletic and many of the minor characters are shown in a fiercely sardonic light. But homily is the coil rather than the core; if such simple moralizing were the main subject, then this would indeed be a naïve and uninteresting work. Incidentally, Shakespeare handles ingratitude far more powerfully in the persons of Regan and Goneril. But the whole concept of Timon as a saintly man who, being wronged, understandably comes to hate mankind, runs quite counter, I am sure, to the actual dramatic impact. In fact, Timon is pictured as flagrantly wrong-headed in both halves of the play. Our untrammelled reaction is surely to feel that at first he is a well-meaning fool, and that later his misanthropy, however provoked, is perverse. Even in the play's still unfinished form, we possess enough to see clearly that such are the effects which Shakespeare intends, and consequently there can be no solemn moralization running counter to this strong dramatic current. I am inclined to agree with J. C. Maxwell that seeing Timon as an embodiment of overtaxed virtue results from a 'subservience to classification and theory—to the traditional classification of *Timon* as a tragedy, and to quasi-philosophical theories...of what tragedy should be.'[2] The critics who were more concerned in attributing parts of the play to various playwrights of their own choice than in assessing it as a whole found a spur to their activities in the obvious absurdities and contradictions inherent in this conventional view.

As I see it, *Timon of Athens* is an investigation of aberrations from natural order in the individual promoted by subtle forms of pride, just as *Troilus and Cressida* concerns itself with similar aberrations in the state. The backbone of Shakespeare's public thinking is the medieval, neo-classical conception of a universal hierarchy, embodied in Ulysses' best-known speech (and perhaps most coherently propounded for later generations in Pope's *Essay on Man*). E. M. W. Tillyard, describing this interpretation of the cosmos in *Shakespeare's History Plays*,[3] quotes a characteristic passage from I.K.'s 1598 translation of Hannibal Romei's *Courtier's Academy*,[4] which conveniently expounds that part of the theory which seems to me relevant to *Timon of Athens*:

Creatures live after the laws of nature: man liveth by reason, prudence and art. Living creatures may live a solitary life: man alone, being of himself insufficient and by nature an evil creature, without domestical and civil conversation cannot lead other than a miserable and discontented life. And therefore, as the philosopher saith very well, that man which cannot live in civil company either he is a god or a beast, seeing only God is sufficient of himself, and a solitary life best agreeth with a beast.

'This passage...', comments Tillyard, 'would have been accepted without question by every educated Elizabethan.' This familiar concept is, I suggest, the framework for *Timon of Athens*. In the first half of the drama Timon plays the god, far above all other men, aloof and indiscriminately munificent; in the second half he becomes the animal, alone and rejecting all fellow contact. In neither case will Timon consider or accept man's real condition. As Alcibiades declares in his funeral speech for Timon:

> thou abhorr'dst in us our human griefs.[5]

The burden of the play, positively expressed in Alcibiades, is the need to accept and love man as he is, and to acknowledge our human condition. Thus *Timon* is closely linked in theme with *Measure for Measure*, in the demand that fallible man shall, without being pandered to, nevertheless be loved and forgiven, a train of thought which eventually leads to *The Tempest*. In *Timon*, however, it is a secondary character who embodies this positive idea, while the protagonist acts out its obverse: Timon is negative. Macbeth too is negative, but *Macbeth* is perhaps Shakespeare's only tragedy of waste (a much abused term) and so the hero remains the controlling figure in presenting the dramatic idea; whereas Timon, when measured against the very different idea which is central to his play, is found wanting. Did this subject, apparently so apt, prove in fact to be too negative to match Shakespeare's dramatic thinking at this time? Was this the reason why his impulse flagged so that he did not finish revising the play? This can be no more than a conjecture.

In the closer analysis of the play which follows I shall not normally distinguish between the polished and unpolished parts of the text. I believe the play can be interpreted as a whole. Those passages which are clearly only in draft form may carry somewhat less weight critically, but they take their place in the general pattern of the play.

As a result of naïve blandness rather than of deliberate presumption, Timon has assumed a god-like status, a role which is clearly reflected in the phrasing and imagery. The poet announces

> I have in this rough work shap'd out a man,
> Whom this beneath world doth embrace and hug.

Timon is irresistible to all men:

> You see how all conditions, how all minds,
> As well of glib and slipp'ry creatures as
> Of grave and austere quality, tender down
> Their services to Lord Timon.

And it is by an act of grace that Timon is seen winning his opponents to join the throng of followers:

> Whose present grace to present slaves and servants
> Translates his rivals.

This line of imagery intensifies, till the sycophants whispering in Timon's ear breathe only by his allowance:

> Rain sacrificial whisperings in his ear,
> Make sacred even his stirrup, and through him
> Drink the free air.

True the painting carries a moral, the warning that pride goes before a fall, but significantly Timon does not consider this when he later receives the work. At the end of the scene the second lord declares that Pluto is merely Timon's steward. The masque symbolically sets Timon again above mere mankind who have to war with the human condition:

The five best senses acknowledge thee their patron, and come freely to gratulate thy plenteous bosom.

The original stage direction tells us that the Lords 'rise from the table, with much adoring of Timon'. And the Steward's bitter regrets carry a double meaning:

> His promises fly so beyond his state.

And even in his long speech at the mock banquet Timon still, by implication but unmistakably, draws a parallel between himself and the gods.

Timon is not discriminatingly or positively generous. The opening of the play presents a repulsive picture of the competing toadies who bask in Timon's favour. They are willing to travesty art to please him, and to fawn on others whom he approves. He is too beneficent to be in real contact with lesser mortals, whom he advances regardless of their worth or worthlessness. And we see him buying a jewel with the same casualness as that with which he relieves a friend. In short, he emulates the indiscriminate generosity of an abstract deity like Fortune. The real difference is that Timon proves to have feet of clay. As Lucius' servant dryly comments:

> You must consider that a prodigal course
> Is like the sun's,
> But not, like his, recoverable.

The only two figures at Timon's court who retain their self-respect are Apemantus, who refuses his gifts, and the Steward, who well earns his comparatively slight rewards.

Timon does not stop to consider the shallowness of the friendship which he virtually buys. Apemantus is unheeded:

> That there should be small love amongst these sweet knaves,
> And all this courtesy!

But Timon is pleasant enough in all his dealings for us to be both disappointed that he should allow himself to be so duped, and chagrined by his blindness. For, however sour his manner, we must surely second Apemantus in

> He that loves to be flattered is worthy o' th' flatterer.

If Timon is easily deceived, the audience is not, and is not meant to be. We mark the warnings that Timon wilfully ignores: 'I take no heed of thee.' He sweeps aside the reasonable considera-tion of his own affairs with an imperious and dramatic selflessness similar to Julius Caesar's:

> *Steward.* . . .it does concern you near.
> *Timon.* Near? Why, then, another time I'll hear thee.

Act I, the act that sets out the situation ends with an authoritative, impersonal rhymed couplet:

> O that men's ears should be
> To counsel deaf, but not to flattery.

Timon allows riches to isolate him in a privileged position, so he remains ignorant of the truth about men, and about himself. 'Why', he vapidly laments, 'I have often wish'd myself poorer that I might come nearer to you.' This is an idle and complacent comment, proper only to hypocrisy or extreme ingenuousness, the more so as the sentence is rounded out with, 'we are born to do benefits': Timon takes it for granted that the traffic between himself and others is in effect one-way. He pays lip-service to community: 'O what a precious comfort 'tis to have so many like brothers commanding one another's fortunes'; but we do not have to await the event to realize what simple self-delusion this is. We can hardly admire a man who cultivates such 'brothers', or who understands so little about men; nor feel unqualified pity when his own conduct overtakes him and he stands aghast in wide-eyed innocence.

The refusal of Ventidius' repayment finally drives home a number of these points. This is an unconsidered demonstration of bounty, part of the culpable display of recklessness that shocks his Steward:

> Takes no accompt
> How things go from him, nor resumes no care
> Of what is to continue.

He is not here doing Ventidius any particular kindness, since we are to understand that Ventidius' father has left him an ample fortune. On the contrary, he is withstanding the one proffered *exchange* of friendship and mutual honourableness, which he talks so much of. This can be nothing but a gesture; a view which is confirmed by Timon's readiness to talk of things which should be unspoken:

> Nay, my lords, ceremony was but devis'd at first
> To set a gloss on faint deeds, hollow welcomes,
> Recanting goodness, sorry ere 'tis shown;
> But where there is true friendship, there needs none.

Timon clearly means well: but that is not enough. His well-meaning favours knaves, smothers real friendship, and ruins his own estate, thus preventing the judicious and constructive generosity he could be offering.

What is the faithful Steward's view of this so-called munificence?

> When all our offices have been oppress'd
> With riotous feeders, when our vaults have wept
> With drunken spilth of wine, when every room
> Hath blaz'd with lights and bray'd with minstrelsy,
> I have retir'd me to a wasteful cock
> And set mine eyes at flow.

The constant impression is that the result of Timon's ready dispensing of cash is drunkenness, debauchery, orgy and waste:

> No care, no stop; so senseless of expense,
> That he will neither know how to maintain it,
> Nor cease his flow of riot.

Timon squanders money to maintain his own conception of himself:

> You may take my word, my lord, I know no man
> Can justly praise but what he does affect.
> I weigh my friend's affection with mine own,
> I'll tell you true. I'll call to you.

This is the vanity of giving:

> I take all and your several visitations
> So kind to heart, 'tis not enough to give:
> Methinks I could deal kingdoms to my friends,
> And ne'er be weary.

Timon's bounty is seen as a 'humour', a wilful obsession: 'There's no crossing him in's humour' declares the Steward. And while Timon thinks himself loved for his generosity, he is despised and made fun of:

> If I want gold, steal but a beggar's dog
> And give it Timon—why, the dog coins gold.

It is impossible to exaggerate the importance of such a line as,

> Never mind
> Was to be so unwise, to be so kind.

The play thus embodies truisms familiar to the neo-classicist. J. C. Maxwell declares that of all Shakespeare's works *Timon* 'falls most easily within the framework of an Aristotelian scheme, and Timon, both before and after his fall, is clearly an example of excess'.[6]

The liberal man [says Aristotle] will give to the right people, the right amounts, and at the right time. . . . Nor will he neglect his own property, since he wishes by means of this to help others. And he will refrain from giving to anybody and everybody, that he may have something to give to the right people, at the right time, and where it is noble to do so.... For as has been said, he is liberal who spends according to his substance and on the right objects; and he who exceeds is prodigal.[7]

Certainly there are important qualifications to be made in Timon's favour: within his own limited vision, he is sincere and constantly imagines himself to be acting idealistically. Shakespeare does not suggest that Timon is always wrong in giving. His brief replies to the Old Man whose daughter he marries to his servant show immediate right feeling. He does indeed in some sort display generous friendship, especially to Ventidius in need, and at an early stage one almost imagines he might be a benevolent despot. There is, again, a certain splendour in his high-minded view of man, even if it rests on a failure to consider the evidence, and on child-like vanity. As Peter Alexander says, he has 'a god-like image of man in his heart'. His behaviour may be culpable, but it is not despicable. He is an 'honest fool'.

And so Timon is, on the one hand, wholly admirable to men who know no intimate facts about him, the strangers; while, on the other, to his Steward, who knows the individual behind the god-like façade, he is truly lovable. If the Steward weeps over Timon's folly, he is weeping for one for whom he feels real affection. Yet the emphasis remains on Timon's lack of self-control. He is indiscriminate. He does good at random; and naïvely squanders more than he wisely distributes. The scene at the end of Act II between steward and master is revealing. With the coming of disaster, Timon abandons all fulsomeness; his tone is now direct and honest; but he is altogether at a loss. He is here like a hurt child beside the sorrowing maturity of his own overseer.

But whatever Timon's limitations, his society has, of course, no justification for treating him as it does: society is, in fact, ruthlessly and painstakingly indicted in the first half of the play. However, in considering Timon himself we are bound to remember that these are the very men he has chosen and fostered with his superficial beneficence, uncontrolled by reason or prudence, blindly presuming beyond man's proper scope to play the role of all-dispensing Fortune. Thus, Timon has no cause to blame Fate or mankind in general for what he wilfully brings on himself: his reaction to adversity is unwarrantably negative, just as his reaction to prosperity has been dangerously irresponsible and presumptuous.

The most difficult role to assess in this first part of the play is Apemantus. He is crabbed and uncouth, but his sour comments come close to the mark. His jibing is sometimes faintly reminiscent of the searching cross-talk from the Fool in *Lear*, who in his asperity also dismisses cliché and conventional attitudinizing:

> *Timon.*   Good morrow to thee, gentle Apemantus.
> *Apemantus.* Till I be gentle, stay thou for thy good morrow,
>   When thou art Timon's dog, and these knaves honest.

Fools in Shakespeare are constantly in league with truth; so that, though the scene is little more than a rough draft, it is not insignificant that Apemantus is on more friendly terms with the Fool when they are together than with any other character. At one point he praises a riposte from the Fool by claiming, 'That answer might have become Apemantus'; and the Fool says immediately afterwards, 'I do not always follow lover, elder brother and woman; sometime the philosopher'.

Critics who have seen Timon himself as a monument of wronged virtue have had to play down the caustic accuracy of Apemantus' social observation; and since he is not a warm or directly likeable character, they have been able to do so by emphasizing his harshness at the expense of his insight. Nevertheless, Apemantus seems to be cast in the philosophical tradition of a Diogenes; he serves as the relentless mentor in the play. He is neither taken in by the glitter of society, nor does he withdraw from it, but stays to warn and moralize. His view of his fellows, if sometimes almost as black as Timon's is at the last, remains philosophic rather than petulant or personal; and he is engaged throughout in moral and prophetic admonition, never in self-glorification or self-pity. Shakespeare, as so often, had set himself a nice problem: how to introduce the voice of reason into the play without hopelessly weakening the protagonist's dramatic status. I do not think he has solved the problem altogether, simply by giving sanity such a rugged exterior. The result is to confuse the issue (as it would have been confused in *Lear* if the king had ultimately resisted the rebukes of the Fool and Kent), since Timon is still necessarily left in a negative position; but by this device Shakespeare at least makes his play viable, however tenuously.

The dividing line between the positions of Timon and Apemantus in the second half of the play is a fine one, a distinction which is not always dramatically clear in detail, though in the main the two voices remain in subtle contrast, except in the apparently unrevised passage wherein Apemantus makes Timon confound himself: here Apemantus' role becomes blurred; but I shall return to this point. In the whole design one can perceive that Apemantus is cast as the homilist: often his words become so impersonal that he seems to speak for the play rather than for himself.

One of Shakespeare's many structural experiments in his later plays was to adopt a simple form divided into two clearly marked halves boldly and significantly contrasted against each other. This is perhaps most subtly effected in *Coriolanus*, and most daringly in *The Winter's Tale*, where the duality is pinpointed in the words

> thou met'st with things dying, I with things new-born.

A similar division is also explicitly summarized in *Timon*:

> One day he gives us diamonds, next day stones.

In his days of prosperity, instead of trying to understand men and work on them positively with his wealth, Timon has lived immoderately: now he flies to the opposite extreme. The malcontent was, of course, a fashionable stage figure at this time; as ever Shakespeare takes the popular fabric and cuts it to his own design.

That Timon's 'love' is so soon converted into hate bespeaks the empty and pretentious nature of his 'generosity'. A truly benevolent man could never be brought deliberately to cry down such vengeance upon his race; anyone might come to say such things in a state of hysteria, but Timon maintains them steadily from now till his death:

> Slaves and fools,
> Pluck the grave wrinkled senate from the bench,
> And minister in their steads! To general filths
> Convert, o'th'instant, green virginity!
> Do't in your parents' eyes! Bankrupts, hold fast;
> Rather than render back, out with your knives,
> And cut your trusters' throats! Bound servants, steal!
> Large-handed robbers your grave masters are,
> And pill by law. Maid, to thy master's bed;
> Thy mistress is o'th'brothel! Son of sixteen,
> Pluck the lin'd crutch from thy old limping sire;
> With it beat out his brains!

The malcontent is also indicting himself—the very excess makes this apparent. There is no poetic conviction in this opening speech of Act IV: compare it with the more savage passages of *The Revenger's Tragedy*. Shakespeare does not seem really to have entered into this wild loathing of mankind. Whatever Timon's state, he has certainly no more grounds for such indiscriminate denunciation than he had for his equally indiscriminate generosity. To underline this fact we are introduced at once to the innocent and open-hearted victims of Timon's excesses—the Steward and his fellows. Timon's unbridled damning of Man must include these patient followers. Their direct feeling and real, simple generosity discredit Timon's megalomaniac ravings. Those Timon has cause to hate, he himself has bred up to it; while he forgets those who patently deserve his consideration. The Steward can see Timon's career in clear perspective:

> Who would be so mock'd with glory, or to live
> But in a dream of friendship...?

But he has no bitter word, only sympathy and affection:

> Poor honest lord, brought low by his own heart,
> Undone by goodness.

And he concludes, 'I'll ever serve his mind, with my best will': here is an unassuming nobility to which Timon cannot aspire.

So when Timon cries:

> Who dares, who dares,
> In purity of manhood stand upright,
> And say this man's a flatterer? If one be,
> So are they all,

we are reminded that his cynicism is culled from narrow and self-induced experience; and when he complains that 'the learned pate Ducks to the golden fool', we remember that such is the conduct Timon has courted. When he concludes,

> all's obliquy;
> There's nothing level in our cursed natures
> But direct villainy,

we ask, 'What of the Steward, of Alcibiades, the servants, the strangers, and their like?' At last we see Timon's fury as a private jaundice resulting from his failure to buy love by means of lavish distribution of favours.

When Timon finds his new supply of gold, his condemnation of the malpractices it could foster is eloquent, but he conveniently overlooks the fact that his own abuse of wealth is to be included in the indictment. To hide the coin is moral escapism, not a solution. Can he conceive it doing no good, simply because it breeds nothing but selfish greed in flatterers? And so Apemantus appears, to shake Timon from his complacent world of private hatred.

The frequency of animal imagery in the play has often been noticed. It should be added that in the early acts it is used almost exclusively by or of Apemantus, his role being contrasted with Timon's superhuman elevation. It is immediately after this dialogue in I, i,

> Second Lord. Away, unpeacable dog, or I'll spurn thee hence!
> Apemantus. I will fly, like a dog, the heels o'th'ass.
> First Lord. He's opposite to humanity,

that Timon is again raised to godhead, the opposite extreme:

> He pours it out. Plutus the god of gold
> Is but his steward.

We are kept aware of the two states outside the human condition. But Timon, when forced to abandon the one, eagerly adopts the other:

> Alcibiades. What art thou there? Speak.
> Timon. A beast as thou art.

Timon turns away friend and enemy alike; and he himself is utterly ungrateful in his petulance, while in the very act of brooding upon the ingratitude of others:

> Alcibiades. Here is some gold for thee.
> Timon. Keep it, I cannot eat it.

The tables are turned: Timon is thankless and incapable of responding to the generosity of others. He has forgotten his own words earlier: 'Oh what a precious comfort 'tis, to have so many like brothers commanding one another's fortunes.'

Apemantus immediately attacks Timon as a fake cynic who has turned misanthrope in an enormous huff because his irrational dreams about human nature have proved false:

Men report thou dost affect my manners...putting on the cunning of a carper....Thou wast told thus....Do not *assume* my likeness.

The argument which Apemantus here presents is often misrepresented. He is not saying that Timon would renounce poverty if he had the chance: we know that he has already found a fresh supply of gold. Shakespeare is not merely concerned to show that Apemantus does not know what he is talking about; far from it. What he says is that Timon, being an escapist from reality, always seeks an extreme, where issues are simplified into being either rosy or without hope:

> Thou'dst courtier be again
> Wert thou not beggar. Willing misery
> Outlives incertain pomp—

in short, in hoping for nothing and dismissing mankind, Timon has found a much more secure retreat than in his previous dream of perfect living. When his glittering world crashed about his ears, he was bound to be involved; when his lonely indulgence in loathing is shown to be ill-founded, he can, and does, shut his eyes, as we have seen. Thus, like Richard II and Coriolanus, though for different reasons, Timon cannot bear mediocrity: he must be all-significant or a cipher; life must appear a Utopia or a Hell. Timon will not accept the human condition with its confusions and compromises. He must be more, or less, than man. If he cannot be a god, he will become a beast.

It is in Act IV that the distinction between Apemantus and Timon, the caustic, satirical philosopher and the spoilt child sulking in the face of a fate he has brought on himself, is most important, and also most difficult to make dramatically. Timon has been 'a madman so long, and now a fool'. In his own defence he enters on a long speech of self-pity, to which Apemantus trenchantly replies, 'Art thou proud yet?' Apemantus exposes the falsity of Timon's values which have led him to confuse gratitude with love, and comes to the heart of the whole play in the sentence, 'The middle of humanity thou never knewest, but the extremity of both ends'. Eventually Apemantus adopts some of Timon's own arguments and attitudes ('Give it to the beasts, to be rid of men', and so on): presumably he is drawing Timon on. Already in the first act Timon has been made to condemn his own future conduct in terms exactly appropriate to the play, when he berates Apemantus' churlishness:

> Fie, th'art a churl, y'have got a humour there
> Does not become a man.

Now, as Apemantus plays devil's advocate, Timon is again made to condemn his own imitation of bestial life in even rounder terms:

What beast couldst thou be that were not subject to a beast? And what a beast art thou already, that seest not thy loss in transformation!

It may seem like special pleading to argue that Apemantus here changes sides to draw Timon out and make him condemn himself. But one should consider that it is in fact Timon who truly adopts the 'solitary life' which 'best agreeth with the beast': it is Apemantus who sought the interview, and it is Apemantus who returns to mankind, to live in society as its moral mentor. His final 'Live and love thy misery' shows him as having accurately sized up Timon's whole situation.

For now Timon proceeds to the final rejection of man. He hates life: 'I am sick of this false world.' And he dedicates the globe to the beasts: 'that beasts May have the world in empire'. He reaches a new pitch of cynicism when he advises the banditti not only to hate others but even to 'love not yourselves'. The climax of this sequence falls in the scene with the Steward. Against all the evidence Timon a first tries to cling to his total rejection of man:

> *Steward.* An honest poor servant of yours.
> *Timon.* Then I know thee not.

> I never had honest man about me, I; all
> I kept were knaves, to serve in meat to villains.

But the play pursues him and pins him down till he is forced to acknowledge 'One honest man'. Is this, we wonder, to be the beginning of a new vision for him? By no means, for it proves the nadir of his wilful introversion. Timon is no longer dealing with men whom he can convince himself are contemptible: but how does he reward this honest man? He offers him gold, the gold which Timon, however wrong-headedly, believes to be evil, and which, as employed in the play, has become the symbol of destructive materialism: he exhorts him to hatred:

> Hate all, curse all, show charity to none;

and ends the act with the ominous words:

> Ne'er see thou man, and let me ne'er see thee.

Shakespeare shows great technical daring in planning the construction of the second half of *Timon* as a series of duologues or interviews. These are not simply repetitive but pile one on top of another to build, as it were, a negative climax. The aim is to achieve a powerful austerity in contrast with the shifting effects of the first half of the play, but also parallel to the successive appeals to Timon's 'friends' in Act III. The manner is severe and classical; but its success is only partial.

There is an attempt to dramatize Timon's last denial of mankind differently and more fully in Act v. This depends on the appeal to Timon by the city of Athens in time of crisis to come and save them, and Timon's refusal. Unfortunately, there is no previous evidence in terms of the play that Timon has ever been a crucial figure in the state. So that, unlike the decision which is forced on Coriolanus, with the whole dramatic weight of the play behind it, the situation in *Timon* appears contrived, and largely fails of its effect. But the dramatic intention is clear enough: Timon's position is now represented by the words 'I care not'. His abandonment of life is negative, the confirmation and consummation of all that has gone before. Timon the absolutist could find no place on earth. This absolutism was at first innocent, and remains sufficiently naïve for him to retain a certain nobility, though a barren and inhuman nobility. In order to strengthen the presentation of Timon's death, his epitaph is introduced twice, not altogether successfully in dramatic terms; but the pattern is now complete.

The action centred on Alcibiades is no mere irrelevant incident. I agree with Peter Alexander that Act III, sc. v is central to the whole play, though I would interpret it rather differently. The Senate admit that Alcibiades' friend has been subjected to wrongs, but they smugly declare, 'He's truly valiant that can wisely suffer', and they advocate the wearing of one's injuries 'carelessly'. Alcibiades then reasonably asks why, if they believe this, they should possess an army instead of being pacifists. The First Senator's reply, 'Nothing emboldens sin so much as mercy', recalls the debate between Isabella and Angelo. This passage is highly relevant to the whole play. The issue is concentrated in Alcibiades' lines,

> To be in anger is impiety;
> But who is man that is not angry?
> Weigh but the crime with this.

In short, he insists that man's fallibility must be taken into account in balancing justice against mercy. Surely there is no doubt that Alcibiades has, and is meant to have, our sympathy in this scene. He is felt to be right because he accepts man as man, with all his limitations and weaknesses. Thus Timon is paralleled with the Senate: each demands or assumes an unattainable absolute standard of conduct. The self-protective canker in the state is legislation by fear; Timon's canker, that of the individual, is fear of living in actuality and facing the complexity of man's condition.

To say this is not to argue that the two plots have been neatly integrated. But it now becomes quite clear why Alcibiades' action is allowed to conclude the play. Alcibiades, like Timon, has been betrayed and has reacted violently, but, unlike Timon, he comes to terms with life. When forced in turn to make his moral choice, his decision is positive; he accepts man and his limitations; and in the light of this acceptance can exercise mercy. The line of argument on which Alcibiades yields is:

> We were not all unkind, nor all deserve
> The common stroke of war,

which forcefully reminds us how oversimplified was Timon's judgement in condemning all men alike by a rule of thumb. 'All have not offended'; and, by corollary, if the state does not consist exclusively either of good or bad members, so the individual is neither perfect nor utterly vile. In burying his anger, Alcibiades acts like a wise, merciful, and humanly inconsistent being, not like a god or a beast. This emphasis on the need to accept, minister to, correct and forgive fallible human nature links *Timon* to a far greater work, *Measure for Measure*, and points the way once again towards the final romances.

So the idea is rounded out. It has been powerfully conceived, but not realized in fully developed dramatic terms. The suggestion, often made both on textual and critical grounds, that we have no more than an advanced draft of *Timon*, seems convincing. It is easy to see why Shakespeare might seize on the subject of Timon in a period of troubled thinking and warring moods, and might modify his material along the lines I have suggested. And it is, further, quite feasible that the reason he failed to finish the work was that, in the event, the hero proved too negative a vehicle for his thinking, and the whole fabric of the play too destructive at a time when his thoughts were slowly gestating the new positive ideas of the final group of plays. It is interesting that Shakespeare's only other fundamentally negative play, *Troilus and Cressida* (though in a much more advanced state of revision than *Timon* and altogether more effective and disturbing), also lacks finish. Perhaps not only the treatment but also the rejection of the Timon motif may contribute to our understanding of the whole body of Shakespeare's thought.

NOTES

1. T. M. Parrott, *The Problem of Timon of Athens* (Shakespeare Association Papers no. 10, 1923), p. 3.
2. 'Timon of Athens', *Scrutiny*, xv, 3 (1948), 196. In reading (and sometimes re-reading) *Timon* criticism, I find that I have agreed fairly closely with J. C. Maxwell on a number of specific points; and elsewhere with O. J. Campbell and A. C. Collins.
3. P. 14. I have adopted Tillyard's modernized spelling and punctuation, except for two commas.
4. P. 247.
5. Quotations are from *Timon of Athens*, ed. H. J. Oliver (Arden Shakespeare, 1959).
6. 'Timon of Athens', *Scrutiny*, xv, 3 (1948), 197.
7. *Ethica Nichomachea*, IV, i, 1020^a, 24–1020^b, 25, translated by W. D. Ross, *The Works of Aristotle* (Oxford, 1915), IX.

WHO STRUTTED AND BELLOWED?

BY

A. J. GURR

Edward Alleyn's reputation as one of the two leading actors of the Elizabethan stage has fluctuated in the last hundred years more or less according to whether critics think Shakespeare disliked his acting or not. William Armstrong's defence,[1] denying that Hamlet's speech to the players was aimed at Alleyn, and quoting praise for him from Thomas Heywood, Nashe, Jonson and Dekker, certainly repolished his reputation for us, by showing that he and Richard Burbage (who played Hamlet) were equally famous in the eyes and ears of Elizabethan theatre-goers. But it does not follow, as Armstrong also claims, that they shared the same manner of acting.

If Alleyn represented a kind of acting quite distinct from that practised by Shakespeare's company and its leader Burbage, then it is possible that what Shakespeare criticized in *Hamlet* was in fact Alleyn's style of acting, which could have been different from Burbage's without in the least affecting his fame, if it stood in a different tradition and was praised from within that tradition.

There is no doubt that two distinct kinds of acting did exist among the adult companies in the early seventeenth century. Thomas Carew attacked a Blackfriars audience for hissing a play of Davenant's, performed there in 1629, in terms which make that quite clear:

> they'l still slight
> All that exceeds Red Bull, and Cockepit flight.
> These are the men in crowded heapes that throng
> To that adulterate stage, where not a tong
> Of th'untun'd Kennell, can a line repeat
> Of serious sence: but like lips, meet like meat;
> Whilst the true brood of Actors, that alone
> Keepe naturall unstrayn'd Action in her throne
> Behold their Benches bare, though they rehearse
> The tearser *Beaumonts* or great *Iohnsons* verse.[2]

It is well known that Shakespeare's company at the Blackfriars had social and intellectual aspirations well above their rivals; as Carew makes clear, their audiences did not always live up to the pretension. The actors, though, certainly did. James Wright's *Historia Histrionica* reports that

Before the Wars, there were in being all these Play-houses at the same time. The *Black-friers*, and *Globe* on the *Bankside*, a Winter and Summer House, belonging to the same Company called the King's Servants; the *Cockpit* or *Phoenix*, in *Drury-Lane*, called the Queen's Servants; the private House in *Salisbury-court*, called the Prince's Servants; the Fortune near *White-cross-street*, and the *Red Bull* at the upper end of St *John's-street*: The two last were mostly frequented by Citizens, and the meaner sort of People. All these Companies got Money, and Liv'd in Reputation, especially those of the *Blackfriers*, who were Men of grave and sober Behaviour.[3]

There are several scornful references to vulgarity at the Fortune, Red Bull and Cockpit in contemporary writing. George Wither in *Abuses Stript and Whipt* (1613), Thomas Tomkis in *Albumazar* (1615)[4] and Carew all give support to Edmund Gayton's sardonic claim to 'have heard, that the Poets of the Fortune and red Bull, had alwayes a mouth-measure for their Actors (who were terrible teare-throats) and made their lines proportionable to their compasse, which were *sesquipedales*, a foot and a halfe'.[5] Other references in Gayton's book prove him to have been familiar with at least seventeen plays and several actors from the Fortune, Red Bull and Globe/Blackfriars companies. Therefore he speaks through the tongue in his cheek with some authority. Richard Flecknoe, writing soon after Gayton, shows what a standard comparison for exaggeration Red Bull acting had become, when he writes (in his Character *Of a Proud [Wo]man*) 'She looks high and speaks in a majestique Tone, like one playing the *Queens* part at the *Bull*'.[6]

It was 'majestick' parts that Alleyn excelled in, according to Flecknoe's contemporary Fuller,[7] and there is reason to believe that Alleyn's violence of voice and gesture in his most famous parts established a tradition of exaggeration which accompanied him with the Admiral's Men to the Fortune, and went from there with Richard Perkins, whom Heywood compared to Alleyn, to the Red Bull, and which contrasted unfavourably in some minds with the moderation of the Blackfriars.

Armstrong is primarily concerned to deny that Alleyn's acting was exaggerated in comparison with Burbage's, but he leaves too many questions unanswered. He quotes Ben Jonson with Heywood as chief witness to Alleyn's quality, even though Jonson revealed in the relative privacy of his *Discoveries* a different opinion about the playing of two of Alleyn's most famous roles:

the true Artificer will not run away from nature, as hee were afraid of her; or depart from life, and the likenesse of Truth; but speake to the capacity of his hearers. And though his language differ from the vulgar somewhat; it shall not fly from all humanity, with the *Tamerlanes*, and *Tamer-chams* of the late Age, which had nothing in them but the *scenicall* strutting, and furious vociferation, to warrant them to the ignorant gapers.[8]

One might almost think he had been reading *Hamlet* ('O there be Players...that neither hauing th'accent of Christians, nor the gate of Christian, Pagan, nor man, haue so strutted and bellowed, that I haue thought some of Natures Iornimen had made men, and not made them well, they imitated humanitie so abhominably'). Armstrong also points out that Alleyn and Burbage were never explicitly contrasted (nor of course were they compared), and that the terms of praise used for both were identical. Each was compared to Roscius as actors and 'Proteus for shapes' at various times. This is hardly surprising, since little else was applicable from classical times. There was very little variation in the terms of praise used for any actor before 1660. Nonetheless, despite this narrow range of possible reference, the praises of Alleyn and Burbage were sung in fact to strikingly different tunes.

Armstrong quotes praise of Alleyn from four major Elizabethan writers. Nashe recorded his high repute in 1592, before Burbage had reached prominence, and in the same year declared that 'Not *Roscius*...could euer performe more in action, than famous *Ned Allen*'.[9] Dekker in 1604 wrote of Alleyn's oration to King James as delivered 'with excellent action, and a well tun'de audible voyce'.[10] Jonson, some time before 1616, said very much the same thing as Nashe:

'others speak, but only thou dost act.'[11] And finally Heywood, in his prologue to the revived *Jew of Malta* written some years after Alleyn's death, compared him to 'Proteus *for shapes, and* Roscius *for a tongue, So could he speake, so vary*'.[12]

When Jonson wrote his praise, the word 'act' still had a residual connotation of the use of (rhetorical) 'Action', and it cannot be insignificant that Jonson joined Nashe and Dekker in applying the term to Alleyn. The 'speaking' with which Jonson contrasted Alleyn's 'Action' seems a term more applicable to what 'the true brood of Actors, that alone Keepe naturall un-strayn'd Action in her throne' were used to practise. Carew contrasted his 'naturall' actors with those who satisfied Cockpit and Red Bull audiences, and it is no coincidence that Heywood's praise of Alleyn was spoken on the stage of the Cockpit. The actor taking Alleyn's old part for the revival of the *Jew*, who was compared in Heywood's prologue to Alleyn, had once acted with him at the Fortune. Heywood himself wrote most of his plays for the Red Bull. Performing 'more in action' seems to have been clearly the aim of only one tradition of acting.

It was the 'naturall unstrayn'd Action' of the Blackfriars which was singled out by those who praised Burbage—not his 'Action', or his majesty, so much as his power of convincing imper-sonation, his acting 'to the life'. His elegist chose not to eulogize the quality of his voice and action but how lifelike he was:

> oft haue I seene him, leap into the Graue
> suiting the person, wch he seem'd to haue
> of A sadd Louer, with soe true an Eye
> that theer I would haue sworne, he meant to dye,
> oft haue I seene him, play this part in ieast,
> soe liuly, that Spectators, and the rest
> of his sad Crew, whilst he but seem'd to bleed,
> amazed, thought euen then hee dyed in deed.[13]

Webster in his Character 'Of an Excellent Actor', generally taken because of the references to his being a painter to be a description of Burbage, after putting forward the standard claims for acting, added, in his praise, that 'what we see him personate, we thinke truely done before vs'[14]. And Thomas May, writing obliquely soon after Burbage's death, in *The Heir* (1620), said almost the same things:

> *Roscio.* ...has not your Lordship seene
> A Player personate *Hieronimo*?
> *Pol(ymetes).* By th'masse tis true, I have seen the knave paint grief
> In such a lively colour, that for false
> And acted passion he has drawne true teares
> From the spectators. Ladies in the boxes
> Kept time with sighs, and teares to his sad accents
> As had he truely been the man he seem'd.[15]

A description of 'painting' grief in one of Burbage's most famous parts, found in a play written within a year of his death, could refer to nobody else. In sum, the correlation between Burbage's and the Blackfriars' 'naturall' impersonations on the one hand, and Alleyn and the Fortune or

Red Bull tear-throat flights on the other seems undeniable. But the most positive evidence of all remains to be considered.

None of Burbage's parts became so synonymous to Elizabethans with noise and violence as Alleyn's Tamburlaine did (his Tamar Cham, Orlando, Cutlack and Faustus were remarked on as noisy too, but his brand image was Tamburlaine). Burbage's lines in *The Spanish Tragedy* were mocked just as Ancient Pistol mocked the pampered jades of Asia, but this was poking fun at famous lines, not violent speech. The only description we have of Burbage's action is something described as a swagger by Samuel Rowland in 1600 (if it does in fact refer to Burbage as Richard III):

> *Gallants*, like *Richard* the vsurper, swagger,
> That had his hand continuall on his dagger[16]

a simple enough trick of characterization, and an isolated reference.

The five known references to Tamburlaine's violence not only reinforce the sneers directed at Red Bull and Cockpit actors, but clinch the theory that it was in fact Alleyn who created the Red Bull style. The first three references were made in 1597, first in a cony-catching tract by one E.S., who wrote 'S. bent his browes and fetcht his stations vp and downe the rome, with such furious Iesture as if he had beene playing Tamberlane on a stage'.[17] Does this not suggest that it seemed exaggerated, or at least was thought of as an apt simile for exaggeration? Joseph Hall gave the same opinion in more eloquent if over-inflated detail, describing Tamburlaine's gait as 'stalking':

> One higher pitch'd doth set his soaring thought
> On crowned kings that Fortune hath low brought:
> Or some vpreared, high-aspiring swaine
> As it might be the Turkish *Tamberlaine*.
> Then weeneth he his base drink-drowned spright,
> Rapt to the threefold loft of heauens hight,
> When he conceiues vpon his fained stage
> The stalking steps of his great personage,
> Graced with huf-cap termes, and thundring threats,
> That his poore hearers hayre quite vpright sets.
> Such soone, as some braue-minded hungry youth,
> Sees fitly frame to his wide-strained mouth,
> He vaunts his voyce vpon an hyred stage,
> With high-set steps, and princely carriage:
> Now soouping in side robes of Royalty,
> That earst did skrub in lowsie brokery.
> There if he can with termes Italianate,
> Big-sounding sentences, and words of state,
> Faire patch me vp his pure *Iambick* verse,
> He rauishes the gazing Scaffolders:
> Then certes was the famous *Corduban*
> Neuer but halfe so high *Tragedian*.[18]

Marston's *Histriomastix* includes a scene where the travelling players on whom Marston tried out his satire are turned perforce into soldiers; and one of them is asked:

Sirha is this you would rend and teare the Cat
Vpon a Stage, and now march like a drown'd rat?
Looke vp and play the *Tamburlaine*: you rogue you.[19]

It can be seen that the role was already proverbial, and yet no more references to it appeared for six years. Alleyn retired from the Admiral's Men at the end of 1597, returning in December 1600 to the new Fortune with a smaller financial interest in the company, and finally retired some time between 1604 and 1606. And so the next group of references to Tamburlaine appeared between 1601 and 1604, when Alleyn was back on stage. Dekker and Middleton both linked 'stalking' with Tamburlaine in 1603, Dekker referring to 'Death (like a Spanish Leager, or rather like stalking *Tamberlaine*)'.[20] Middleton said that 'the Spindle-shanke Spyders which showed like great Leachers with little legges, went stalking ouer his head, as if they had been conning of *Tamburlayne*'.[21] And during the same year this writer used a different simile which seems to refer to Alleyn's new financial arrangements at the Fortune:

the whole Neast of Ants...made a Ring about her and their restored friend, seruing in stead of a dull Audience of Stinkards sitting in the Penny Galleries of a Theater, and yawning vpon the Players, whilst the Ant began to stalke like a three Quarter sharer.[22]

Finally, in the second period Anthony Scoloker used the term 'furious' of another of Alleyn's roles, alluding to the acting as well as to the story:

thus did he act yᵉ tragical Sceanes who onlye pend the Comicall, Became, if not as brutish as *Acteon*, as furious as *Orlando*, of whose humours, and Passions, I had rather you should read them, then I Act them.

It is inconceivable that such a renowned player could have appeared for the Admiral's Men without taking the leading roles, especially those he was most famous for, and it is hard to believe that these six writers could have had anyone but Alleyn in mind. Certainly no reader would have taken the allusions to refer to anyone else. And if further proof is needed to link Tamburlaine's stalking with Alleyn, we need only take one more quotation from the end of the earlier period (1597), which actually speaks of someone with Alleyn's gait as 'stalking and roaring':

Clodius me thinkes lookes passing big of late,
With *Dunstons* browes, and *Allens Cutlacks* gate:
What humours haue possest him so, I wonder,
His eyes are lightning, and his words are thunder:...
Stalking and roaring like to *Iobs* great deuill.[24]

All these references to Alleyn's characteristics, in four of his seven known parts, give rise to some uncertainty whether Armstrong is right in dismissing the claim that Hamlet was attacking him. It is true that Pistol's parody of *Tamburlaine's* verse does not prove that Hamlet was referring to the actor of *Tamburlaine*. It is equally true that Shakespeare's bad actor *struts*; in *Hamlet* it is the Ghost who has a 'martial stauke' ('with solemne march...slowe and stately'). But the robustious periwig-pated fellow who has the gait of neither 'Christian, pagan, nor man' may have been meant to suggest 'that atheist *Tamberlane*' as much as any other monster (Jonson seems to have made the association), and he is periwigged like the Tamburlaine of Laurence Johnson's 1603 portrait, which is believed to have been modelled on Alleyn.[25] And what role of the time was better calculated to 'spleet the eares of the groundlings'? If the 'fellow' was not Alleyn, he certainly came close with his strutting and bellowing to Alleyn's stalking and roaring.

The chief counter-argument, that Shakespeare would not attack the only other adult company at the same time as he was attacking the rival children's companies, collapses if the 'little eyases' passage be accepted for a late insertion, as E. A. J. Honigmann contends.[26] But of course if it does refer to Tamburlaine, then it is the only one (apart from Jonson's late entry) made at a time when Alleyn was not on view. And above all, the references seem deliberately oblique.

I think both Dover Wilson and Armstrong miss the point in arguing either that the 'Trage-dians' of the City in *Hamlet* were meant to parody Alleyn's company, or that Hamlet admired his 'old friends' too much to draw a picture of their First Player in his strictures. Their function in the play is much more complex than that. Their first appearance and the 'rugged Pyrrhus' speech which is then spoken serve primarily to prepare Hamlet's mind for the soliloquy that follows. There Hamlet admits himself confronted by the 'fiction', the 'dream of passion' in the Player which mocks the reality of his own situation—this being the climax of the act. The Players here serve as catalysts for Hamlet's emotions, no more. Their leader, in giving a patently poetic piece of declamation, simply provides a contrast with Hamlet, who gives a performance of his own much more realistic passion immediately afterwards. That is, the actor of the First Player provides a level of recitation in comparison with which the actor of Hamlet seems completely natural.

When the Players appear again, and Hamlet delivers his admonitions, they are still supposed to be people behaving normally, not yet acting, and cannot be taken as the butts of Hamlet's attack. He had not objected to the First Player's Pyrrhus speech, although when it was spoken the Player's manner of delivery must have been different from his original manner when he was just a First Player being himself. Hamlet makes no reference at all to his earlier speech. The 'robustious perwig-pated fellow' is surely therefore held up at this point simply as a horrible example. The occasion is ripe for the lordly (but far from majestic) amateur to hold forth on what the earlier soliloquy following the First Player's recitation had put in his mind: the whole question of feigning reality in acting. Nothing could be better calculated than these strictures to make the audience conscious of the Players as actors and unconscious of the underlying fact that the play to come is itself part of a play and that everyone else is of course acting too. The effect is to lose the audience in the Hamlet level of the play, leaving them conscious not of their own level of reality in relation to the play they are watching, but only of Hamlet's level in relation to the further level which the Players are to supply.

It is natural that in doing this Shakespeare should put the audience in mind of another, readily recognizable style of acting, since his chief purpose was to distract attention from the style of his own actors at the Hamlet level, which ought not to be recognized as acting at all. A purpose like this requires a second style far from parody (which would be a distracting amusement), and it is worth noting how carefully it is introduced to the audience in four slow steps. First we are given just the Players as themselves, and one piece of deliberately archaic verse for one of them to recite; this is followed by a comment on the falsity of recited passion; not until some scenes later comes the picture of an overdoing actor (one which the First Player evidently recognizes, since he declares that his company has reformed the faults Hamlet mentions); and more of the play proper intervenes before the final step to the acting of the Play within the play.

In the Play-scene the Players show that they have indeed reformed their acting only indifferently. Where before they were players acting Players, now they appear as players acting Players acting. Therefore the Player Queen '*makes passionate action*' in an all too explicable dumbshow, imitating the robustious fellow whose tricks Hamlet had reprehended; and so they at the same time offset the 'Play' from the play proper, and by increasing the layers of 'feigning' make Hamlet/Burbage and the rest of the cast seem natural in comparison. Though naming no names too loudly Shakespeare did use Alleyn's distinctive style, not for parody, but to give his own more restrained players more credibility.

If Shakespeare actually did have Alleyn in mind, then, he left him condemned only by implication, no more than shadowed in Hamlet's airy words, a foil primarily for Burbage's virtuosity. The condemnation of 'a strutting player' spoken to some Inns of Court audience in *Troilus and Cressida* a couple of years later, when Alleyn was back on stage, is still less specific. Nonetheless, *Hamlet* and *Troilus* do show that Shakespeare considered Burbage to be more restrained, less exaggerated in his acting than some of his profession, and there is plenty of evidence from outside the Globe to prove that Alleyn's virtuosity was as 'a stalking-stamping Player, that will raise a tempest with his toung, and thunder with his heeles'.[27] Alleyn and Burbage were equally praised by posterity partly because they were the leaders of the two companies which first purged the theatres from the 'barbarisme' of the 1580's and raised it to 'the perfection it now shines with', as Richard Brome put it in 1638.[28] The same two leaders created the divergence of style which led the pretensions of the King's Men at the Blackfriars to differ so clearly from those of the Fortune and Red Bull companies through the seventeenth century.

NOTES

1. W. A. Armstrong, 'Shakespeare and the Acting of Edward Alleyn', *Shakespeare Survey* 7 (1954), 82–9.

2. Prefatory verses to Davenant, *The Just Italian* (1630), A3ᵛ–A4ʳ.

3. *Historia Histrionica* (1699), B3ʳ.

4. *Abuses Stript and Whipt* (1613), D2ᵛ, and *Albumazar* (1615), C1ʳ. Each of these passages jibes mainly at the audiences.

5. *Pleasant Notes upon Don Quixote* (1654), 24.

6. *Ænigmatical Characters* (1658), B1ᵛ.

7. *The History of the Worthies of England* (1662), Fff2ᵛ.

8. *Works*, ed. Herford and Simpson, VIII, 587.

9. *Pierce Pennilesse* (1592), F4ᵛ.

10. *The Magnificent Entertainment* (1604), C1ʳ.

11. 'To Edward Allen', *Works*, VIII, 56–7.

12. Marlowe, *The Jew of Malta* (1633), A4ᵛ.

13. Third funeral elegy, 2nd version (1619). Cf. C. M. Ingleby, *Shakespeare, the Man and the Book* (1881), II, 169–77.

14. Overbury, *New Characters* (1615), M6ʳ.

15. *The Heir* (1620), B1ʳ.

16. *The Letting of Humours Blood in the Head-Vaine* (1600), A2^r.
17. *The Discovery of the Knights of the Post* (1597), C2^v.
18. *Virgidemiarum* (1597), B4^v–B5^r.
19. *Histriomastix* (1610), G1^r.
20. *The Wonderfull Yeare* (1603), C4^v.
21. *The Blacke Booke* (1604), D1^r.
22. *Father Hubburds Tales* (1603), B4^r.
23. *Daiphantus* (1604), B1^v.
24. Everard Guilpin, *Skialetheia* (1598), B2^v.
25. Cf. Martin Holmes, 'An Unrecorded Portrait of Edward Alleyn', *Theatre Notebook*, v (1950), 11–13.
26. 'The Date of *Hamlet*', *Shakespeare Survey* 9 (1956), 24–34.
27. W.S., *The Puritan* (1607), F2^v.
28. *The Antipodes* (1638), D3^v.

SHAKESPEARE IN PLANCHÉ'S
EXTRAVAGANZAS

BY

STANLEY WELLS

James Robinson Planché (1796–1880) was a man of varied talents: on the one hand, a Fellow of the Society of Antiquaries, instrumental in the founding of the British Archaeological Association, Rouge Croix Pursuivant of Arms and later Somerset Herald, author of books on heraldry, *A History of British Costumes* (1834) and *A Cyclopaedia of Costume* (1876–9); on the other hand a practical man of the theatre—musician, designer, translator and adapter of many plays from the French, and author of innumerable pantomimes, burlesques, burlettas, melodramas and other stage works. His output was prodigious; but scarcely a line of it is remembered. If we hear anything that he wrote, it is as likely as not to be in the German translation of his libretto for Weber's opera *Oberon*. True, he has his place in theatrical history; but he is remembered less for his original writing than as a campaigner for reasonable copyright laws for the protection of the rights of librettists and playwrights, and as the man whose work on the history of costume had a profound influence on the staging of Shakespeare and other 'historical' dramatists. His best work for the stage is undoubtedly in the forty-four extravaganzas, published in a Testimonial Edition in 1879.[1] A number of writers have demonstrated W. S. Gilbert's indebtedness to these works,[2] but Planché was a Gilbert without a Sullivan. The extravaganzas are no longer read or performed. Indeed they, along with the rest of his output, have been declared unreadable.[3] But this is a harsh judgement; I feel more sympathy with that expressed by Allardyce Nicoll, who describes some of Planché's earlier writings as 'among the most delightful things the early nineteenth-century theatre produced. Trivial they may be, but they have a grace and a lightness of touch which makes us esteem more highly this prolific Somerset Herald.'[4]

Those who condemn and those who praise have alike recognized that Planché's writings are highly informative about the stage of his time. As Dougald MacMillan has shown, his intentions were not always trivial.[5] He was genuinely concerned about the future of the English theatre, anxious to raise the standards of both the 'legitimate' and the 'illegitimate' drama, and this concern is evident even in many of his lightest works. Writers such as Allardyce Nicoll and George Rowell[6] have quoted from Planché's works in general surveys of the Victorian stage. My object here is the more limited one of looking at the extravaganzas to see what they have to tell us about Shakespeare.

I

In the preface (published in 1879) to the first of his works to be called an extravaganza—*High, Low, Jack, and the Game*, first performed in 1833—Planché explained that he had used blank verse instead of the rhyming verse normal in pieces written, as this was, for the Olympic Theatre: 'There was some risk in departing from a style which had become identified with the popular little theatre; but it was favourably received by the audience, the ears of the play-going public being more accustomed to the heroic measure in those days than they are at present, and thoroughly familiar with all the quotations from, or parodies on, passages in Shakespeare and other of our elder dramatists with which the dialogue was copiously interlarded.' There seems no need to question the assumption that his public would recognize allusions to Shakespeare.[7] Indeed it might reasonably be argued that Shakespeare's plays—in however debased versions—were more truly a part of the living theatre a century ago than they are today. Henry Morley, for instance, wrote of a production in 1853: 'The "Midsummer Night's Dream" abounds in the most delicate passages of Shakespeare's verse; the Sadler's Wells pit has a keen enjoyment for them; and pit and gallery were crowded to the farthest wall on Saturday night with a most earnest audience, among whom many a subdued hush arose, not during, but just before, the delivery of the most charming passages.'[8] And the actor John Coleman, writing of the early Victorian theatre, says that even 'country audiences were as familiar with the standard plays as the actors themselves; indeed, it is upon record that in his youth, when [Charles] Kean broke down in the last act of *Macbeth* at Newcastle-on-Tyne, the "King of the gallery" "gave him the word" in the euphonious dialect of the district, and that Charles readily accepted the help of his rough and ready prompter, bowing his grateful acknowledgment'.[9] The reason for this familiarity is a matter of theatrical rather than educational history. Familiarity with Shakespeare was bred in the theatre, not in the classroom. This was the age of the Great Actor; and the prevailing repertory system made it possible for a regular theatregoer to become a connoisseur of performances in a way that is scarcely possible today. For instance, *Who's Who in the Theatre* (1961) lists eight *important* revivals of *Richard III* in London between 1833 and 1838: Warde, Vandenhoff, Denvil, Wallack, J. B. Booth, Edwin Forrest, Phelps and Charles Kean played the title-role; and between 1850 and 1855 you could have seen, among others, Phelps, C. Kean, Wallack, G. V. Brooke and James Anderson as Macbeth. If you were a keen theatregoer you probably did see them all, and discourse on their relative merits, just as a music-lover of today will compare different conductors' interpretations of a Beethoven symphony.

No precision is possible, of course, in the attempt to determine the degree to which Victorian audiences were familiar with Shakespeare: and it seems fairly clear that as the 'long-run' came to prevail over the repertory system this familiarity gradually diminished. But it is certain that Planché felt able to slip in a Shakespearian allusion or quotation with the assurance that at any rate a fair proportion of his audience would recognize its aptness. True, some of the quotations that he used are very obvious ones. In *The Drama's Levée* (1838), for instance, 'Drama', exasperated by the quarrelling of Legitimate and Illegitimate Drama, exclaims:

> Hence both and each who either cause espouses!
> You'll drive me mad! a plague on *all* your houses!   (II, p. 13)

No great familiarity with *Hamlet* would be required to give point to the exclamation 'Dead for a ducat, dead' in *Fortunio* (1843; II, p. 208) when a dragon is killed. Only slightly less obvious, though entirely unforced in its application, is another allusion to *Hamlet*, also in *Fortunio*:

> *Boisterer.*   Lightfoot has hit upon a rare invention.
> *Fortunio.*   What is't?
> *Fine-ear.*   A flying steamcoach!
> *For.*   Ha!—indeed!

> *Strongback.* Built on a principle that must succeed.
> *Marksman.* Just like a bird—with body, wings, and tail.
> *Tipple.* Or like a fish—
> *For.*   Aye—very like a whale.
> *Marks.* You think we're joking, sir.
> *For.*   In truth, I do.   (II, p. 217)

But it may be doubted whether many members of a modern audience would know *Richard III* well enough to see the point of the following:

> *Duke.* ...what's o'clock?
> Who's there?
> *Staffhold.* 'Tis I! the early village cock
> Hath thrice done salutation to the morn!
>
> (*The Prince of Happy Land*, 1851, IV, p. 200)

Somewhat elusive, too, is the reference to *The Merchant of Venice*, II, ii, in *The King of the Peacocks* (1848):

> *Poo-lee-ha-lee.* I am a chap—chap fall'n—with Fortune out,
> Who's conscience hanging his heart's neck about,
> Like Gobbo junior's, would the owner strangle,
> If at the yard-arm he'd no right to dangle.   (III, p. 303)

These allusions are not, it is true, of the first importance. They are made in passing; they would raise hardly more than a smile of recognition, and if they went unnoticed little would be lost. More important, and far more extensive, are those passages in which Planché consciously parodies lines, speeches and sometimes whole scenes from Shakespeare. The brilliant pun in the following lines from *Once Upon a Time there were Two Kings* (1853) would be quite lost if the audience did not remember its *Hamlet*:

> *Pastora.* ...a piano you're not born to play.
> Oh, there be misses, I have here and there heard,
> Play in a style that quite out Erard's Erard.
> Pray you avoid it....   (IV, p. 343)

A longer passage from *High, Low, Jack, and the Game*, in which the characters are members of a pack of playing cards, is based on *Macbeth* (with a glance at *Hamlet*), and gains its point from the witty and sustained word-play linking card-terms with the original:

> *The Ghost of the King of Hearts appears.*
> *King of Spades* (*starting*). Mother o'pearl! What *carte-blanche* have we here?
> *Ghost.* I am the *ombre* of the King of Hearts.
> *Queen of Hearts.* My husband!
> *Knave of Hearts.* My late King!
> *King of Spades.* Avaunt and quit my sight—let the earth hide thee!
> There is no speculation in those eyes
> That thou dost glare withal!
> *Ghost.* I do not play
> At speculation.

Knave of Hearts. (No; he plays at fright.)
King of Spades. What game is now a-foot?
Ghost. Whist! whist! oh whist!   (I, p. 131)

Planché's own definition of the extravaganza was a 'whimsical treatment of a poetical subject' as distinguished from 'the broad caricature of a tragedy or serious opera, which was correctly termed a "Burlesque"'.[10] But this did not prevent him from including in a 'fairy extravaganza' passages, at least, of 'broad caricature'. In *The Fair One with the Golden Locks* (1843), for instance, King Lachrymosa is rejected by his beloved, Queen Lucidora; he bemoans his fate in lines obviously inspired by *Othello*:

> Haply, for I take snuff, she thinks me dirty;
> Or, for I'm on the shady side of thirty.
> But that's not much, I'm only thirty-four.   (II, p. 260)

However, he decides that in order to improve his chances he will take a draught of an 'elixir, that can youth restore!' He goes to get it, slightly misquoting *Macbeth*, IV, i:

> This deed I'll do before this purpose fail.

And at his next appearance the hint of *Macbeth* burgeons into a full-scale burlesque of the dagger soliloquy:

> Is this a corkscrew that I see before me?
> The handle towards my hand—clutch thee I will!
> I have thee not—and yet I see thee still!
> Art thou a hardware article? or, oh!
> Simply a fancy article, for show.
> A corkscrew of the mind—a false creation
> Of crooked ways, a strong insinuation!
> I see thee yet, as plain as e'er I saw
> This patent one, which any cork can draw!
>   (*shewing patent corkscrew*)
> Thou marshal'st me the way that I should choose,
> And such an instrument I was to use!
> There's no such thing; 'tis what I steal to do,
> That on my fancy thus has put the screw.
> I go, and it is done. (*going*) Confound it! there's
> That stupid Mollymopsa on the stairs.   (II, p. 262)

He drinks poison by mistake, and *Macbeth* is further recalled in a few slight and subtle echoes of wording and dramatic technique:

> *King* (*within*).   Help, there, ho!
>   (*Exit* Viscount)
> *Queen.* What voice was that?
> *Grace.*   My royal master's surely.
>
>   Re-enter Viscount.
> *Vis.* Run for a doctor, the King's taken poorly.

106

Exeunt Officer *and* Viscount.

Queen. The cramp has seized his conscience, I presume.
What business has he in my dressing-room?

Re-enter Viscount, *with bottle.*

Vis. Oh, horror! horror! Madam—

Enter Courtiers *from different entrances.*

Queen.   Well, proceed.

Vis. His Majesty is very ill, indeed.   (II, p. 263)

Many examples of this sort of thing could be cited: *Fortunio* has a parody (II, p. 223) of a speech from *Macbeth*; in *Graciosa and Percinet* there is a lengthy parody (II, pp. 324–5) of the closet scene from *Hamlet*; *King Charming* has a long sequence (IV, pp. 100–11) based, often closely, on *Romeo and Juliet*, as well as references to *Macbeth*, 1 *Henry IV*, *Hamlet* and *Twelfth Night*; in *Once Upon a Time There Were Two Kings* (IV, pp. 329–31) there are parodies of speeches from *Hamlet* and *Romeo and Juliet* (quoted by Granville-Barker, *op. cit.* pp. 114–16); and *The Yellow Dwarf* has a wooing scene (V, pp. 59–60) based on that in *Richard III*, as well as parodies and quotations of parts of *Othello*, *Macbeth*, *The Merchant of Venice*, *A Midsummer Night's Dream* and *Romeo and Juliet*. Many of the parodies are still entertaining; Planché punned with less strain than many of his contemporaries. Even the skit, in *The Island of Jewels*, on a scene of *King Lear* is inoffensive and sometimes funny. Laidronetta's father, a King, is wandering in a storm in a Rocky Pass, with his Queen, Tinsellina; his son, Prince Prettiphello; his daughter, Princess Bellotta; and Count Merecho:

Prince. As to the King, who thought such wealth to sack,
The blow has given his cranium quite a crack;
His talk is all of money, but so queer,
I really think he must have seen King Lear.

Enter King, Queen, *and* Count.

King. Blow winds and crack your cheeks, the clouds go spout!
To raise the wind, and get a good blow out.
Rain cats and dogs, or pitchforks perpendicular,
The sky's not mine, and needn't be particular.
I tax not you, ye elements, you pay
No duty under schedules D or A,
You owe me no subscription. Funds may fall,
It makes no difference to you at all.

Bel. Gracious, papa! don't stand here, if you please.

Queen. 'Things that love night, love not such nights as these.'
Persuade him to move on, Prince Prettiphello.

Prince. Are you aware, sir, you have no umbrella? (*rain*)

King. A thought has struck me, rather entertaining,
I am a King more rained upon than reigning.
My wits are going fast!

Queen.   I fear 'tis so.

Prince. Take comfort, ma'am, there are so few to go.
Would that our loss was nothing more, alas!
   King. What, have his daughters brought him to this pass?
   Count. He has no daughters, sir.
   King.   'Sdeath! don't tell fibs!
He must have one who won't down with the dibs,
Although she's made of money! Nothing I know
Bothers your gig so much as want of *rhino*.
   Prince. His head's quite turned with losing all that pelf.
   King. For coining they can't touch the King himself.
   Queen. Here's a dry cavern, if he would but cross over.
   King. I'd talk a word with this philosopher!
What is the price of stocks?
   Prince.   Mine are but low.
Suppose you just walk in, some here may know.
   King. A famous dodge! For ninety millions draw
A bill at sight upon my son-in-law,
And then—bolt—bolt-bolt-bolt.

                   (*Exeunt* King *into cavern, followed by* Queen, *&c.*)
                                 (IV, pp. 41–2)

It is interesting to learn that in performance some of Planché's parodies retained a measure of the force of their originals. The following lines from *The Yellow Dwarf* (1854) read like a vulgarization of their model in *Othello*:

   Haridan. Monster, what means this tragical tableau?
You've killed the little King on whom I doted.
   Dwarf. And caused her death to whom I was devoted.
Oh heavy trial! Verdict—Serves me right!
Whip me ye devils—winds come, blow me tight!
Roast me in flames of sulphur—very slow!
Oh Allfair—Allfair!—Dead—O, O, O, O!   (V, p. 72)

But the dwarf was played by that very remarkable actor, Frederick Robson, of whose performance Planché wrote: 'So powerful was his personation of the cunning, the malignity, the passion and despair of the monster, that he elevated Extravaganza into Tragedy. His delivery of the lines, slightly parodied from the wail of Othello over the dead body of Desdemona, moved Thackeray, "albeit unused to the melting mood", almost to tears. "This is not a burlesque," he exclaimed, "It is an idyl!"' (V, p. 37). *The Illustrated London News* in its review confirms this, saying that the Shakespeare parodies 'told exceedingly well, and proved, what has often been asserted, that, notwithstanding his minute size, Mr Robson's power in a legitimate tragic part would be great indeed'. The work was 'not merely a burlesque, but a poem'.

    Planché's light-hearted variations upon Shakespeare suggest a less solemn attitude than might be inferred from the general trend of Shakespearian production during the century. The comic effect of some Shakespeare skits of our own time is based upon incomprehension: our sympathetic laughter is invited for someone who is trying unsuccessfully to master a seemingly confused plot, to understand half-forgotten allusions or to explain in realistic terms the conventions and motives of poetic drama. This is not Planché's way. Nor does he write critical burlesque; his is not the searching parody of a Beerbohm, drawing attention by imitation and concentration to the stylistic mannerisms of the author parodied. Planché's is the humour of the consciously absurd; he plays tricks with the original, he exercises his ingenuity upon it, but he leaves it intact. He felt able as it were to say to his audience 'You all know Macbeth's dagger soliloquy; let's see how we can apply it to this ridiculous situation'. The audience's respect for, and understanding of, the original is urbanely taken for granted; consequently, there is no cheapening.

II

Besides providing general evidence on the attitude of Planché and his audiences to Shakespeare, the extravaganzas also yield interesting information on specific points of the staging of Shakespeare's plays over a wide period of time.

In *Olympic Devils, or, Orpheus and Eurydice*, first performed on Boxing Day 1831, Orpheus and Eurydice are pleading to Pluto:

> *Orpheus.* I kneel to you—the son of great Apollo
> Kneels—who ne'er knelt before—I—me—like Rolla.
> *Eurydice.* I kneel—like Miss O'Neill—in Desdemona,
> 'Let me go with him.'
> *Orpheus.* Oh, be mercy shown her!
> To ransom her I'd give my best Cremona. (I, p. 75)

In his first speech, Orpheus refers to a climactic moment in Sheridan's *Pizarro*, v, ii; the mention of Eliza O'Neill's Desdemona is particularly striking in that she had retired from the stage in June 1819—eleven years before this was written. True, her name is introduced partly for the sake of a pun; but the quotation from *Othello* suggests that Planché had in mind a particular theatrical effect. I know of no evidence that Miss O'Neill knelt on the line 'Let me go with him' (I, iii, 260); but Oxberry's acting edition dated 1822, which lists her as Desdemona at Covent Garden, makes her kneel at her father's exit in the same scene:

> *Brabantio.* Look to her, Moor; have a quick eye to see;
> She has deceived her father, and may thee.
> (*Desdemona follows her father and kneels to him,*
> *he puts her from him.—The Moor raises*
> *her. Brabantio and Gratiano go off,* R.H.)

Planché's reference to this kneeling[11] may suggest that it was a memorable effect, worthy of record.

In *The Camp at the Olympic* (17 October 1853) Planché goes into more detail in a scene (IV, pp. 304–6) that reflects his interest in the costuming of historical drama. Tragedy enters 'in the costume of Lady Macbeth, 1753'—there is no especial significance in this date, which is simply a century before the date of Planché's work. Fancy says:

First in the field, old English Tragedy
In stately hoop and train 'comes sweeping by'!
As in the British Drama's palmy day,
When people took an interest in the play!

It is only by the letter in her hand that she is recognized as Lady Macbeth. Mrs Wigan (she and her husband were playing themselves) exclaims 'Lady Macbeth! In Dollalolla's dress!', and her husband comments

That must have been a hundred years ago,
To judge from a costume so rococo!

Tragedy delivers an impassioned attack on the degeneration of the stage that has occurred since her time (see below, p. 113). In retaliation Fancy speaks:

The times have changed; but there is still a stage,
And one on which Macbeth has been the rage.

There is then discovered '"*The Blasted Heath*", *same as at the Princess's Theatre, with the Three Witches*—Macbeth *and* Banquo *in the costume worn at that theatre*—*Temp.* 1853'. Charles Kean's production of *Macbeth* in February 1853 had been attended by some controversy about the costumes used. Kean, with his usual passion for archaeological accuracy, had been worried by 'the very uncertain information...which we possess respecting the dress worn by the inhabitants of Scotland in the eleventh century'. He therefore 'introduced the tunic, mantle, cross gartering, and ringed byrnie of the Danes and Anglo-Saxons, between whom it does not appear any very material difference existed; retaining, however, the peculiarity of "the striped and chequered garb", which seems to be generally admitted as belonging to the Scotch long anterior to the history of this play; together with the eagle feather in the helmet, which according to Gaelic tradition, was the distinguishing mark of a chieftain.'[12]

This spectacle astonishes Tragedy:

...'Great Glamis! worthy Cawdor!'
Can that be he?
Fancy.   In heavy marching order.
Not as when Garrick used to meet the witches—
In gold-laced waistcoat and red velvet breeches...

whereupon 'Garrick *appears as* Macbeth *with the daggers*'. (Garrick's typically eighteenth-century appearance as Macbeth is illustrated in Plate I B.) Fancy continues:

Nor as in Kemble's time, correct was reckoned,
Accoutred like 'the gallant forty-second',

and 'Kemble *appears as* Macbeth, *with target and truncheon*' (see Plate I C). An officer of 'the forty-second' wore 'bonnet, plaid, red jacket faced with blue, the philibeg [kilt] and tartan hose'.[13] Fancy concludes her speech with:

But as a Scottish chieftain roamed scot-free—
In the year one thousand and fifty-three.

PLATE I

A. Mrs Yates 'in Dollalolla's dress'

B. David Garrick

c. John Philip Kemble

D. Charles and Ellen Kean

'MACBETH' COSTUMES

There follow various comments on what has been seen. Mr and Mrs Wigan with Fancy sing, to the tune of 'Auld Lang Syne':

> My auld acquaintance I've forgot,
> If ever he was mine;
> Is that the way they clad a Scot
> In days o' Lang Syne.

Tragedy expresses her surprise in words aptly chosen from *Macbeth*:

> *Tragedy.* 'My countryman—and yet I know him not!'
> *Mr W.* More like an antique *Run'un* than a Scot!
> *Trag.* A Scotchman, and no kilt?
> *Mrs W.*   Don't Macbeth say,
> 'We've *scotch'd* the snake, not *kilt* it!'

And finally Fancy sings:

> Through their habits conventional managers broke,
> To make old plays go down they new habits bespoke;
> The old-fashioned Scotchman no longer we see,
> Except as a sign for the sale of rappee.
> So pack up your tartans, whatever your clan,
> And look a new 'garb of old Gaul' out, my man;
> For the stage in its bonnet has got such a bee,
> It's all up with 'The Bonnets of Bonny Dundee'.

This curious piece of dramatized stage-history reflects the surprise of Kean's audiences at his break with tradition: it also shows Planché's own awareness of the rapid changes in theatrical fashion over the preceding century—changes he himself had helped to bring about. It was perhaps a little unfair to suggest that the new costumes were adopted 'to make old plays go down'; though Kean's productions were on the whole very popular, his innovations were not universally approved, and he complained in his farewell speech that he had 'been blamed for depriving Macbeth of a dress never worn at any period, or in any place, and for providing him instead with one resembling those used by the surrounding nations with whom the country of that chieftain was in constant intercourse'.[14] Nearer the mark was Planché's reference to the bee in 'the stage's' bonnet.[15]

III

Planché's concern with the staging of Shakespeare is a reflection of his faith in Shakespeare as the cornerstone of the British stage, a faith which finds expression in a *Tableau Vivant* at the end of *The New Planet* (1847). Juno sings:

> See of Britain's stage the splendour;
>   Not for ages, but all time,
> Wrote the bard whose form we render;
>   Who shall reach his height sublime?

> Till the earth to circle ceases,
> Till no eye his scenes can trace,
> Spite of fashion's wild caprices,
> He will ne'er be out of place. (III, p. 179)

A similar note was heard in a patriotic passage of *The Drama's Levée* first performed on 16 April 1838. Victoria had come to the throne in the previous year and, as Planché notes, 'was a constant visitor to the theatres, and at this period attended nearly all the farewell performances of Charles Kemble at Covent Garden'. Her interest in the theatre seemed like a portent of better days ahead.

> ...whatso'er may be the moment's rage,
> The British public love the British stage,
> And days as bright as when thy [i.e. Drama's] birth was seen,
> Are dawning 'neath another British Queen.
> To thine old temples she hath led the town,
> With garlands fresh thy Shakespeare's bust to crown;
> Richard, Coriolanus, Hamlet, Lear,
> In splendour worthy of themselves appear;
> And by their Sovereign's gracious smile inspired,
> Shall British bards with nobler ardour fired,
> Strike chords which find their echoes in the heart,
> And make the muses from their slumber start. (II, p. 22)

As things turned out, the muses had their full quota of sleep for some considerable time after this was written; and it is not long before Planché is complaining that Shakespeare's heroes do not 'in splendour worthy of themselves appear'.

The Drama at Home (8 April 1844) presents a vision of Drury Lane: 'as soon as the building is up, the portion beneath the portico opens, and the stage is seen with a tableau from the play of "Richard III", as lately performed there [by Charles Kean].' Drama is delighted at the sight.

> Vision of glory!—I'm at Drury Lane
> With Shakespeare—'Richard is himself again!'

But the statue of Shakespeare over the portico speaks, Commendatore-like:

> Awake! Beware of fibbers!
> That Richard's none of mine—'Tis Colley Cibbers!

Puff, who has been trying to impress Drama, is annoyed:

Rot that Shakespeare, he always speaks the truth! I wonder what the devil they stuck him up there for. There was a leaden Apollo, with a lyre in his hand, on the top of the old building—much more appropriate to the new one—where William Tell[16] draws more than William Shakespeare (II, pp. 297–80).

Planché's voice may thus have been one of those that encouraged Samuel Phelps, less than a year later, to stage Shakespeare's, instead of Cibber's, *Richard III*—not, as it happened, with any lasting result.

In the same piece is a passage in which we see famous Shakespearian characters out of work:

Othello is a sandwich-man advertising Warren's Blacking; Macbeth has 'set up a cigar divan, And stands at his own door as a Highlandman', and Shylock has 'opened a slop shop in the Minories' (II, pp. 284–7). But again the note of hope is sounded. Portia and Nerissa enter and tell Drama, who feels that 'they've ceased to care for me at home': 'Then you've not heard the news—the Drama's free!' The allusion is, of course, to the Theatre Regulation Act of 1843, by which the monopoly of the patent theatres had been abolished. As a sign of what has already been achieved, the principals from *The Merry Wives of Windsor* and *The Taming of the Shrew* appear, representing the important Haymarket productions of these plays: the first had an exceptionally long run, and the second was a very remarkable, and successful, attempt, suggested and designed by Planché himself,[17] to produce a full text of Shakespeare's play (instead of Garrick's *Katherine and Petruchio*, which went on being performed throughout the century), and to present it in conditions approximating to those of the Elizabethan theatre. There were, then, fair reasons for hope.

One of the results of the Theatre Regulations Act was that the serious drama tended to move out of the large patent theatres, to which it had been for too long confined, into smaller theatres in which an actor had a better chance of making an effect without coarsening his style. This was in many ways a good thing; but naturally some regret was felt at the consequent degeneration in the state of Covent Garden and Drury Lane. Planché reflects this regret in *The Camp at the Olympic* (1853) where Tragedy asks how she can fail to be in a passion

> when I see the State
> Of Denmark rotten! When I hear the fate
> Which hath befallen both the classic domes,
> 'Neath which my votaries once found their homes!
> Where Garrick, monarch of the mimic scene,
> His sceptre passed from Kemble down to Kean;
> Where Cibber's silver tones the heart would steal,
> And Siddons left her mantle to O'Neil!
> The Drama banished from her highest places
> By *débardeurs* and 'fools with varnished faces',
> Sees foreign foes her sacred ruins spurning,
> Fiddling like Neros while her Rome is burning. (IV, p. 304)

The author's own awareness that there is another side to the question is suggested by Fancy's reply, which begins 'The times have changed'.

The move to smaller theatres did nothing to lessen the increasing emphasis on the spectacular in Shakespearian productions. Planché deplored this. In *Mr Buckstone's Ascent of Mount Parnassus* (28 March 1853) he has a dig at the elaborate productions of Shakespeare then being given by Phelps at Sadler's Wells and by Charles Kean at the Princess's Theatre. Melpomene asks for news of Shakespeare, and Mr Buckstone replies:

> Shakespeare! We call him the illustrious stranger;
> He has been drooping—but he's out of danger,
> And gone to Sadler's Wells and the Princess's
> For change of air—I may say scenes and dresses. (IV, p. 289)

Later in the same year, in *The Camp at the Olympic*, a similar complaint is voiced in more general terms. The somewhat didactic tone suggests that Planché is here expressing strong personal feelings:

> *Tragedy.* Has not immortal Shakespeare said 'tis silly,
> 'To gild refinèd gold—to paint the lily?'
> *Spectacle.* Immortal Shakespeare! come, the less you say
> The better on that head. There's not a play
> Of his for many a year the town has taken,
> If I've not buttered preciously his bacon. (IV, p. 317)

And a few lines later Fancy says:

> What's to be done when the immortal names
> Of Shakespeare and of Byron urge their claims
> In vain to popularity, without
> Spectacle march all his contingent out?
> Not mere Dutch metal, spangles, foil, and paste,
> But gems culled from authority by Taste;
> Until, reflecting every bygone age,
> A picture-gallery becomes the stage;
> And modern Babylon may there behold
> The pomp and pageantry that wrecked the old! (IV, p. 318)

It is worthy of note that Planché is attacking, not merely tawdrily decorated productions, but also those which employ 'gems culled from authority by Taste'. He had culled such gems himself. We may remember his work with Charles Kemble, his pride in the 'roar of approbation, accompanied by four distinct rounds of applause', which in 1823 greeted the sight of 'King John dressed as his effigy appears in Worcester Cathedral, surrounded by his barons sheathed in mail, with cylindrical helmets and correct armorial shields, and his courtiers in the long tunics and mantles of the thirteenth century'. Charles Kean was to some extent his disciple. But half a century later he wrote:

if propriety be pushed to extravagance, if what should be mere accessories are occasionally elevated by short-sighted managers into the principal features of their productions, I am not answerable for their suicidal folly....I can perfectly understand 'King John' or any other historical play being acted in plain evening dress without any scenery at all, and interpreted by great actors interesting the audience to such a degree that imagination would supply the picturesque accessories to them as sufficiently as it does to the reader of the play in his study.[18]

He wrote similarly of his revival of *The Taming of the Shrew*; it was 'eminently successful, incontestably proving that a good play, well acted, will carry the audience along with it, unassisted by scenery; and in this case also, remember, it was a comedy in *five* acts, without the curtain once falling during its performance'.[19] This production was fifty years before the founding of the Elizabethan Stage Society. It is paradoxical that Planché has claim to be remembered as the forerunner of both the elaborately pictorial school of Shakespeare production and of the simplicity of William Poel.

IV

During the fifties the rage for burlesque drama was at its height, and Planché depicts what he saw as the battle between burlesque and tragedy. In *The Camp at the Olympic* he hints, rather subtly, that the decline of tragedy is due to a lack of great actors: on Burlesque's approach, Tragedy calls for support, but Mr Wigan asks 'where's the actor strong enough?' 'Then I shall fall!', says Tragedy, sinking into a chair (IV, p. 308). It is somewhat curious that Frederick Robson was playing Burlesque; curious because he was probably the greatest English burlesque actor, and curious too because a common reaction to his performances in travesties of Shakespeare was a comment deploring the fact that he was not playing the role 'straight'. Burlesque sings:

> Your Hamlet may give up his Ghost,
> Your Richard may run himself through,
> I'm Cock-of-the-Walk to your cost,
> And I crow over all your crew!
> For Burlesque is up! up! up!
> And Tragedy down! down! down! O!
> Pop up your nob again,
> And I'll box you for your crown, O!

In the words of Macbeth to Banquo's ghost, Tragedy bids Burlesque depart, but is met with a seriously argued self-defence:

> ...I fling your follies in your face,
> And call back all the false starts of your race
> Shew up your shows, affect your affectation,
> And by such homoeopathic aggravation,
> Would cleanse your bosom of that perilous stuff,
> Which weighs upon our art—bombast and puff.

He cites *Tom Thumb*, *The Critic* and *Bombastes Furioso* as evidence that burlesque can have a serious purpose, and claims that

> When in his words he's not one to the wise,
> When his fool's bolt, *spares* folly as it flies,
> When in his chaff there's not a grain to seize on,
> When in his rhyme there's not a ray of reason,
> His slang but slang, no point beyond the pun,
> Burlesque may walk, for he will cease to run.

He begs however that his claims to sense will not be spread abroad:

> If once of common sense I was suspected,
> I should be quite as much as you—neglected.   (IV, p. 309)

This is admirable dramatic argument; Planché triumphantly succeeds here in presenting a serious case with urbanity and wit. The pun in 'for he will cease to run', for instance, lightens a passage that might without it have appeared unduly homiletic.

In *Love and Fortune* (1859) comes Planché's final defence of the liberties he and other dramatists have taken with Shakespeare. The piece was presented at the Princess's Theatre, in which Charles Kean's Shakespeare productions had been so successful. Augustus Harris had just followed Kean in the management of the theatre, and Fortune says:

> Oh, don't name Shakespeare—of his awful shade
> The new lessee is horribly afraid.
> Here in such state he lately wore his crown.
> His spirit on us fatally may frown.

But Love reassures him:

> What, gentle Shakespeare? pleasant Will, who'd run
> Through a whole page to make a shocking pun!
> Who shed a glory round things most grotesque?
> Who wrote for Grecian clowns the best burlesque?
> He look on harmless mirth with angry eyes?
> No, no, he is too genial and too wise.
> His heart was e'en his matchless mind above—
> He nothing owes to Fortune, much to Love!

(v, p. 203)

The extravaganzas preserve for us something of the Victorian attitude to Shakespeare; they should also remind us that their author, in his vigilance for high standards of production, a vigilance which often rose above the prevailing standards of his time, served Shakespeare well. The Victorian attitude has developed into our own, and Planché was one of its shaping forces.

NOTES

1. *The Extravaganzas of J. R. Planché, Esq., 1825–1871*, edited by T. F. Dillon Croker and Stephen Tucker; 5 vols. (1879). All references to Planché's dramatic works are to this edition.

2. E.g. H. Granville Barker, 'Exit Planché—Enter Gilbert', in *The Eighteen-Sixties*, edited by J. Drinkwater (Cambridge, 1932), pp. 102–48; Sir St Vincent Troubridge, 'Gilbert and Planché', *Notes and Queries*, CLXXX (22 March and 12 July, 1941); H. H. Tilley, *J. R. Planché, Reformer* (1951; unpublished M.A. dissertation in the library of the University of Birmingham).

3. *The Oxford Companion to the Theatre*, edited by Phyllis Hartnoll (1951).

4. *A History of English Drama, 1660–1900*, IV (Cambridge; 2nd ed., 1955), p. 151. See also G. Wilson Knight, *The Golden Labyrinth* (1962), pp. 273–6.

5. 'Some Burlesques with a Purpose, 1830–1870', *Philological Quarterly*, VIII (1929), 255–63.

6. *The Victorian Theatre* (Oxford, 1956); see especially pp. 68–9.

7. MacMillan, *loc. cit.* p. 259, writes: 'Fitzgerald says that his plays, which were full of delicate conceits and classical allusions, "supposed a too high state of culture in the audience"; and the producers cut and hacked them, inserting "wheezes" and "bits of fat". We know that there were exceptions to this rule, especially in the parts acted by Mathews and Robson, and Planché enters no complaints against his producers on this account.' This is based upon a misunderstanding of Fitzgerald, who wrote, not of Planché's 'plays', but of *one* play written at the end of his career. Fitzgerald's statement implies that an audience of the 1870's was less cultured than one of the 1840's: 'I remember him in great elation at being called upon to supply a piece for Covent Garden—the strange "Babil and Bijou" venture; and the old writer concocted one of his literary burlesques of the old pattern in the Vestris days—full of delicate conceits and classical allusions. This kind of wit seems now very ponderous, and is all but

unreadable—it supposed a too high state of culture in the audience. The business men of the speculation treated his work *sans ceremonie* [sic]—hacked and hewed it mercilessly, suppressed about half, and stuffed it with "wheezes" and bits of "fat"' (*The Garrick Club*, 1904, p. 43). *Babil and Bijou* was Planché's last work for the stage.

8. *The Journal of a London Playgoer* (1866), p. 69.

9. *Fifty Years of an Actor's Life* (1904), I, 194.

10. Preface to *The Sleeping Beauty in the Wood*, II, 66.

11. It is not recorded in A. C. Sprague's *Shakespeare and the Actors* (1948).

12. Quoted from W. M. Merchant's *Shakespeare and the Artist* (1959), pp. 102–3, where there is a longer quotation from Kean's playbill discussing this topic.

13. J. R. Planché, *A Cyclopaedia of Costume*, II, 360. The 'target and truncheon' were also used by Macready: see Sprague, *op. cit.*, portrait facing p. 230.

14. Reprinted in A. M. Nagler's *Sources of Theatrical History* (1952), p. 489, from J. W. Cole's *The Life and Theatrical Times of Charles Kean F.S.A.*, edition of 1860, II, 379–82.

15. Charles Kean is referred to again in *Mr Buckstone's Voyage Round the Globe* (17 April 1854; V, 23–4), where there is a passage concerning his rivalry, particularly as Richard III, with G. V. Brooke (cf. W. J. Lawrence, *The Life of Gustavus Vaughan Brooke* (Belfast, 1892), p. 142).

16. Rossini's opera *William Tell* had recently been performed with great success at Drury Lane.

17. *Recollections* (1872), II, 83–6. Writing of the Induction, Planché says 'My restoration of this "gem" is one of the events in my theatrical career on which I look back with the greatest pride and gratification'. An engraving of a scene from this production is reproduced by R. Mander and J. Mitchenson in *A Picture History of the British Theatre* (1957), no. 262. G. C. D. Odell reprints part of *The Times*' report in *Shakespeare from Betterton to Irving* (New York, 1920), II, 313.

18. *Ibid.* I, 56–9.

19. *Ibid.* II, 85.

'OUR WILL SHAKESPEARE' AND LOPE DE VEGA: AN UNRECORDED CONTEMPORARY DOCUMENT

BY

PAUL MORGAN

In 1562 a famous poet, Lope de Vega, was born in Catholic Spain; two years later another famous poet, William Shakespeare, was born in Protestant England. Any fresh documentary record concerning either of these writers would, of course, have its own value; that value would be increased if the names of the two authors were linked; and the document's value would become still more if it were found to have been penned by a man intimately associated with the one or the other. The possibility of finding such a document today might well seem to be remote, yet it has been my good fortune to unearth a hitherto unrecorded note which does precisely this.

The library of Balliol College, Oxford,[1] possesses a copy of the third edition of Lope de Vega's *Rimas*, a duodecimo printed at Madrid in 1613.[2] On the fly-leaf at the front of this copy is a short inscription which apparently has so far escaped notice. It reads as follows:

> Will Baker: Knowinge
> that Mr Mab: was to
> sende you this Booke
> of sonets, wch with Spaniards
> here is accounted of their
> lope de Vega as in Englande
> wee sholde of o^r: Will
> Shakespeare. I colde not
> but insert thus much to
> you, that if you like
> him not, you muste neuer
> neuer reade Spanishe Poet
> Leo: Digges

The writer of this note was Leonard Digges, the son of the mathematician and astronomer Thomas Digges. Born in 1588, he was the 'L. Digges' who provided for the First Folio one of two sets of verses written in Shakespeare's memory. The other set was signed simply 'I.M.', initials which are now generally thought to indicate James Mabbe, fellow of Magdalen College, Oxford, from 1594 to 1633—and he is the 'Mr Mab' referred to in the inscription. Thus the document not only associates the names of Lope de Vega and Shakespeare, it also draws together Shakespeare and the two men who commemorated him in 1623.

The close connections of Leonard Digges with the Stratford district have been fully explored by Leslie Hotson.[3] His mother's second husband was Thomas Russell, overseer of Shakespeare's

PLATE II

DIGGES'S REFERENCE TO SHAKESPEARE

will, so it seems certain that Digges was personally acquainted with his great contemporary. He matriculated at University College, Oxford, on 1 July 1603, at the age of fifteen and took his B.A. in 1606.[4] Then, as Anthony à Wood reports, he first went to London and later 'travelled into several countries, and became an accomplish'd person'; after some time he returned to Oxford, where 'he was esteemed...a great master of the English language, a perfect understander of the French and Spanish, a good poet and no mean orator'.[5] His chief works were translations, and among these was one, *Gerardo, the Unfortunate Spaniard* (1622), adapted from an original by Cespedes y Meneses.

James Mabbe was also a Spanish scholar; in his version of Mateo Aleman's *The Rogue* (1623) the connection between himself and Digges is further attested by the fact that the latter contributed some congratulatory verses to his friend's volume.[6] Mabbe was a traveller too, and Wood records that 'he was taken into the service of Sir John Digby knight [afterwards earl of Bristol] and was by him made his secretary when he went ambassador into Spain; where remaining with him several years, improved himself in various sorts of learning, and in the customs and manners of that and other countries. After his return into England he...was esteemed a learned man, good orator and a facetious conceited wit.'[7] It seems clear that, when the little volume of Lope de Vega's sonnets was sent to 'Will Baker', these two friends were together and the implication is that they were in Spain, which seems to confirm Leslie Hotson's conjecture that 'Leonard Digges went along to Madrid with his friend Mabbe in the train of James's ambassador, Sir John Digby', in 1611.[8]

The identity of the volume's recipient, Will Baker, is obscure, but it appears probable that he was the one of this name who was an exact contemporary of Digges at University College. A Devonshire man, he matriculated on 29 July 1603, took his B.A. in 1607 and his M.A. in 1609.[9] Furthermore, he was possibly the 'Gulielmus Baker' who contributed two sets to the mass of 'Panegyricke Verses' prefixed to Thomas Coryate's *Crudities* (1611);[10] if this is the case, then the beginning of the second set has a more subtle meaning in the light of Digges's inscription:

> Ovr trauelling frie, liquorous of Nouelties,
> Enquire each minute for thy *Crudities*;
> And hope, that as those haddocks tooke refection,
> Cast from thy sea-sicke stomacks forc't eiection,
> And straight grew trauailers, & forsook our Maine,
> To frolicke on the grau'ly shelues of Spaine:
> So they by thy disgorgement, at their will
> Shall put downe *Web*, or Sir *Iohn Mandeuil*.

As *Coryats Crudities* was published at the end of March 1611[11] and Sir John Digby arrived in Madrid in June[12] the same year, the travellers, Mabbe and Digges, would presumably have been preparing themselves at the same time that Coryate was gathering his 'Panegyricke Verses'.

From the inscription in this copy of Lope de Vega, it may be presumed that Mabbe, the oldest, was sending a present to one who may have been a former pupil and that Digges seized the opportunity of enclosing a message, letting a fellow student know about the current literary rage in Madrid and giving the contemporary reputation of Shakespeare's *Sonnets* as a yardstick. Especially important is the evidence provided in this message that in 1613 or 1614 men interested in literature regarded Shakespeare's poems as the supreme achievement in contemporary poetry.

How this particular book came to Balliol is not known; it is entered neither in the manuscript catalogue of 1721 nor in the Donors' Book, but it is recorded in the printed Bodleian Catalogue of 1738 annotated with the College library's shelf-marks. Apart from Digges, no one has written in it or left a mark, and as there are so many possibilities it is unprofitable to guess its provenance.

NOTES

1. I wish to express my thanks to the Master and Fellows of Balliol College for their kind permission to reproduce and comment on this document.

2. Y. Palau y Dulcet, *Manual del Librero Hispano-Americano*, VII (1927), 133–4. The first edition was printed in Lisbon in 1605 and the second in Madrid in 1609 by Alonso Martin, who also printed the third.

3. Leslie Hotson, *I, William Shakespeare, do appoint Thomas Russell, Esquire...* (1937), pp. 237–59.

4. *D.N.B.*; J. Foster, *Alumni Oxonienses*. Early series, I (1891), 403.

5. Anthony à Wood, *Athenae Oxonienses*, new edition by P. Bliss, II (1815), cols. 592–3.

6. *D.N.B.*; J. Foster, *op. cit.* III, 956; E. K. Chambers, *William Shakespeare* (1930), II, 234; A. W. Secord, 'I.M. of the First Folio Shakespeare and other Mabbe Problems', *Journal of English and Germanic Philology*, XLVII (1948), 374–81. P. E. Russell, 'A Stuart Hispanist: James Mabbe', *Bulletin of Hispanic Studies*, XXX (1953), 75–84.

7. Anthony à Wood, *op. cit.* III, col. 53.

8. Leslie Hotson, *op. cit.* p. 238.

9. J. Foster, *op. cit.* I, 59.

10. On leaves *g*2 recto to *g*3 recto; I am indebted to I. A. Shapiro for this reference.

11. Boies Penrose, *Urbane Travellers* (1942), p. 95.

12. J. W. Stoye, *English Travellers Abroad, 1604–1667* (1952), p. 358.

SHAKESPEARE AND THE MASK

BY

PHILIP PARSONS

Man's profound self-identification with the face he wears is reflected in a dozen different cultures, both ancient and modern, where the dead are given masks to help them make their return to earth at the appropriate time. By the same token, to assume a new face is to assume a new personality—the mask imposes its role upon the wearer. But what happens to the wearer of a blank mask? Symbolically, it throws open the whole question of identity. The old self is blotted out and the way left clear for a new to manifest. The blank mask imposes the most challenging role of all, signalling a death and an enigmatic rebirth. Something of this feeling appears in Shakespeare's handling of the black masquing visor in two early plays, probably written within a year of each other, *Love's Labour's Lost* and *Romeo and Juliet*. At their very different levels, each play shows the mysterious unfolding of personal destiny, a creative development from which emerges a deeper and more vital self-awareness. And at the beginning of that journey stands the mask.

The black visor is a visual image of the theatre, easily overlooked in the study; but it takes its place among the opposed images of darkness and light, night and day, death and life, that run through both plays, infusing the sugared conceits with warmth and substance. In *Romeo and Juliet* this dark-light imagery rises almost to conscious level by its insistent presence in almost all the memorable lines:

> Come night, come Romeo, come, thou day in night,
> For thou wilt lie upon the wings of night
> Whiter than new snow upon a raven's back:
> Come, gentle night, come loving black-brow'd night,
> Give me my Romeo, and when he shall die,
> Take him and cut him out in little stars.

In *Love's Labour's Lost* the same themes are muted; but they give a sad gravity to the Queen's 'Dead for my life' when the news is brought of her father's death and in one phrase she gathers up the sunlight and the shadow.

The two plays show surprising similarity of theme, imagery, even of tone. The claims of death in love are brought home, gently in the comedy, insistently in the tragedy. In both the lover stands for humanity at its most vital; but that vitality is fully realized only when it embraces a sense of death. In *Love's Labour's Lost* the imagery of darkness is felt only in the last act and the lovers are left with the promise of fully realized life rather than the thing itself. But Shakespeare brings Romeo to this point by the end of Act I. Darkness and light dominate the whole play as death searches through youthful love, clothing it first with a mature dignity, then transforming it into an intense, ethereal passion.

Within this developing theme the mask holds an identical position. In *Love's Labour's Lost* it appears at the point where the lords begin to realize that love demands something more than a sugared sonnet, and in *Romeo and Juliet* it marks the far clearer division between the infatuated boy and the young man who loves, marries and dies with Juliet. Shakespeare chooses the moment when Romeo puts on the black visor to sound, through mysterious fears, the first note of tragedy, and it is through these eye-holes that he sees, quite literally, his fulfilment and his fate. The tragedy takes up, explores and develops the lightly hinted theme of the earlier play, so that it seems a fair conclusion that in 1595, when Shakespeare's 'Pleasant Conceited Comedie Called, Loves labors lost' was published, a part of his mind was already preparing for 'an Excellent conceited Tragedie' in the following year.

In *Love's Labour's Lost* the themes of love, death and self-realization run through a full circle in the course of a summer's day. The play begins and ends with a vow of mortification in order to find wisdom, but while the first is taken in the bliss of ignorance, the second springs from sadness and understanding. Youth, summer, light and gaiety surround the vow at the opening of the play, with the King of Navarre looking forward lightheartedly to that Fame which shall

> Live register'd upon our brazen tombs,
> And then grace us in the disgrace of death.

The light conceit conveys the care-free mood, when death is very far away and quite unreal. The King and his lords have taken a three-year vow to 'war upon' their 'own affections', for-swearing women, eating little and sleeping less, 'living in philosophy': and the grand purpose of all their study is, rather vaguely, 'that to know which else we should not know'. But when the Princess of France arrives with her ladies, the young men discover that wisdom is taught not by books but by life itself. They have vowed to ignore their own true nature.

> Let us once lose our oaths to find ourselves,
> Or else we lose ourselves to keep our oaths.

Their decision to break the vow, marked by Berowne's great panegyric on love, is the serious centre in a comedy of self-realization. And from this moment the dark images begin to gather.

The first hint of darkness arrives with the princess, on embassy from her 'decrepit, sick, and bed-rid father', demanding payment of a debt that the youthful king has forgotten. It is developed in her hunting expedition 'to spill The poor deer's blood' and completed when she makes the King her prize under the shadow of her father's death. Only then do the lords begin to realize that death is life's creditor, and the audience to see the dead husk at the root of the young green plant. The barren vow of the opening scene and Costard's sentence to bran and water for consorting with a woman are transformed in the last act into the penances imposed on the lords to win the ladies. Berowne's forswearing of 'three-pil'd hyperboles' for 'russet yeas and honest kersey noes' is a turning to reality that helps prepare for the harsh intrusion of death into the summer enchantment. The broken vow has, after all, shown the young men 'that which else we should not know'—that 'to find ourselves' brings the solid joy of fulfilment, but only through the painful discipline of the real world. And so the play ends, with words of Mercury after the songs of Apollo.

The black mask belongs with the imagery of darkness and cloud which is associated with the themes of death and self-realization. Having decided to 'find themselves', the lords' first thought is to court the ladies in a masque. 'Blackamoors with music' go before them as they advance through the park, masked and disguised as men from the wintery north, come to be thawed by beauty. The ladies, forewarned and suspecting mockery, have put on black visors to receive their Muscovite guests and of course the whole plan miscarries. The lords court the wrong ladies unknowingly, and unknowingly the ladies reject sincere advances.

That masquing has to be seen. The predominant tone will be one of witty contrariness and each figure will be a little unfamiliar and strange. Things are not what they seem, the summer scene is flecked with black. 'Vouchsafe to show the sunshine of your face', asks Berowne, 'that we, like savages, may worship it'. 'My face is but a moon', he is told, 'and clouded too.' Even the King's request for the 'bright moon' and 'these stars to shine, (Those clouds removed)' is to no avail. Not only do the ladies deny the masquers the traditional courteous welcome. When the lords ask to 'tread a measure with you on the grass'—the essence of every masque— they wittily decline, and the omission of this exercise of love and joy points up the frustrated wooing. By all the rules, the scene ought to be the perfect conventional setting for love. But despite the summer's day, youth, and masquing in the park, it all comes to nothing. The truth of each lover is hidden from his lady, the identity of each lady is hidden from the men, and the real demands of love have yet to appear. The slightly sinister black visor fitly dominates a scene where the reality is disguised by appearance.

So much for the place of the mask in the imagery pattern of *Love's Labour's Lost*. It brings a feeling of the unknown, and its association with winter imagery and darkness connects it with death. But it is also connected with self-realization, a fact which is underlined not only by the imagery but also by the striking position of the masquing theme in the play. When the lords decide to find themselves, they believe the search is already at an end. They need only break their vows, court the ladies and marry them. They are mistaken, yet their decision does lead to self-realization, through a series of quite unforseen events. Those events are causally unrelated— the king's death and the ladies' misunderstanding are matters of chance—but all are touched with the same darkness. And the first sign of this intangible movement towards reality comes with the masquing.

The confrontation of light-hearted youth with death and the need for deeper self-awareness also mark the second masque, or rather pageant, in which the amiable eccentrics present the Nine Worthies for the ladies' delectation. The lords, brilliant, unperceptive and a little cruel in their youthful confidence, revenge their failed masque by making this old-fashioned entertainment a butt for their modish wit. The show comes at the end of the long afternoon, and this sadly burlesque offering for a young princess catches somehow a momentary gleam of the late golden light. It falls kindly on Pompey, 'travailing along this coast' to make his devoir and lay his 'arms before the legs of this sweet lass of France'. It touches with pathos this Alexander, who begins 'When in the world I liv'd...'. As the odd, shambling figures relate their legends, they serve only to remind us how long ago, and in how remote a world, they lived.

This sense of things vanished and forgotten is sharpened by the wit of the court into something harsher, a sense of mortality. The liveliness of the lords turns again and again to death. They will have Judas Maccabeus to be Judas Iscariot, a kissing traitor who hanged himself; and the face lent him by Holofernes is a death's face in a ring, the face of an old Roman coin, scarce seen. Their laughter puts him to flight in the dusk, with the boy Moth crying after him 'A light for monsieur Judas, it grows dark, he may stumble'. The echo is a little macabre. The jest will turn back on the lords in a few moments when news arrives from France. Don Armado's gentle rebuke in defence of Hector comes through the shadows with a piercing sadness:

> The sweet war-man is dead and rotten,
> Sweet chucks, beat not the bones of the buried.

The Nine Worthies are presented, of course, as a companion piece to the masque made by the lords. But although one entertainment is graceful and the other ludicrous, this difference is less striking than their similarity. Both are laughed at, both are failures, and, as we have seen, the darkness imagery runs through both. Berowne's dismissal of the pageant—'Worthies away, the scene begins to cloud'—recalls faintly the fair moon clouded in the masque. If the Muscovites brought a hint of the coming winter, the Nine Worthies give it weight. The surprising thing is that Don Armado should be allowed to utter words of this peculiar resonance, that the comic characters should carry so grave a meaning. The bones of the buried Hector have the impact of a *memento mori*, and in them the serious undertones of the pageant break through the burlesque. Behind the fantastic costumes the dead have come to speak to the young, and as their mouth-piece Don Armado finds a touching, utterly unexpected dignity. Both here and in the Musco-vite costumes that expressed more truth than the wearers knew, there is something of the feeling for disguise as a form of possession by unknown powers—a feeling which the Elizabethans never quite lost.

Love's Labour's Lost may be left with a brief reference to Shakespeare's curious hint that light is not necessarily associated with love. The first half of the play is full of light and gaiety but that light is gradually streaked with shadow as the young men come closer to a sober realization of love. Yet the ladies, for all their darkness, seem to move in a peculiar light of their own. Berowne swears that Rosaline is 'born to make black fair'. His argument, as the King ob-serves, seems a paradox, and Dumaine adds mockingly 'Dark needs no candles now, for dark is light'. When it is remembered that all the ladies have in fact come out of dying France, a sugges-tion arises that love is somehow inherent in death, that the true light burns invisibly within darkness. Sunlit Navarre must then appear a land of wanton desire, not of love, a place to be rejected, not transformed. There the cuckoo sings on every tree, unpleasing to a married ear; but in true-loving France, Marion's red and raw nose is not unattractive by twilight. In Navarre, the eye is dazzled by a false light which blinds it to the true—or as Berowne remarks in another context, 'Light seeking light, doth light of light beguile'. This hint of a dual concept of light is so slight as to have little bearing on the interpretation of the play, but it is interesting as a premoni-tion of the imagery pattern in *Romeo and Juliet*, where we shall find that love is entirely a thing of the night, a secret rite which, as Juliet says, lovers perform by the light of their own beauties. And in both plays the black masquing visor is one of love's dark images, an element in the creative pattern of self-discovery.

Romeo and Juliet may be seen as a tragic battle between the lovers and the world. To think of Romeo and Juliet is to think of the night; the day belongs to Verona where Escalus rules, where Montagues and Capulets go about their business, arranging marriages, entertaining at banquets or brawling in the streets. These block terms are imposed from the moment of the opening scene, with its hierarchic building up of the Verona world through all its degrees—servants, then sons of the houses, then masters and their wives, then the prince and his train; and Romeo and Juliet are absent. Immediately afterwards we have a picture of Romeo, locked up in the dark, unreal world of his own melancholy from which he is to emerge—by night—into the reality of his love for Juliet. The separation of the lovers from the world is in fact the pivot of the whole play. Romeo must cease to be a Montague and Juliet a Capulet if they are to love each other—they must renounce their public selves. When Romeo is forced to resume his public self, saying 'O sweet Juliet, thy beauty hath made me effeminate', the two worlds are brought into a collision that destroys the lovers. But it cannot destroy their love. It seeps into the sun-lit world of Verona, reconciling its factions, honoured and made memorable in golden statues. When Romeo is drawn back so violently into the world of Verona 'the day is hot, the Capulets abroad'; when Verona is drawn down to the dark world of the lovers, 'a glooming peace this morning with it brings, The Sun for sorrow will not show his head'.

Romeo and Juliet, then, have their being in a secret kept darkly from the world. Only two people share it, and they both stand apart from the public life of Verona. They are the Nurse and Friar Lawrence. These two counsellors are placed to the right and left of the lovers, rather like the good and evil angels in *Dr Faustus*. But though the Friar draws near the divine, the Nurse is, of course, by no means evil. She merely speaks for the natural will of the flesh which brings the lovers together, while the Friar speaks for the gracious spirit by which Holy Church incorporates two in one.

Through Friar Lawrence the tragic action is related to the abiding structure of truth as Shakespeare would have us see it in this play. This Franciscan friar, dedicated like his patron to the divine love for all created things, is a thorough neo-Platonist, adept at natural magic, attuned to the mysterious affinities and correspondences that unite the universe—for love is the power of union, a fact central to neo-Platonic teaching. Shakespeare goes out of his way to drive the point well home by first introducing the Friar in his garden gathering herbs and expounding in a lengthy soliloquy their secret virtues—a scene which holds up the action while we are made to listen. For Friar Lawrence this world shadows and is informed by the divine, eternal world of the spirit. He finds the spiritual world more immediate than an Aristotelian divine such as Hooker would allow, let alone a modern theologian. Yet Hooker and Friar Lawrence would join in declaring the general immanence of the spiritual world, both divine and satanic. The reader can only feel how inadequate is the modern concept of religion to interpret the amalgam of Plato, Aristotle, magic and theology which informed the Elizabethan world with spirit.

> O mickle is the powerful grace that lies
> In plants, herbs, stones, and their true qualities.

The powerful grace that Friar Lawrence finds in his garden is divine grace, the work of the Holy Ghost.

The effect of this explicit cosmological statement is to emphasize the immediate yet secret quality of the spirit in the world of the play. The common eye sees the simple herb, but only the initiate knows of its secret virtue; and the common eye sees nothing of the secret love which unites Romeo and Juliet. More important, the neo-Platonic sense of secret spiritual life infuses with a deeper seriousness the Petrarchan mood which colours so deeply the love of Romeo and Juliet. The raw Romeo of Act I had told his tale of leaden feathers, bright smoke, cold fires and sick health, no doubt charming the audience with his fashionable Petrarchan cast of feature;

when the lovers shared a sonnet at their first meeting the audience had not missed the more serious note as the saint gravely accepted her palmer; but now, with the entry of Friar Lawrence, the audience is to feel a firmer religious implication in this Petrarchan worship of beauty. If the lover finds a divine beauty shadowed in a face, the Church affirms the immanence of the divine in the world. *Romeo and Juliet* appeals to the spirit of *Astrophel and Stella*, or of Spenser's *Four Hymnes*, published in the same year. And that appeal would have evoked a wide response. When Romeo whispers at night 'it is my soul that calls upon my name', it should be remembered that even the tough Ben Jonson in a Florentine mood could pronounce for the divine nature of beauty, making women the souls of men in the *Masque of Beauty*.

It will be noticed that Friar Lawrence himself directs us to draw the parallel between his occult garden and the world of men:

> Two such opposed kings encamp them still
> In man as well as herbs—grace and rude will;
> And where the worser is predominant,
> Full soon the canker death eats up that plant.

The First Folio reads *Enter Romeo*, apparently unobserved, just as the Friar holds up a flower, and from its medicinal smell and deadly taste proceeds to this parallel. There is reason to accept the Folio reading rather than the emendation which delays Romeo's arrival until the end of the speech. For the progress of the whole tragedy shows grace informing and correcting rude will as the lovers enter more and more deeply into the experience of love.

Here we take up the significance of the lovers' second confidant, the old Nurse. If Friar Lawrence speaks the character of grace, she is the rude will of the flesh personified. Kindly in her nature, she is dangerously innocent of any moral sense. She listens appreciatively to the Friar's homily on Romeo's despair:

> O Lord, I could have stay'd here all the night,
> To hear good counsel. Oh, what learning is!

The waters of grace run off her duck's back as she goes her cheerfully amoral way. In her view of marriage she differs greatly from the Church—though it has clearly never occurred to her that the Church holds any views at all. Paris, Romeo, or a husband by any other name amounts to much the same thing:

> Your first is dead, or 'twere as good he were,
> As living here and you no use of him.

At this point the rude will of nature becomes sin, not by any deliberate choice, but merely for lack of wit and grace. She ministers to the body—the soul is no concern of hers. Our abiding picture of her is that given in her first scene—of an old woman, garrulous and full of her fourteen-year-old memories, telling of the day when she weaned the baby Juliet—'sitting in the sun under the dove-house wall'—and cracking the same bawdy jest time and again. There is a ripe, fruity quality about her that comes from the kitchen—'they call for dates and quinces in the pastry'—and for all her complaints of aches and pains, it is quite clear that she will live for ever, nursing babies up to manhood or womanhood, and bedding them to beget more babies:

> I am the drudge, and toil in your delight,
> But you shall bear the burthen soon at night.

That is the 'sentence' both of Juliet's Nurse and of her cosmological type, Nature, who is our ancient foster-mother, persistent, unbaptized, devious in her endless effort to rear all the children of creation and make them multiply.

Guided by the Nurse, Romeo and Juliet come together in the flesh; guided by the Friar, they adventure beyond it, finally beyond him. The action of the play sharply divides the lovers, as lovers, from the world, and as the play progresses they tend more and more to leave the physical behind them. Romeo begins the play as a Petrarch saddled with an unsatisfactory Laura. Lacking a mistress who will 'stay the siege of loving terms', he cannot realize himself in his chosen role. He can only make himself 'an artificial night' until he finds the true night with Juliet. In the meantime he is out of contact with the real world:

> Tut, I have lost myself, I am not here,
> This is not Romeo, he's some other where.

The transformation comes after he has donned the black visor:

...now art thou sociable, now art thou Romeo: now art thou what thou art, by art as well as by nature....

The world sees the new and real Romeo, but it cannot see the secret cause that has brought him into being. He has seen 'true beauty' and the saint has accepted her palmer. Again, however, devout and true religion will have to make provision for the rude will of the flesh:

> ...vestal livery is but sick and green,
> And none but fools do wear it; cast it off.

From this point onwards the Nurse plays her part in bringing the lovers together, and in their secret marriage Holy Church incorporates two in one. Gracious wit gives permissive sentence to the flesh. But the insistent secrecy has already made it clear that this will prove no ordinary marriage. What has been hidden from the world now dies to the world with Romeo's banishment and Juliet's 'death', showing quite literally their passing from the land in which they have lived.

Juliet's journey to the Capulet tomb is, of course, explicitly a form of death, by which she casts off the body, symbol of rude will:

> Ancient damnation, O most wicked fiend!...
> Go, counsellor,
> Thou and my bosom henceforth shall be twain:
> I'll to the Friar to know his remedy.
> If all else fail, myself have power to die.

She will save her soul alive, be loyal to the spirit of love, no matter whether the Friar can help her or not:

> God join'd my heart and Romeo's, thou our hands.

And so she finds grace to 'die' through the occult ministrations of the Friar; her life is now a secret hidden from the world.

Romeo's banishment is charged with overtones of death from the moment it is pronounced. He himself makes them explicit:

> Hence banished is banish'd from the world,
> And world's exile is death.

And the lovers part under the same shadow:

> *Juliet.* O God! I have an ill-divining soul!
> Methinks I see thee, now thou art so low,
> As one dead in the bottom of a tomb.
> Either my eyesight fails or thou look'st pale.
> *Romeo.* And trust me, love, in my eye so do you:
> Dry sorrow drinks our blood. Adieu, adieu.

Juliet's fear both foretells their final death and sends Romeo off into his death-in-banishment. But in succeeding lines her premonition acquires a peculiar emphasis. First Juliet is made to give apparent consent to her mother's murderous intentions:

> Indeed I never shall be satisfied
> With Romeo till I behold him—dead—
> Is my poor heart so for a kinsman vext.

(The double meaning of the speech includes a double meaning of 'with'—'in the company of'.) Then, shortly afterwards, the hint is developed:

> My husband is on earth, my faith in heaven;
> How shall that faith return again to earth,
> Unless that husband send it me from heaven
> By leaving earth?

Through her pathetic fears for herself and Romeo comes a suggestion that her faith in heaven, her spiritual life and love, can be preserved only by Romeo's death. And by some agency that suggestion reaches Romeo, though in a different form.

> If I may trust the flattering truth of sleep,
> My dreams presage some joyful news at hand.
> My bosom's lord sits lightly in his throne,
> And all this day an unaccustom'd spirit
> Lifts me above the ground with cheerful thoughts.
> I dreamt my lady came and found me dead...
> And breath'd such life with kisses in my lips
> That I revived and was an emperor.

The speech gives ironic point to the news from Verona of Juliet's death and that is its chief dramatic function; but the first part of the prophecy is fulfilled in the Capulet tomb when Juliet wakes to find Romeo dead beside her, and kisses the poison from his lips in hope to 'die with a restorative'. It remains an open question whether Romeo is alive in the next world and watching her as in his 'strange dream that gives a dead man leave to think'.

This hint of enduring life in the luminous, real, and eternal world of the spirit is given weight by the dark and light imagery. It will be recalled that in *Love's Labour's Lost* the sunny light of the first four acts is opposed to the darkness and clouds of the last. The position is much the same at the beginning of *Romeo and Juliet*. 'The worshipped sun', 'the all-cheering sun', is contrasted with Romeo's 'artificial night' for which he 'locks fair day-light out'. Old Montague fears that 'black and portentous must this humour prove', and the audience is clearly meant to agree with him. Light betokens life and darkness death.

But from this point onwards the emphasis changes. The lovers invoke darkness as a friend at some of the most memorable moments of the play, and daylight comes increasingly to suggest danger and death. The disasters all take place by day and only the night brings happiness:

> Then, window, let day in and let life out.

And the warring, street-brawling qualities of daylight are appropriated by death in Juliet's tomb. 'Thou art not conquer'd...Death's pale flag is not advanced there.' The reversal of the customary day-life and night-death associations is, of course, only one strand in a tissue of paradoxes woven about the loving enemies.[1] But the effect is to disturb the common-sense point of view, preparing the audience to accept a suggestion that darkness and even death may bring a more vivid life.

But, though the lovers 'pay no worship to the garish sun', their love is itself a thing of light. It fills their speech with images of things luminous and touched with mystery—stars in a night sky, a rich jewel in an Ethiope's ear. The sun and moon send forth rays to betray secrets, but love is a light contained, visible only in a setting of darkness or the mysterious and friendly night. There was a hint of this dual concept of light in *Love's Labour's Lost*. There the light of common day was opposed to the true light of love—brought by the ladies from the land of death—which burns invisibly in darkness. The images of love in *Romeo and Juliet* tend in this direction and sometimes achieve it:

> Lovers can see to do their amorous rights,
> ...by their own beauties—

and again, in Juliet's tomb,

> ...her beauty makes
> This vault a feasting presence full of light.

These images of the invisible light of beauty gather a strength of impression greater than their own from the central theme of secret love and from the neoplatonic magic of Friar Lawrence, which reminds the audience of secret, divine and powerful virtue in the world, undiscovered by the common eye. The tomb image just quoted has peculiar force, partly because it comes at the climax of the whole play, but also because the light of beauty shines mysteriously, unseen by any but Romeo, in the very stronghold of death. It is as if Romeo has moved so far towards the other side of the grave that he can see a glory visible only there. This and other features of the play support a suggestion that, in their death, the lovers have indeed 'breathed in their lips such life by kisses' that they have revived as emperor and empress in a kingdom of divine love. The audience has seen Romeo and Juliet die in the eyes of the world and yet remain alive; it has felt the immanence of the spirit throughout the play; it has been reminded constantly of the divine in the person of Friar Lawrence. An Elizabethan audience, in which almost every man took for granted a life continuing through death, would certainly assume that only now have Romeo and Juliet found their full realization. A modern audience is left with a sense that all the cards are not on the table, or if they are, that there are not enough of them—and this, I suggest, has a good deal to do with the feeling that the play does not quite 'come off'.

The masquing scene may well be considered in the context of the whole play. The black visor itself is, of course, part of the darkness imagery; in Shakespeare's mind it suggests the night— probably because of its colour and because masquing visits were usually made at night. The two are connected in Juliet's speech from her window:

> Thou know'st the mask of night is on my face....

As part of the night imagery, the mask is associated with secrecy, with love, with spiritual life and with death. The first two are obvious associations of the masquing visor in its own right, and the last is a primitive association of the simple mask which Shakespeare takes up in *Love's Labour's Lost*. The third—spiritual life—is the most interesting suggestion and invites closer examination.

In Act I, sc. 4, the masquers appear before Capulet's house and put on their visors. Romeo is depressed:

> ...we mean well in going to this masque,
> But 'tis no wit to go.

He has had a foreboding dream, and, though Mercutio counters it with his Queen Mab speech, the fears persist:

> ...my mind misgives,
> Some consequence, yet hanging in the stars,
> Shall bitterly begin his fearful date
> With this night's revels, and expire the term
> Of a despised life clos'd in my breast,
> By some vile forfeit of untimely death.
> But He that hath the steerage of my course,
> Direct my sail. On, lusty gentlemen.

And without more ado they go in to the feast.

After Mercutio's light-hearted speech, Romeo's insistent return to his original mood has all the more weight. The sense of misgiving is more than superstition in the modern sense. For the Elizabethan, dreams are often significant because the spirit is free to roam while the body sleeps, and the dreamer may see events of this temporal world prefigured in the timeless reality of the next. But dreams are not always to be trusted. Many of them are so confused that they reveal nothing. However, Romeo's dream has suggested that his masquing visit will prove to be one of those events in the visible world that impinge on the invisible. Not a capricious fate, but necessity—the stars—will make him suffer. The vague presentiments of the earlier speech are here sharpened into a fear of inevitable death. Romeo's impulse must be to turn back. Instead he commits himself blindly into the hands of Him who 'hath the steerage of my course', and the self-abandonment brings a lightening of the mood into 'On, lusty gentlemen'. The words convey not defiance, nor a weighing of probabilities, but acceptance of whatever fate providence may allot.

It will be seen that Shakespeare has given a very considerable weight to this moment in the play. The audience sees a Romeo whose identity has disappeared behind a black visor. In this, the last speech of the old, unrealized Romeo, it hears him commit himself to the spiritual power of the stars despite a fear of death. The mask is at the centre of an association of fear, death, mystery, the unseen powers and acceptance of their will. These are clearly designed to point forward to Romeo's death, while underlining the imminent meeting with Juliet and the coming self-realization. In this, his first death, Romeo loses a despised—and rightly despised—life closed in his breast to find a new, real life in the love of Juliet. The mask itself is, of course, merely an external instrument in the process of self-realization; but here, as in *Love's Labour's Lost*, it is clearly associated in Shakespeare's mind with the idea of such a process—an association underlined by its place in a coherent imagery pattern of creative darkness. It is through a mask that Romeo first sets eyes on Juliet, and it is through a mask that the lords of *Love's Labour's Lost* first discover that love is not a simple matter of asking and getting. In each play the mask appears at the inception of a progressive movement towards reality and a more mature, more spiritual self-awareness. It would be a gross exaggeration to suggest that Shakespeare actually thought of the mask in these terms, but the evidence does indicate that he felt the black visor to be a mysterious, even creative thing.

NOTE

1. It will be noticed that the central paradox of the lovers lends weight to the Petrarchan paradoxes (O brawling love, O loving hate). Or perhaps it would be more accurate to say that the ideal and spiritual love of Romeo and Juliet, the recurrent paradoxes (a damned Saint, an honourable villain) and the highly formal, symmetrical structure are all appropriate to an extended Petrarchan sonnet in five acts.

INTERNATIONAL NOTES

A selection has been made from the reports received from our correspondents, those which present material of a particularly interesting kind being printed in their entirety, or largely so. It should be emphasized that the choice of countries to be thus represented has depended on the nature of the information presented in the reports, not upon either the importance of the countries concerned or upon the character of the reports themselves.

Australia

In 1961 an Old Vic Company presented in the Australian capital cities three plays, of which one was *Twelfth Night* (with Vivien Leigh as Viola). Sydney had also what was called, perhaps optimistically, the 'First Sydney Shakespeare Festival', when John Alden Shakespeare Productions Ltd, with the assistance of the Australian Elizabethan Theatre Trust, gave performances of *Othello*, *Macbeth* and *The Merchant of Venice*, in at least three different theatres. *Macbeth* and *The Merchant* were well received but not *Othello*.

Melbourne and Brisbane also saw performances of *Macbeth*, by the Union Theatre Repertory Company and the Twelfth Night Theatre respectively. (The Melbourne Company used an Elizabethan type stage.) In Brisbane the Arts Theatre presented *Julius Caesar*, and the Repertory Theatre, *Twelfth Night*. In Victoria, there was a second production of *Macbeth* by the Morwell Players, in modern dress (technical school students being co-opted for crowd scenes and to make scenery and properties).

Details of productions in other States have not been made available. What can be added, however, is that for many Australians the most impressive Shakespeare productions of 1961 were the scenes from the Histories, televised and recorded by the B.B.C. as 'The Age of Kings'. This gave rise to more discussion of Shakespeare than one remembers hearing for many a long day.

H. J. OLIVER

Austria

The most important event among the performances of Shakespearian plays in Austria was the production at the Burgtheater, Vienna, of *Henry V*. The play had not been acted there since 1904, when it was staged in a production dating back to 1875. This 1961 Vienna production of *Henry V* by Leopold Lindtberg is part of a plan to play all of Shakespeare's histories between now and 1964. In that centenary year all the histories will each be acted five nights in succession, with two parts of *Henry VI* and the two parts of *Henry IV* being performed in shortened versions.

Henry V was favourably received, and some critics reviewed the performance in terms of highest praise. It is interesting to note, however, that quite a number of critics felt that the producer and his excellent actors had made the play seem better than it really is. The interpreters of *Henry V* thus received much more attention than its author, a situation that once again, the present writer feels, indicates the current overemphasis upon interpretation and the underrating of dramatic creation.

There was only one other production of a Shakespeare play in Vienna, that of *The Taming of the Shrew* at the Akademietheater, for which the producer, Josef Gielen, chose the fine and efficient translation of Richard Flatter instead of the commonly used version by Wolf Graf Baudissin.

The Austrian provincial theatres were more active in this field than Vienna. *Troilus and Cressida* was played in the translation by Richard Flatter in Linz, Upper Austria, and *The Merchant of Venice*, which had not been performed in Salzburg since 1925, was put on by the Landestheater, a production which overemphasized the tragic traits of Shylock. Shakespearian plays also constituted the core of various festival programmes in Austrian provincial towns, including the standard performance of *A Midsummer Night's Dream* in the park of Graz-Castle, Styria, *Twelfth Night* in the courtyard of the baroque Melk monastery, Lower Austria, and *The Comedy of Errors* at the Castle of Porcia, Spittal, Carinthia.

SIEGFRIED KORNINGER

INTERNATIONAL NOTES

Czechoslovakia

If we look at the repertoire of the Czechoslovak theatres in the past two seasons, we hesitate to say that there have been more plays by Shakespeare put on than usual, though no doubt most of these productions already form a nucleus of the repertoire to be played in the jubilee year of 1964. Most popular were *A Midsummer Night's Dream* and *Much Ado About Nothing* (at four theatres); then follow *The Merry Wives*, *Twelfth Night*, *Romeo and Juliet* and *Hamlet* (at three), *Othello* (at two), *The Comedy of Errors*, *A Winter's Tale*, *Richard II*, *Julius Caesar*, *Coriolanus* and *King Lear* (each at one).

All these plays are produced in modern translations by E. A. Saudek, Zdeněk Urbánek, Aloys Skoumal, Frank Tetauer, Jaroslav Kraus, Zora Jesenská, František Nevrla and others. A promising dramatist, Josef Topol, has recently translated *Romeo and Juliet*, so that there are now three modern translations of this play. The public may easily assess the merits of the new translations by comparing them with the classical renderings of J. V. Sládek. His translations of Shakespeare's tragedies (in two volumes) are published by the State Publishing House KLU, edited by O. Vočadlo; Saudek's translations have notes and comments by Z. Stříbrný. Artia have brought out *The Dream* with stills from Jiří Trnka's puppet-film version of the play. This book, as well as a students' edition of *Twelfth Night*, published by the State Pedagogical Publishing House, were edited by myself.

All theatres and publishing houses are now looking forward to 1964 and a meeting has already taken place at which the nine Prague theatres made their bids for Shakespeare's plays.   BRETISLAV HODEK

France

The Merchant of Venice was produced last winter by Marguerite Jamois at the Odéon-Théâtre de France. The choice of Claude-André Puget's 'adaptation' was perhaps not very fortunate, and the interpretation was not striking, if we except Daniel Sorano as Shylock. Performances were dramatically interrupted by the sudden death of this dedicated artist, who was still young. The cause, as in the case of Gerard Philipe, was strain and overwork. Sorano had begun his career at the Grenier de Toulouse, a Dramatic Centre devoted to the comedies of Molière and Shakespeare, and later joined the Théâtre National Populaire (he was the Porter in Vilar's *Macbeth*). Originally a comic actor, he was later attracted by serious and even tragic parts. Born in Africa, he had some negro blood in his veins, and was unusually aware of the racial conflict in *The Merchant*. This may have accounted for the intensity of his interpretation of the Jew's part, which was, however, a carefully thought piece of acting, doing justice to all the facets of this controversial character.

Gabriel Monnet, who was responsible for a fascinating production of *Hamlet* at the Festival d'Annecy, has become director of the new Dramatic Centre in Bourges. Significantly he chose, for his first programme, *Timon of Athens*, a play which is rarely, if ever, performed in France, and besets the producer with a series of difficult problems. The play was well received when the young company visited Paris, and Monnet met deserved success in the leading part. New provincial Centres are still being created. André Reybas is now at the head of the Centre Dramatique du Nord (Lille and its industrial area) where he has staged *Hamlet* in a new version by José Axelrad.

Edward II, as it was played by the company of the Théâtre de la Cité in Villeurbanne (an industrial suburb of Lyons) and in Paris, should be mentioned here as a further development along the lines indicated by René Planchon's stimulating and controversial production of *Henry IV*. The Elizabethans and Brecht have been decisive influences with Planchon. On the whole it was wiser to write a new play 'after Marlowe's' than just to tamper with the original. In spite of some clumsy didacticism it was impressive for the intensity of its feeling of the ruthless pressure of history upon man. The solidity it possessed was undoubtedly due to what was retained of the structure of the old play. Scenography, *décor* and costumes were by René Allio, an exceptionally gifted artist, who was perhaps unable, this time, sufficiently to discipline his exuberant wealth of invention.   JEAN JACQUOT

Germany

It is remarkable that in a survey of last year's performances of Shakespeare *Hamlet* predominates much more than in previous years. There were no less than fifteen new productions of *Hamlet*, comprising 305 performances in seventeen different theatres. Of these productions the one by Kurt Meisel at the Residenztheater, Munich, was particularly successful and impressive. Thomas Holtzmann, who played Hamlet, emphasized the dynamic, energetic and almost threatening element in Hamlet's character, while Christa Keller gave relief to Ophelia's tenderness, innocence and purity. On other stages, too, as at Konstanz, Wiesbaden, Aachen, Bautzen and Weimar, Hamlet appears to have been conceived as a man of action, an 'angry young man' rather than the hesitating delicate intellectual.

On the old 'Burg' of Dinkelsbühl a noteworthy open-air performance of *Hamlet* took place. An old-fashioned Thespian cart was drawn by a pony through the torch-lit alleys of the old town to the square in front of the castle; the actors, after unloading the cart, mounted guard on the castle wall.

In a new and interesting production of *Othello* by Hans Schalla (with Erich Aberle in the title-role) at Bochum a clown was introduced who arranged the regrouping of the scene between the acts and drew the curtain; apparently this was meant to suggest the tragic paradox of chance and fate. Of Shakespeare's less-known tragedies a new production of *Timon of Athens* by Fritz Kortner at the Kammerspiele, Munich deserves special mention. This difficult play turned out to be of great symbolic impact, of human intensity and of perennial significance in Kortner's original and moving production.

Another successful revival of a less-known play was that of *King John* in Hans Schalla's production, which was performed both at Bochum and at Berlin. A second production of *King John* at the Staatstheater, Kassel, emphasized the pageantry and the great political issues of this history play.

Of the comedies, *Twelfth Night* was performed in more than eighteen theatres. Whereas most stages used the older translations by Schlegel, Benda and Eschenburg, the Staatstheater, Schwerin, made a successful attempt at introducing Rudolf Schaller's new translation, which lends itself to fluent delivery by the actor.

Among several new productions of *A Midsummer Night's Dream*, that of Karl-Heinz Stroux at the Schauspielhaus, Düsseldorf, revealed an interesting tendency to increase the effect of romantic enchantment. Puck, discovering that the two pairs of Athenian lovers are again coupled in the wrong way, raises them as with an invisible thread and leads them in a kind of ballet to their right partners. Jean Pierre Ponelle's sets considerably added to the charm of this performance. Benjamin Britten's new opera *Midsummer Night's Dream* had its German first performance at the Staatsoper, Hamburg, and won warm response from the audience. At the festival of Schwetzingen this opera was performed with the original English text, John Gielgud being the producer and Meredith Davies the conductor.

Of the apocryphal plays, *The London Prodigal* was again—as in 1960—produced, this time in an open-air performance at Stromberg on the staircase of the Gothic church. The emphasis was on the comic scenes, which were made more effective by the introduction of a draper speaking Westphalian dialect.

It is again revealing to compare the total number of Shakespeare performances in 1961 with those of other popular dramatists. While there were altogether 2556 performances of twenty-six plays by Shakespeare, there were only 1436 by Lessing, 1396 by Goethe, 1168 by Schiller, 1249 by Bert Brecht and 1230 by Gerhart Hauptmann.

On the Free Berlin Television screen Ludwig Berger's adaptations of *The Taming of the Shrew*, *Much Ado about Nothing* and *Measure for Measure* reappeared.

The President of the German Shakespeare Society, Rudolf Alexander Schroeder, was honoured by the award of the translator's prize of the 'Deutsche Akademie für Sprache und Dichtung'. His translations include, besides Homer, Horace, Racine, T. S. Eliot and others, nine plays by Shakespeare.

KARL BRINKMANN
WOLFGANG CLEMEN

Greece

Oddly enough, fewer plays of Shakespeare's than usual were performed in Greece during 1961: in all no more than three productions. These were *Romeo and Juliet* at the National Theatre, an amateur production of *A Midsummer Night's Dream* organized by the Dramatic Club of Anatolia College, Salonica, and *Twelfth Night* by the Arts Theatre of Cyprus. Of these, the first was of course the most important.

The producer of *Romeo and Juliet* was Alexis Solomos, who emphasized the lyrical aspect of the work. The quality perceptibly lacking was that of tragic grandeur, both in the acting and, in general, in the course of the action. Dimitri Papamichail's interpretation of Romeo was distinguished by a tendency to facile sentimentality. As for the Juliet of Antigone Valakou, although she showed all the girlish qualities demanded of the role in the first part of the play, she lacked the courage to make a frontal attack on the great moments offered her by the playwright and the power to scale truly dramatic heights. The magnificent soliloquies evaporated in a kind of flat naturalness. Of the other actors, those who came nearest to what was demanded of their roles were Stelios Vocovits as Mercutio, Lycurgus Callerghis as Capulet and Nico Papaconstantinou as Tybalt. The crowd scenes were brilliantly managed.

The stage designs by George Vacalo were picturesque but lacked any dramatic quality. Andonis Phocas' costumes were magnificent. ANGHELOS TERZAKIS

Hungary

In the 1961-2 theatrical season there was no falling off in the popularity of Shakespeare in Hungary. Of the plays that had a run a year earlier, *Othello* and *Twelfth Night* continued to be performed by the National Theatre in Budapest. To these were added a successful revival of *All's Well That Ends Well* in the small J. Katona Theatre of Budapest. Zoltán Várkonyi, one of our most experienced Shakespeare directors, emphasized the comic and fairy-tale-like elements of the play, ably assisted by I. Köpeczi-Bócz's ingenious costumes and scenery as well as by Gy. Ránky's incidental music. The two gifted young actors, Mari Törocsik as the patiently wise and poetically modest Helena, and Lajos Cs. Németh, a pert teenagerish Bertram, were more than matched by the brilliant Parolles of Ferenc Kállai, whose self-conceited stupidity was sharply contrasted by the pitifulness of his almost tragic downfall, by the broad humour of János Rajz as Lavache and by Lajos Mányai's carefully modelled Lafeu.

Another success of the year was the long run of *Hamlet* in the new Madách Theatre in Budapest, directed by L. Vámos and presented on a curtainless open stage. The strongly intellectualized Prince, as played by M. Gábor, with his soberly sincere sadness seemed occasionally to lack fire and passion. Sándor Pécsi presented a most convincing Polonius. The entire performance, with its multitude of carefully wrought figures, was characterized by conscious restraint, eschewing all possibilities of colourful exaggeration and directorial experimentation to which the play on Hamlet has been exposed all too often in the past.

The theatres in the country followed the lead given by the capital in the previous seasons. Thus *The Taming of the Shrew* was given in Békéscsaba, *Much Ado* in Eger, *The Merry Wives* in Miskolc, *Twelfth Night* in Debrecen and *Romeo and Juliet*, that perennial favourite of the Hungarian stage, in Kaposvár, Kecskemet, Pécs and Szeged. In each locality there were at least six or eight performances of each play, often considerably more. The performance of *Romeo and Juliet* in Szeged, directed by J. Szendro, emphasized the rapidity of the dramatic events and the inevitability of conflicts in feudal society. Against the cast of predominantly young actors the mature humanism of Friar Lawrence (played by that excellent old-timer Ferenc Kiss) stood out.

Twelfth Night had a run of over thirty performances in Debrecen, the third largest town of Hungary, and in its neighbourhood. The director, Gy. Lengyel, by giving the play a touch of carnival gaiety, underlined the comic elements of the plot.

The Hungarian Broadcasting Company, in a series of studio broadcasts, made accessible to the public several dramas that are very seldom or never seen in Hungarian

theatres, such as *King John*, *Coriolanus*, *Henry V* and *A Winter's Tale*. These somewhat abridged broadcast versions were played by the best Shakespearian actors of Hungary.

The popularity of Shakespeare was reflected in the field of book-publishing as well. The complete dramatic works in Hungarian translation, as published in 1955, were brought out again in 1961–2, with only minor changes. This time, however, a seventh volume was added, containing the *Sonnets* (in the translation of Lörinc Szabó), the *Rape of Lucrece*, *Venus and Adonis* and even some minor poems of doubtful authorship.

LADISLAS ORSZÁGH

India

This year, the Shakespeare Society of St Stephen's College, Delhi, the only institution to keep Shakespeare alive on the Indian stage, produced *Romeo and Juliet*, under the direction of William Jarvis and David Summerscale. The stage consisted of a single set without the proscenium curtain, and with light arrangements dexterously used both to set off the costumes and make-up of the actors and to mark changes in time and place. Zafar Hai played Romeo and Dakshu Bhavnani Juliet. The play ran for three nights and attracted well over a thousand visitors.

At my instance, Prime Minister Nehru has established an Indian National Theatre at Delhi and other similar theatres in the capital cities of other Indian states, and this is likely to lead towards the production of new and authentic translations of Shakespeare's dramas into simple Hindi.

H. S. D. MITHAL

Italy

The Venetian Festival of the Prose Theatre, which was started in 1934 in the courtyard of Ca' Foscari (the Venice University College) with the performance of *Romeo and Juliet*, opened in September 1961 with *Romeo and Juliet* again as acted by the Old Vic Company and produced by Franco Zeffirelli: this time the stage was that of the Venice theatre, but though the public greeted the performance with five minutes' applause, the praise of the critics was not unqualified. Opinion has been divided also regarding *Twelfth Night* (*La Notte dell'Epifania*), produced by Giorgio De Lullo at the Roman Teatro Eliseo in January 1962. Following an innovation now more than twenty years old, originality was sought in a medley of costumes, most of them inspired by the early thirteenth century, some of them Victorian, and only here and there a touch of Elizabethan fashions.

Yet, if there is a Shakespearian play which demands its proper period setting, it is *Twelfth Night*, whose language and type of dialogue can be fully appreciated only within its historical framework. Giorgio De Lullo wore the garb of a Byronic hero in the role of Orsino, Rossella Falk (Viola) and Claudio Camaso (Sebastiano), though their fancy dresses were alike reminiscent of those of early nineteenth-century jockeys, were so shockingly unlike each other in appearance as to make the acceptance of any mistaken identity impossible. Feste's acting was mediocre, and the magic of the songs vanished in the flat translation by Fantasio Piccoli. Romolo Valli was a plausible Malvolio, though the caricature he presented was certainly not soft-pedalled. Annamaria Guarnieri interpolated a Biedermeier Olivia who fitted least of all into a performance in which everything was at sixes and sevens. The costumes, far from making up for the lack of atmosphere consequent on the translation of the play into a foreign language (Shakespeare's comedies lose much more in translation than his tragedies), increased the general sense of disharmony.

The theatrical season on television began in November 1961 with *Enrico IV*, with Carlo d'Angelo as Enrico IV, Tino Buazzelli as Falstaff, Giancarlo Sbragia as the Principe Enrico, and Raoul Grassilli as Lord Percy. Gabriele Baldini, who is planning a complete prose translation of Shakespeare's theatre for 1964, has given this year new translations of *Measure for Measure*, *Twelfth Night*, and the *Comedy of Errors*: in most cases he has not attempted to give Italian equivalents for the puns, as the complete translation published years ago by Sansoni under my editorship tried to do, though, of course, rather lamely. Baldini's complete translation will not be the only Italian tribute to the Shakespearian centenary. A suggestion by the present writer has been made in the stamp-collectors' periodical *Il Collezionista* (April 1962): 'In 1964 the fourth centenary of Shakespeare's birth will be celebrated. Many Shakespearian plays have Italian towns as backgrounds. Stamps might be issued in which Shakespeare's portrait would appear side by side with views of Venice, Verona, Padua, and even Florence, Milan and Messina, though these latter towns are hardly more than conventional place-names. One could make these stamps similar to the English ones in which the portrait of the sovereign appears at the side of a view: this would be a hint to the English P.O. that the effigy of the King or Queen is not the only one which is worthy to appear on a stamp, according to an English tradition which has had no exception so far. Until now the only stamp in the world commemorating Shake-

speare is an ugly Hungarian stamp. On the other hand, how many stamps have been issued to commemorate Goethe, Mozart, Pushkin, Chekhov, etc., etc. !'

MARIO PRAZ

Japan

Shakespeare is now a favourite with Japanese theatre-goers. The Bungakuza and the Haiyuza, two of the three main theatrical companies concerned with modern drama, have given numerous productions of Shakespearian plays: indeed, the former, led by Tsuneari Fukuda, a translator and producer, includes one in its repertory every year. In 1961 *Julius Caesar* was performed by the younger members of the Bungakuza at Toshi Centre Hall in Tokyo. The Roman tragedy is the earliest play of Shakespeare's rendered into Japanese and has been popular for nearly eighty years. In the present production traditional black-and-white characterization was replaced by modern psychological presentation. Although perhaps not a perfect representation of the producer's intention, the twelve nights' full-house performances were the principal topic in Tokyo's theatrical circles.

JIRO OZU

Poland

The tenth anniversary of the State Publishing Institute of Warsaw, publishing a series of new Shakespeare translations, has been marked by the appearance of *The Winter's Tale* in a fresh Polish rendering by the founder of the series, Włodzimierz Lewik, critic and poet.

Jan Kott, Professor of Comparative Literature at Warsaw University, at the same time published a book entitled *Szkice o Szekspirze* (*Essays on Shakespeare*), printed by the same Warsaw firm. Well known as a widely-read connoisseur of modern West-European drama and theatre, the author analyses the meaning of political power in Shakespeare's history plays, the imperial theme in *Antony and Cleopatra*, the class struggle in *Coriolanus*, the problem of war in *Troilus and Cressida*. In two important chapters dealing with *King Lear* and *The Tempest* new hints of a fresh theatrical approach are presented from the point of view of twentieth-century historiosophy.

This volume by Jan Kott is being translated into French and English so as to make it accessible to Western scholars. STANISŁAW HELSZTYŃSKI

Sweden

A first performance for Sweden can be reported, namely *King John*, staged at the Dramatiska Teatern. This was one of the most interesting productions of the last decades. Alf Sjöberg, the producer, assisted by

INTERNATIONAL NOTES

Lennart Mörk (decorations and costumes) and Birgit Akesson (dances), created a fascinating scenic setting. He showed his inventive power especially in the use of dances, particularly those concerned with the changing of masks in the opening scene and a soldiers' 'war dance', which replaced one of the battlefield episodes. Karl Ragnar Gierow translated the play, which, in the preface to the programme, he compared with the scenes of the Bayeux tapestry. Dag Wirén's music made a good accompaniment to the action of the play.

In the Göteburg Stadsteater, Johan Falck produced *Romeo and Juliet* with Tommy Berggren and Jane Friedmann in the leading parts. Although costumes and decorations were interesting, this was on the whole a rather lack-lustre performance, relieved by the excellence of Berta Hall as the Nurse.

Frank Sundström—now in Uppsala—presented a *Romeo and Juliet* in the best traditional style. Göran Graffman as Romeo and Bibi Andersson as Juliet found genuine expressions for youthful love.

At the Vasateatern in Stockholm, Per Gerhard chose *The Taming of the Shrew* to celebrate the Theatre's seventy-fifth anniversary. It proved a great success and had 170 performances. Sture Lagerwall was Petruchio and Maj Britt Nilsson Katherina. Spectacular decorations by Yngve Gamlin added to the successful entertainment.

Björn Collinder has continued his work at translating Shakespeare's tragedies. With *Macbeth* and *King Lear*, the latest volumes published, he has brought this task to an end. We are now in the fortunate position of possessing a number of first-rate translations to choose from.

Meanwhile, another great event is drawing near—a new translation of Shakespeare's plays, carried out by Ake Ohlmarks. The comedies will be published this year. The intention is that the entire translation will be available in the Jubilee year of 1964. NILS MOLIN

Turkey

Towards the end of the theatre season, last spring, the younger group of the Municipal Theatre of Istanbul performed *Hamlet* under the direction of Muhsin Ertuğrul, who used Orhan Burian's Turkish version. The production was carried to the fifteenth-century castle of Sultan Mehmet II, a large fortress on the European side of the Bosphorus.

This production is noteworthy for having been the first play performed within the picturesque walls of an old fortress in Turkey. Due to the lack of experience for such performances, the gigantic battlements and

huge towers overlooking the audience were never used; the players hardly left the circular orchestra area recently built in a form similar to that of the ancient Greek theatres. Large spotlights, used to impersonate the invisible Ghost, could not be concealed from the eyes of the spectators. Yet the lofty walls and the lapping of the Pontic Current just out of the iron gates could have offered the most suitable surroundings for a Shakespearian Ghost with a transparent grey cloak flapping in the North wind, prepared to beckon Hamlet up the long flights of mysterious stairs to the top of most ghostly battlements. The play as a whole lacked the professional touch necessary for a castle setting. Polonius, played by Mucip Ofluoğlu as a gentleman hardly older than a middle-aged courtier and Abdurrahman Palay, as a kind-looking Claudius with a devil's heart, were convincing enough with their resonant baritone voices and mature attitudes, but Engin Cezzar as Hamlet was not even audible in the open air.

At the National Theatre of Ankara *Hamlet* opened on 27 October 1961 with Cüneyt Gökçer in the title-role. Gökçer, Turkey's leading Shakespearian actor, was also responsible for the production. In this second portrayal of his Hamlet he preferred to have a simpler and more concentrated environment which largely dispensed with objects on the stage. There was, indeed, not a single seat except those for the King and the Queen—part of the revolving steps in the centre. This was a daring innovation, which in the experienced hands of its performer and with his expressive face, ideal physical stature and high quality of bodily and vocal control won great success. Mrs Gülsen Almaçik (formerly Miss G. Tunççekiç) was also noteworthy for her delicate and impressive Ophelia. Her witty tones in the first act and her pensive mood in the jewel scene harmoniously contrasted with her sprightly innocence in her final madness. Sahap Akalin as Claudius was at his best. Ahmet Evintan's Polonius, in spite of his hoary hair, was far too energetic for the conventional character, although convincing as a good father and a devoted courtier. Asuman Korat and Muzaffer Gökmen as the Grave-diggers were typically Elizabethan and received most hearty applause at the curtain call. On the first night the curtain rose more than twenty times. The play is still on and will continue during the 1962–63 season.

A third impression of my translation of *A Midsummer Night's Dream* has just come out. NUREDDIN SEVIN

U.S.A.

In the United States as in the rest of the world, Shakespeare has become the concern of the dedicated drama lover more than the staple of the professional stage. Today it is the summer festival, the community theatre, the repertory company, the theatre workshops, the equity groups, and the speech and drama departments of universities that offer Shakespeare to the great audiences that never tire of his works, that do not see one *Hamlet*, but every *Hamlet* they can.

With more than a dozen regular festivals in operation and a host of other theatres offering occasional productions, Shakespeare was available in regular theatres, from Maine to Hawaii, on open stages, in parks, in Globe replicas, on showboats in Indiana, in collegiate gymnasiums.

The realization that Shakespeare provides edification as well as entertainment has stimulated, as in the past, large appropriations by civic bodies to bring his plays to student audiences. The Board of Education of New York City in 1961 appropriated $50,000 to bring *Romeo and Juliet* to thousands of High School students and has put up the same sum for 1962. The American Theatre Wing and the Helen Hayes Equity Group, also with subsidies, presented *As You Like It* and *Twelfth Night* to many thousands more. Theatre in Education toured much of Connecticut with scenes from several plays, and more than 80,000 young folk attended reduced-rate performances of *Twelfth Night* at the American Shakespeare Festival Theatre in Stratford, Connecticut.

The American Shakespeare Festival offered a fourteen-week season of *As You Like It, Macbeth* and *Troilus and Cressida*—the last achieving some notoriety for its being transposed from the Trojan War to the American Civil War period of 1861-5. With the conclusion of the seventh season Jack Landau ended his reign at this playhouse: for the eighth season, the American Allen Fletcher and the English Douglas Seale have been engaged as directors. The American Shakespeare Festival was honoured in 1961 by being requested to give a command performance at the White House on 4 October, the first performance of Shakespeare in the history of the presidential mansion.

The New York City Festival had its early hopes dashed when its new festival amphitheatre could not be opened in time, but a stage and seating area was improvised over the Woolman Memorial Skating Rink nearby and a nightly audience of 3000 brought the season total to well over 160,000.

The Oregon Festival in its 21st year scored 99 per cent. of capacity for its forty-two performances, with B. Iden Payne scoring the greatest triumph with his *Midsummer Night's Dream*. *All's Well*, and *1 Henry IV*, and Ben Jonson's *Alchemist* were also on the programme. San Diego's 12th National Festival entertained more than 36,000—98 per cent. of capacity—in ninety-one performances of *Twelfth Night, The Merchant of Venice*, and *Richard III*.

Among the newcomers to the Festival orbit was the Summer Shakespeare Festival organized by Ellie Chamberlain in the nation's capital. Miss Chamberlain, a disciple of Joseph Papp—organizer of the free New York City Festival—has also managed to get enough government support to offer free admission in a 1500 capacity outdoor theatre only a stone's throw from the Washington Monument.

With so much being produced, the inevitable distortions and unusual productions occur. At the Dallas Theatre Centre in Texas the role of Hamlet—in a production reminiscent of one at Baylor University six years ago—was distributed to three different actors, each exhibiting a different facet of his personality. A *Richard III* at Goucher College had all the roles but that of Richard played by women. A Fairmont State College production of *Julius Caesar* was set in the modern dress of revolutionary Castro-Cuba. A professional New York group has prepared, but not yet presented, another version of the play with the title *Julius Castro*! Perhaps even more extraordinary was the widely toured Canadian Players' *King Lear*, staged in Eskimo dress, the director having decided on a primitive setting and having eliminated the American Indian and the Mexican as possibilities!   LOUIS MARDER

U.S.S.R.

During the season of 1961-2 the Moscow theatres have disappointed Shakespeare-lovers: not a single new Shakespearian production was staged by any of the companies. The explanation given by the directors is that they are accumulating their creative energy for the coming anniversary of Shakespeare; but it is more than doubtful that the audience can be satisfied by such an explanation.

It was only in summer that Moscow theatregoers were recompensed for this silence, when a series of Shakespeare productions were brought to the capital by provincial theatres. A great success was scored by the new production of *Richard III* staged by P. Monastyrsky at the Kuybyshew Theatre, with N. Zasukhin in the title-role. Of other artistic achievements the acting of L. Shutova as Cleopatra (Saratov Theatre) and V. Rezepter as Hamlet (Tashkent Theatre) should be mentioned.

It is, indeed, the various national theatres which have been most active in producing Shakespeare. For example, in the Daghestan Autonomous Republic Shakespeare's plays are staged in three languages—Avar, Darghin, Lezghin; it is perhaps worth pointing out that the written languages of these nationalities have appeared only after the October Revolution.

A Shakespeare conference was held at the All-Russia Theatre Society in April, which was addressed by A. Anikst, N. Zubova and G. Kosintzev. In May a meeting was called by the Ministry of Culture in commemoration of Prof. M. Morozov, a prominent Soviet Shake-spearian, former correspondent to the *Shakespeare Survey*.

YURI SHVEDOV

Estonia. Seng Meri has now completed a four-volume Estonian translation of the Histories, and other volumes including the Comedies are promised for publication in 1962. Although three editions of the complete works in Russian have appeared since 1917, this Estonian edition is the first attempt to publish the whole of Shakespeare's plays in any other language spoken in the Soviet Union.

SHAKESPEARE PRODUCTIONS IN THE
UNITED KINGDOM: 1961

A List compiled from its Records by the
Shakespeare Memorial Library, Birmingham

JANUARY

16   *The Merry Wives of Windsor:* Civic Theatre, Chesterfield. *Producer:* ANTHONY CORNISH.

23   *As You Like It:* The Playhouse, Sheffield. *Producer:* DAVID PAUL.

FEBRUARY

14   *Antony and Cleopatra:* Birmingham Repertory Theatre. *Producer:* BERNARD HEPTON.

14   *Henry IV, Part I:* The Old Vic Company, at the Old Vic Theatre, London. *Producer:* DENNIS VANCE.

22   *Richard II:* Oxford University Dramatic Society, at the Playhouse, Oxford. *Producer:* MICHAEL CROFT.

25   *Henry IV, Part I:* Eton College. *Producers:* E. P. HEDLEY, R. J. G. PAYNE, R. PRIOR.

28   *Macbeth:* Ispwich Theatre. *Producer:* GEOFFREY EDWARDS.

MARCH

6   *Twelfth Night:* New Theatre, Bromley. *Producer:* DAVID POULSON.

6   *A Midsummer Night's Dream:* Everyman Theatre, Cheltenham. *Producer:* DAVID GILES.

7   *Richard III:* The Playhouse, Nottingham. *Producer:* VAL MAY.

14   *Alarms and Excursions (Henry VI, Parts 2 & 3):* The Marlowe Society, at the Arts Theatre, Cambridge. No Producer named.

14   *Macbeth:* The Belgrade Theatre, Coventry. *Producer:* GEORGE ROMAN.

14   *The Merry Wives of Windsor:* Theatre Royal, Northampton. *Producer:* LIONEL HAMILTON.

14   *Coriolanus:* Dulwich College Dramatic Society, London. *Producer:* J. A. PALMER.

20   *Twelfth Night:* Theatre Royal, York. *Producer:* DONALD BODLEY.

22   *Henry IV, Part I:* The Playhouse, Salisbury. *Producer:* IAN MULLINS.

APRIL

4   *Much Ado About Nothing:* Royal Shakespeare Theatre, Stratford-upon-Avon. *Producer:* MICHAEL LANGHAM.

11   *Hamlet:* Royal Shakespeare Theatre, Stratford-upon-Avon. *Producer:* PETER WOOD.

18   *Twelfth Night:* The Old Vic Company at the Old Vic Theatre, London. *Producer:* COLIN GRAHAM.

19   *As You Like It:* Fylde College Theatre Group, at the Tower Circus, Blackpool. *Producer:* FRANK WINFIELD.

25   *Richard II:* Bristol Old Vic Company, at the Theatre Royal, Bristol. *Producer:* JOHN HALE.

MAY

1   *As You Like It:* Theatre-in-the-Round, Pembroke Theatre, Croydon. *Producer:* ELLEN POLLOCK.

SHAKESPEARE PRODUCTIONS IN THE UNITED KINGDOM

1   *Twelfth Night:* Richmond Theatre. *Producer:* ALEXANDER DORE.

8   *Hamlet:* Meadow Players, Oxford, at the Arts Theatre, Cambridge, in London and at the Playhouse, Oxford. *Producer:* FRANK HAUSER.

19   *Hamlet:* The Maddermarket Theatre, Norwich. *Producer:* IAN EMMERSON.

24   *Richard III:* Royal Shakespeare Theatre, Stratford-upon-Avon. *Producer:* WILLIAM GASKILL.

30   *Macbeth:* The Renaissance Theatre Company, Her Majesty's Theatre, Barrow-in-Furness. *Producer:* DONALD SARTAIN.

30   *The Merchant of Venice:* The Old Vic Company at the Old Vic Theatre, London. *Producer:* PETER POTTER.

JUNE

2   *The Tempest:* Royal Academy of Dramatic Art, at the Vanbrugh Theatre, London. *Producer:* JOHN FERNALD.

12   *Twelfth Night:* The Century Theatre Company at the Kemble Theatre, Hereford, and at Keswick. Producer not known.

13   *Romeo and Juliet:* Rugby School. *Producer:* N. A. H. CREESE.

27   *Macbeth:* Ludlow Summer Festival, at Ludlow Castle. *Producer:* DAVID WILLIAM.

29   *The Merchant of Venice:* Oxford Stage Group at the Playhouse, Oxford. *Producer:* RICKY SHUTTLEWORTH.

30   *Love's Labour's Lost:* Bristol University, Department of Drama, at Dyrham Park House. *Producer:* CAMPBELL ALLEN.

JULY

No date given   *Macbeth:* Stowe School. *Producers:* W. L. MCELWEE, R. M. CAMPBELL, T. W. J. WAINE.

4   *As You Like It:* Royal Shakespeare Theatre, Stratford-upon-Avon. *Producer:* MICHAEL ELLIOTT.

11   *As You Like It:* Birmingham University Guild Theatre Group at the Civic Theatre, Cheltenham. *Producer:* JOHN R. BROWN.

13   *The Merry Wives of Windsor:* The National Trust at Polesden Lacey. Surrey. *Producer:* ELSIE GREEN.

17   *A Midsummer Night's Dream:* The White Rose Company, at the Opera House, Harrogate. *Producer:* ROBERT CHETWYN.

AUGUST

2   *Richard II:* The Youth Theatre, at the Apollo Theatre, London. *Producer:* MICHAEL CROFT.

14   *Henry VI, Part II:* Hovenden Theatre Club, London. *Producer:* VALERY HOVENDEN.

15   *Romeo and Juliet:* Royal Shakespeare Theatre, Stratford-upon-Avon. *Producer:* PETER HALL.

22   *Henry IV, Part II:* Youth Theatre, at the Apollo Theatre, London. *Producer:* MICHAEL CROFT.

28   *King John:* Old Vic Company at the Edinburgh Festival and at the Old Vic Theatre, London. *Producer:* PETER POTTER.

SEPTEMBER

13   *The Taming of the Shrew:* Royal Shakespeare Theatre Company at the Aldwych Theatre, London. *Producer:* MAURICE DANIELS.

18   *The Merchant of Venice:* Colchester Repertory Theatre. *Producer:* PETER POWELL.

26   *Macbeth:* Bristol Old Vic Company at the Theatre Royal, Bristol. *Producer:* VAL MAY.

OCTOBER

2   *As You Like It:* The Playhouse, Derby. *Producer:* CLIVE PERRY.

2   *Twelfth Night:* The Old Vic Company at the Old Vic Theatre, London. (Revival.) *Producer:* COLIN GRAHAM.

3   *The Taming of the Shrew:* The Arts Theatre, Cambridge. *Producer:* TREVOR NUNN.

3   *Macbeth:* The Playhouse, Nottingham. *Producer:* FRANK DUNLOP.

10 *Romeo and Juliet:* The Citizens Theatre, Glasgow. *Producer:* CALLUM MILL.

10 *Othello:* Royal Shakespeare Theatre, Stratford-upon-Avon. *Producer:* FRANCO ZEFFIRELLI.

16 *The Merchant of Venice:* The Connaught Theatre, Worthing. *Producer:* GUY VAESEN.

23 *King Lear:* Guildford Repertory Theatre. *Producer:* HARRY LOMAX.

31 *Much Ado About Nothing:* The Library Theatre, Manchester. *Producer:* DAVID SCASE.

NOVEMBER

4   *Henry IV, Part I:* The Questors Theatre, Ealing, London. *Producer:* ALFRED EMMET.

7   *Othello:* The Marlowe Theatre, Canterbury. *Producer:* KENNETH PARROTT.

13 *Julius Caesar:* Civic Theatre, Carlisle. *Producer:* DAVID MCDONALD.

13 *Twelfth Night:* Leatherhead Repertory Company, at the Leatherhead Theatre Club. *Producer:* ROBERT TRONSON.

17 *Henry IV, Part II:* The Maddermarket Theatre, Norwich. *Producer:* IAN EMMERSON.

20 *Much Ado About Nothing:* The Civic Theatre, Chesterfield. *Producer:* ANTHONY CORNISH.

27 *Julius Caesar:* Oldham Repertory Company at the Coliseum, Oldham. Producer not known.

DECEMBER

4   *The Tempest:* Fylde College Theatre Group, at the Tower Circus, Blackpool. *Producer:* FRANK WINFIELD.

7   *As You Like It:* The People's Theatre, Newcastle-upon-Tyne. *Producer:* ARTHUR KAY.

19 *Macbeth:* The Old Vic Company, at the Old Vic Theatre, London. *Producer:* OLIVER NEVILLE.

ACTING SHAKESPEARE TODAY:

[*A Review of Performances at the Royal Shakespeare Theatre, August 1962*]

BY

JOHN RUSSELL BROWN

> It takes most young actors but five years' acute suffering to become effective, to become
> theatrical....Beware of this and rather be ineffective. G. Craig, *On the Art of the Theatre*
> (ed. 1957), p. 40.

Gordon Craig's advice has been on record since 1907, and in England it has been disregarded. Rarely can an actor prepare a masterpiece. For the neophyte, training is huddled into two or three years and then he must make his name and establish himself as the man to be called upon for this type of role, or this kind of play. He cannot expect benefactions like a young painter and therefore he does not travel in pursuit of new ideas and experience, nor become a kind of apprentice to a master-craftsman. He cannot learn the rudiments of his art while practising it in a continuous but humble and responsible way, like a young poet, singer or dancer. Nor can an established actor plan his career to allow two or three years' study and experience of a major role before showing his interpretation to a wide public. In England today an actor does not find a suitable environment for full artistic development: he must choose continuous publicity or the forced pace of weekly or fortnightly changes of programme at a repertory theatre. (The few monthly repertory companies aspire to national publicity and so provide no true alternative.) An actor must become effective quickly and, if he wishes to continue to act, must always be effective.

Few people would argue that these conditions are conducive to the development of an actor's talents, but it is obvious that some plays are well served. Whole productions are vital, vigorous, straightforward, unified, inventively effective: this is the style associated with Joan Littlewood's Theatre Workshop. Still more are discreet settings for one, two, or three easily appreciated 'star' performances: this is the style of Shaftesbury Avenue. Some plays, chiefly newly written ones, show to best advantage in these kinds of presentation: it is the undeniably great play that suffers from English acting today. The Royal Shakespeare Company at Stratford-upon-Avon in the summer of 1962 had many effective actors and their performances were justly praised for modern virtues. But the eulogies were often tempered by the thought that something had been missed or a suggestion that the play itself was unsatisfactory: *Measure for Measure* and *Cymbeline* were said to be muddled in thought and feeling, *Macbeth* poorly planned, *A Midsummer Night's Dream* an obviously 'early' work. But these excuses for the absence of great art leave Shakespeare unscathed: each of these plays has been produced on other occasions when critics were so caught by its power, eloquence, entertainment or beauty that they had no leisure for finding fault with the writing or construction. Even the limited experience of reading Shakespeare's texts or accounts of earlier performances is sufficient to turn these strictures on his plays into criticism of the prevailing style of acting and prevailing conditions of work. Shakespeare's roles were giants' clothes upon the obvious effectiveness of many of the Stratford interpretations.

A revival of the 1960 production of *The Taming of the Shrew* showed the talents of the company to best advantage. Elaborate comic business obscured the dramatic line of the play as a whole but provided many farcical incidents that could be played vigorously and ostentatiously. Doors were slammed, heads slapped, plates tossed, postures held, lines underlined or thrown away with controlled gusto. This was a competitive style of production in which everyone was allowed to be assertive and single minded. *Cymbeline*, in contrast, was Vanessa Redgrave's play. As Imogen she varied hasty speech with credible pathos. She always used the simplest means, moving as little as possible and avoiding modifications of pitch or tone even in long speeches. For the rest, the broadest stroke in the text of the play, the appearance of Jupiter, was notably well done: John Corvin, in gold costume and make-up, descended on a wide-winged copper eagle and spoke his lines with deliberated force; here simple effectiveness was wholly appropriate.

In *Measure for Measure*, Marius Goring seemed to isolate himself from every other player in creating a straight-backed, tight-skinned Angelo: he concentrated on the expression of suffering by physical tensions. Tom Fleming as the Duke used sharp turns of head and eyes and a vocal decisiveness to represent authority, and Judi Dench as Isabella aimed as consistently for ardour, often narrowing the range of her voice and using gestures repetitively in her search for emphasis. In general the production was remarkable for the way in which the three main characters all used pauses to give an impression of profundity. They were empty pauses, for during the silences the figures on the stage often did not move so much as an eyebrow to express feeling and sometimes they walked across stage as simply as possible. The device was used to direct attention to single lines of the text or to placings on the bare set.

As Macbeth, Eric Porter husbanded his resources. In his first scene he gave little outward sign that a 'horrid image' shook his 'single state of man'. The dagger-soliloquy was accompanied by long and impressive pauses, but the first major climax was the banquet scene that concluded the first half of the performance. Here he was a tired and desperate man, and for the end Porter seemed to add only anger. It was a strong, consistent, closely observed, and limited, portrayal.

In a revival of the 1959 production of *A Midsummer Night's Dream*, the farcical performance of *Pyramus and Thisbe* and the Burgomask made the largest impression at the close. And elsewhere there was a marked tendency to choose one of several possible impressions and to work wholeheartedly for that: broad coltish humour in the lovers, an endearingly simple simple-mindedness in the mechanicals, and verbal beauty in the fairies. This last attempt was a modification of the previous showing of this production and entailed still moments when Titania, Oberon or the first Fairy stood facing the audience, out of contact with other persons on the stage, to speak lines in a studied manner that was out of tone with the giggles, pouts and posturing of the rest of their fussy performances. The speeches gave great delight, especially to the verbally conscious among the audience.

Undoubtedly the actors can feel gratified by the 1962 season, for they were often effective; several of them will have enhanced their reputations and can proceed to more and perhaps bigger roles. But if we ask how well they served Shakespeare's plays, their success will appear far smaller. Perhaps the most noticeable failure was an inability of many to give the impression of intelligence. Shakespeare often requires an actor to speak as if he were thinking quickly, cun-

PLATE III

A. Eric Porter as Macbeth and Irene Worth as Lady Macbeth

B. After the Banquet

'MACBETH', ROYAL SHAKESPEARE THEATRE, 1962

Directed by Donald McWhinnie, setting by John Bury, costumes by Annena Stubbs

PLATE IV

A. The Sleep-walking Scene

B. The Last Scenes

'MACBETH'

PLATE V

A. The Bedchamber: Eric Porter as Iachimo and Vanessa Redgrave as Imogen

B. Imogen by Cloten's Corpse

'CYMBELINE', ROYAL SHAKESPEARE THEATRE, 1962
Directed by William Gaskill, setting and costumes by René Allio

PLATE VI

A. John Corvin as Jupiter
'CYMBELINE'

B. The Bargaining: Ian Holm as Gremio, Ian Richardson as Tranio, and Paul Hardwick as Baptista

'THE TAMING OF THE SHREW', ROYAL SHAKESPEARE THEATRE, 1962
Redirected by Maurice Daniels, setting and costumes by Alix Stone

ningly or subtly; sometimes he must say one thing and seem to think about another, sometimes he must seem to enjoy alacrity of mind, or to turn desperately to it because his passions have been inexplicably aroused. On such occasions the pursuit of effectiveness betrays the actors to clumsiness. If a Malcolm punches home his points and tries to appear vigorously concerned when he is falsely describing himself as a tyrant and beast, he will find it very difficult to make it appear that he is using his wit to test Macduff. Yet this is how Brian Murray endeavoured to make the scene effective; and when the audience response slackened he sometimes redoubled his efforts. Gareth Morgan as Lennox tried to be intense and urgent in order to impress his subtle and intelligently ironic speech to the Lord at the beginning of III, vi: but it is surely written to heighten the sense of danger by alert caution and requires subtle speaking. When Posthumus has been persuaded that Imogen has been false, he returns to the stage for a soliloquy which moves rapidly from the general to particular, from the present moment to the past and future, from others to his lady and himself; but Patrick Allen played it for forcefulness. He showed no intellectual energy or insecurity in his passion, but placed his foot upon a table, and pointed towards the audience to make his 'points' with emphasis. He then strode back and forth with firm tread until he stopped with 'Yet' and paused with his finger authoritatively raised before rounding the phrase out with ''tis greater skill In a true hate...'. The soliloquy was 'big', as actors sometimes call such renderings, but it was not sharp and varied as the writing, and it was not a revelation of a man at his wits' end, a man who, according to the text, is prepared to 'write against' women as a last resort. As we have seen, in *Measure for Measure* there was a general attempt to give an impression of thought by introducing pauses; but this gave a portentous impression, not that of quick intelligence. And for Lucio another method had to be found; for his most acerbic scene (III, ii) he excused himself from suggesting an intellectual edge and involvement by pretending to be drunk.

The shortcomings of the effective actor can be put more simply by saying that he is afraid of subtlety. How else can we account for the protracted moment at the end of the first scene between Petruchio and Katharine in the Stratford *Taming of the Shrew*? This was played so broadly for sentiment, the lovers gazing in each other's eyes while Petruchio strokes his lady's calves, that the whole 'game' of the play was given away: of course, these two would have to love-ever-after. It gave a strong moment of feeling at the beginning of the play and engrossed the audience's interest, but Katharine's final victory was shorn of all its surprise and much of its pleasure. The Queen in *Cymbeline* also lacked subtlety, she was presented as obviously wicked in appearance and manner; her 'glozing' words were spoken to sound malicious, not to show feigned friendship, and no attempt was made to show 'Who is't can read a woman' or how she made the king believe at the end:

> Mine eyes
> Were not in fault, for she was beautiful;
> ...it had been vicious
> To have mistrusted her.

Snow White would not have been deceived for a moment.

Yet this fear of subtlety and the failure to show intelligence are symptoms of a more basic failure. Shakespeare was surely an effective dramatist, but the closely wrought texture of his writing and the development of ideas and characterizations from play to play show that he sought other qualities as well. His art is in all senses humane—we must praise him as all ages have done for his 'humanity', for it is still the best description—and he did not achieve this by pursuing effectiveness for its own sake. In little ways and large our present-day actors fail to see quite obvious devices by which Shakespeare gave his plays this quality of humanity, or seeing them they reject them because they detract from a single effective impression. Our actors are so afraid of not being strong, that they are often needlessly limited, presenting silhouettes instead of Shakespeare's 'human' characters, momentary excitements instead of a coherent, expressive whole.

The restricted aims of effective acting are most apparent in characterization. Shakespeare often gave two faces to one *dramatis persona* so that an actor can suggest different levels or areas of consciousness; but his interpreter today is likely to seize on one only. In small scale, this technique is seen in Imogen's speech on reading Posthumous' letter in III, ii. Here the text alternates between an extreme practicality that inquires about distances, feigns a sickness, thinks of a franklin's housewife, and a sweeping fancy that travels on a winged horse more nimbly than the sands in an hour-glass. At Stratford Miss Redgrave subdued the first impression in favour of the second, in a rendering that did not swerve from a lightly urgent raptness; she also did not seem to catch at the almost unspoken instability or insecurity which the speech can also suggest, especially towards its close.

On a grander scale, the conclusion of Macbeth's role alternates between angry, valiant resolution and deep reflection, between:

> Bring me no more reports; let them fly all:...
> The mind I sway by and the heart I bear
> Shall never sag with doubt nor shake with fear...

and

> ...Seyton!—I am sick at heart,
> When I behold—Seyton, I say!—This push
> Will cheer me ever, or disseat me now.
> I have lived long enough....

Sometimes one mood overwhelms another in an instant, as Macbeth's mind is turned to a new object; so:

> it is a tale
> Told by an idiot, full of sound and fury,
> Signifying nothing.

is followed by '*Enter a* Messenger' and Macbeth leaps to hear *this* 'tale':

> Thou comest to use thy tongue; thy story quickly.

He answers what it 'signifies' with 'sound and fury', with the wrathful 'Liar and slave!' And then, his passion being spent, he reverts to the wider view: 'I 'gin to be aweary of the sun....' Faced by Macduff and knowing he was 'not of woman born' but ripped from his mother's womb, he momentarily tries to escape and then finds from within himself a deep-seated pride:

> I will not yield,
> To kiss the ground before young Malcolm's feet.

From this, the last transition takes him back to his vaunting resolution: 'And damn'd be him that first cries "Hold, enough!"' Faced by these diverse demands, Eric Porter at Stratford underplayed the reflective passages and concentrated on presenting furious desperation. He shouted 'I have lived long enough', made an angry point of 'There would have been a *time* for such a word', and directed 'A tale Told by an idiot, full of sound and fury' in large exasperation to 'the Idiot', some god imagined for the moment above his head. 'I 'gin to be aweary...' was spoken in order to show how strongly and vehemently he repudiated life; it was another out-burst of anger. With sure consistency his death was that of a tired, angry, disarmed fighter: to make this clear he was killed on stage after he had been encircled by the entire army and had lost all his weapons.

As Iachimo in *Cymbeline* Porter again simplified his role. He taunted Posthumus with relish and in Imogen's bedchamber he noted particulars with an amused and watchful exactness. This was all played with a nice and appropriate sense of timing. But Shakespeare presents another face of Iachimo, which is clearly revealed for the first time at the end of the bedchamber scene. This villain realizes that there is no need to write down particulars: as Hamlet knows that Claudius' crime is written in the tables of his mind and heart, so Iachimo says that Imogen's beauty is 'riveted' and 'screw'd' to his memory. Next he is aware of the 'dragons of the night' and wishes for day; this echoes Achilles' evocation of 'the dragon wing of night' after the assassination of Hector in *Troilus and Cressida*, but this villain wishes them to be gone. Certainly, Iachimo's soliloquy at last makes an explicit statement of fear and guilt, sharply expressed as so many of the deepest feelings in *Cymbeline*:

> I lodge in fear;
> Though this a heavenly angel, hell is here.

To give credibility to this line and a half, the actor needs to begin to suggest an uneasiness under the busy concerns of the rest of the soliloquy; in this way the brief phrases can seem to be the necessary resolution of an earlier lack of conviction. If the actor strives to make these final lines ring true from deep within his consciousness, he will be supported by the stage device, appro-priate to what is called today a 'comedy of menace' and already used memorably in Marlowe's *Faustus*, of an immediate striking of a clock. The audience is alerted and Iachimo seems to accept the sound as a sign of completion, for he says only 'One, two, three: time, time!' and returns to the trunk. Porter let all this go by unmarked: to give a slight prurience to his expert stealth was the limit of his objective. He made the scene effective but far from complete, and not so exciting as it might be. His last lines gave the impression that he thought his task had been neatly done, not that he felt a deep and true response which revalued the entire preceding soliloquy and prepared for the time when conscience brings him to his knee, rather than the 'force' of a sword (v, v, 412–14).

It seemed almost a rule at Stratford that the actors should choose only one face of the character they portrayed. After the example of Zeffirelli's *Romeo and Juliet* the lovers in *A Midsummer Night's Dream* might have shown more than coltish energy. In this revival they were allowed to speak the lines of awakening in the wood that had been cut from the original production, but they could only sound sturdy as spoken within these forceful and farcical interpretations. In

Measure for Measure a portentous stress upon key lines often robbed them of more delicate or affecting nuances. Juliet's:

> I do repent me, as it is an evil,
> And take the shame with joy

was bold and sure, missing the deep involvement with Claudio and the modesty which is implied by her access to such a response—an attitude which even stops the Duke's stream of good advice. Yvonne Bonnamy's Mariana pleaded earnestly in the last scene, as of course she should, but not at all pathetically or at a loss for words. Surely such affecting impressions are required by the broken, repetitive phrasing of:

> Isabel,
> Sweet Isabel, do yet but kneel by me;
> Hold up your hands, say nothing; I'll speak all.
> They say, best men are moulded out of faults;
> And, for the most, become much more the better
> For being a little bad: so may my husband.
> O Isabel, will you not lend a knee?

On occasion the direct description of a character by others on the stage was neglected because this 'face' would detract from the one that had been chosen for emphatic presentation. So Clive Swift made Cloten the clotpoll, the coarse, slow-witted buffoon; but he did not attempt to live up to Pisanio's description of his sudden passion for the loss of Imogen's presence at court, nor did he show what drove him alone to the forest, a deed which Belarius says he could not have attempted even under the influence of 'frenzy' or 'madness'. In reading their own lines or considering the effect they have on other characters, these actors seemed to search for what could make a strong impression, at the cost of complexity or depth of characterization; and in so doing they often lost the means which Shakespeare has cunningly and usefully provided for developing the audience's impression of a character. The play had less to reveal, less to awaken expectation and hold interest.

It is not unusual for actors to present less than Shakespeare has provided for them. What is comparatively new is satisfaction with a readily effective reading. It is possible to imagine this company at rehearsals and, faced with two ways of reading a line, choosing the most immediately effective without further consideration. But their predilection goes further than that, for several major roles were consistently portrayed, and talent, invention and originality spent on rigorously limited interpretations.

Perhaps no way of acting Shakespeare is without its rewards. Certainly the 1962 Stratford season brought its own special pleasures.

One of these was Irene Worth's Lady Macbeth. It was a simple reading in keeping with the bias of the whole company: determined and egocentric ambition, leading to a struggle with guilt and weakness. One 'face' succeeded the other during the discovery of Duncan's murder at the moment when, very effectively with a movement down centre-stage, she fainted; on her next appearance, and even when she appeared crowned for the first time, Lady Macbeth was physically weakened and mentally strained. The sleep-walking scene was no surprise, for as she had spoken 'A kind goodnight to all', on the departure of the thanes from the disordered banquet, she had already shrunk in stature within her great robes, and her mind controlled her voice only by a great, dying effort; she stood a long time without moving and then went slowly to her throne from which she did not rise until after the scene had finished with a black-out. Her few brief words while Macbeth played out the scene were uncalculating responses when speech, of some sort, became unavoidable. Miss Worth had decided on an effective interpretation and she presented it in clear lines. In the earlier passages, she made little of those reactions which contrast with willed ruthlessness:

> Had he not resembled
> My father as he slept, I had done't

and:

> I have given suck, and know
> How tender 'tis to love the babe that milks me

were both too tense with determination to suggest, as they did for Mrs Siddons and many Lady Macbeth's after her, the gentler impulses that are for most of the time subdued by cruelty. Nor did Miss Worth show the wife in Lady Macbeth: she was closest to her husband, but still not intimate, when she lent upon him for support, becoming dependent in a simply physical way, at the end of the scene before the banquet, after she has asked 'What's to be done?' and has been answered by Macbeth's invocation of 'seeling night' and the assertion 'Things bad begun make strong themselves by ill'. In the sleep-walking scene, Shakespeare has directed that Lady Macbeth is concerned first with her own guilt, then mocks her husband for being afraid, then remembers the dead man who had resembled her father, and so is led back to imagine that earlier moment of horror; this raises a profound and inarticulate sigh, and then after a silence almost all her thoughts remember her husband, and her last speech is chiefly spent urging him to come with her, asking for his hand:

To bed, to bed! there's knocking at the gate: come, come, come, come, give me your hand. What's done cannot be undone.—To bed, to bed, to bed!

Here, however, Miss Worth continued the single line of her portrayal: 'What's done...' was emphasized by a held, crucified attitude, and on leaving she went towards Duncan's room and not the conjugal bed; and then, realizing her mistake, she turned in horror and ran out. Guilt was the last impression; 'To bed, to bed, to bed!' spoken only for fearful haste.

The remarkable achievement was the refinement of the performance, the varied vocal technique and fresh invention which were brought to it. And they showed all the more brilliantly for the simplicity of her interpretation and the predilection of most of the company towards broader and more obviously strong effects. Her vocal control and range were shown, for example, in her quite low pitched 'You must leave this'; she was not urging and encouraging her husband as most actresses play this moment; rather it was followed by a turn away from him, and suggested by its terseness a determination (and a failing power) to find new ways of confronting danger for herself. More strongly but still precisely controlled, 'Stand not upon the order of your going, But go at once', was spoken as two phrases, the first a courtesy assumed with difficulty and the second a betrayal of inner tension, pain and hopelessness, a loud and curt

'AT ONCE!' If Lady Macbeth was not fully presented in this performance, the actress' powers shone within the limits she had chosen. Her originality was nowhere more apparent than in 'Give me the daggers!': this was said with nothing of the usual, obvious drama, but with a rapid, quiet simplicity which spoke eloquently for self-reliance and its limitations.

Another success of the season was a more general achievement, though it was most noticeable in Miss Redgrave's Imogen. This was a direct result of the pursuit of effectiveness and showed that in a few contexts this is a quite appropriate approach: some moments do need a simple, unreflecting strength. Sudden expressions of sentiment require this, and when Imogen greets Guiderius and Arviragus in the last scene, her:

> O my gentle brothers,
> Have we thus met? O, never say hereafter
> But I am truest speaker: you call'd me brother,
> When I was but your sister; I you brothers,
> When ye were so indeed

held the audience by its large impression of new-born wonder and spontaneous joy: broad acting, if it is also unaffected, can transform such a moment giving to the brief words of recognition the emotional authority sufficient to resolve the many confusions of the narrative. The grief of Tony Steedman's Siward for the death of his son and the last blessing on his foster children of Paul Hardwick's Belarius were also unusually affecting by clear and large transitions of mood.

This effective acting was also useful in scenes which even a few years ago were customarily played with some awkwardness. Possibly new plays like Ionesco's *Rhinoceros* or Pinter's *The Dwarfs*, which use fantastic happenings to present the fantastic realities of half-conscious thought, have accustomed actors to playing unrealistic situations boldly. No tricks of lighting or trap-doors presented Banquo's ghost at Stratford, for its phantom presence and power needed no more reality than the new intensity it brought to Eric Porter's acting of Macbeth. Jupiter's eagle was supported on a solid and obvious steel pole, but this did not detract from his supernatural reality because of the actor's firm and simple acceptance of unhurried, formal speech. And, although Cloten's headless body was an object which raised the nervous laughter which normally greets a too-obvious disturbance of the accepted mode of illusion in a play, the audience was held in rapt belief and concern as Imogen was roused from her drugged sleep to feel it at her side. Miss Redgrave carried this scene by boldly accepting the improbability of her half-conscious thoughts; even as she said:

> it is
> Without me, as within me; not imagined, felt

she was still half unconvinced. She touched the stuffed and painted canvas which represented the bloody neck and said 'A headless man!' as a quiet, flat recognition, such as comes before full realization. She did not gain a fully responsive consciousness until she cried 'Murder in heaven?' The other major difficulty of the soliloquy:

> Where is thy head? where's that? Ay me! where's that?
> Pisanio might have kill'd thee at the heart,
> And left this head on

was met with comparable clarity, for the question which sounds absurd in considered or temperate speech was spoken in full flight of passion, and gave to that expression of feeling the recklessness and directness of imagination, and of thought which is too rapid and instinctive to be sensible.

Imogen's reawaking to hear Lucius questioning her was similarly affecting by a simple and convinced performance. She gazed at him unmoving while he slowly asked:

> What's thy interest
> In this sad wreck? How came it? Who is it?
> What art thou?

and without changing this impression of inward involvement she then spoke slowly, one broken word at a time: 'I am nothing.' Only by telling her story did she seem to gain a full knowledge of what she was speaking. Miss Redgrave's performance in this scene was judged by an artistic sense that responded to both fantasy and pathos as manifestations of a mind overmastered by feeling, and it had the strength and simplicity to carry conviction in every change of consciousness.

A further achievement of the season was not gained by its general pursuit of effectiveness. This was the playing of Derek Godfrey, Paul Hardwick and Ian Holm in *The Taming of the Shrew*, as Petruchio, Baptista and Gremio. Occasionally they all acted too broadly and were too indulgent in accepting details of comic business, but this was the second or third season in which these players had appeared in these roles, and effective acting had been refined by practice. Many points that were once too simple were now rejudged by instinct or vigilant self-criticism, and in experienced playing seemed to gain new meaning and deeper effect. Derek Godfrey's

> O, how I long to have some chat with her!

could now suggest both assurance and something like self-mockery. Both Ian Holm and Paul Hardwick could turn a jest so that it aroused pity as well as laughter, and by making their two old men draw together in adversity they gave another 'face' to their parts and enhanced the whole play by a comic demonstration of a coupling of interests to offset the various couplings of love. This was not superimposed on the text, but a revelation of a part of Shakespeare's play which would be missed in less subtle performances and probably in the most painstaking reading of the words alone. As the plot unfolds, these two characters do, in fact, speak in new agreement and the text does imply that they should stand or sit by each other's side. At the latest possible moment in the comedy, Baptista gives money to Katharine as Gremio had offered money at his instigation to purchase Bianca, but now the money is a gift without conditions. These actors had had practice to make perfect their effective characterizations, and they sometimes used it to add subtlety and discover the various 'faces' of their roles; so they were able to give an impression of a character responding to various levels of consciousness and to contribute to the general wit and enjoyment of the play. In their roles the 1962 Stratford season was not without the Shakespearian quality of 'humanity'.

CANADA'S ACHIEVEMENT

BY

ARNOLD EDINBOROUGH

Canada's Shakespeare Festival at Stratford, Ontario, celebrated its tenth season last summer. In more sophisticated countries, where the tradition of theatre runs deeper, there would be little to crow about in a mere ten-season record. But when the first Stratford season opened in a big-top circus tent, there can have been only a few visionaries who thought that such a venture in Canada would last as long as ten years.

The first season, in the Coronation time of 1953, was dominated by three people: Sir Tyrone Guthrie, who directed *Richard III* and *All's Well That Ends Well*; Tanya Moiseiwitsch, who designed them and, with Guthrie, designed the stage too; and Alec Guinness, who played a traditional Richard Crookback and a modern-dress King of France in *All's Well*.

Guthrie and Moiseiwitsch still dominate the Festival—Miss Moiseiwitsch because she has designed at least one play each season, and Guthrie because no one can direct a play at Stratford without its being moulded to some degree by the exigencies of the stage which he had such a hand in designing.

The stage was not, and was not intended to be, a replica of any specific shape which Hotson or Cranford Adams or Hodges or anyone else thought the Globe might have been. It was a stage designed, as Guthrie said at the time (*Shakespeare Survey 8* (1955), pp. 127–31), merely to 'offer the facilities of an Elizabethan stage'; a stage, in other words, on which a play might be mounted as it might have been in the earlier Elizabethan age.

This stage is constructed on eight different levels, including three workable balconies or balcony alcoves. It juts out into the audience so that no one of the 2300 people in the audience is farther than 65 feet from it. There are entrances from above and below the stage, as well as from the back and sides. There are two tunnel entrances from under the audience and four aisles regularly used for entry through the audience.

Above the balcony—in the roof of the theatre—is the musicians' gallery and behind the stage are grouped dressing rooms, wardrobe areas and property racks which are elaborate enough to give the actors the best possible service for quick entries in changed costumes or changed circumstances.

Just how well-designed this stage is can be deduced from the fact that twenty-three different plays of Shakespeare have been enacted thereon, mounted according to the varied theories of nine different directors. This past season it was enlarged and reshaped to give it a more massive appearance at the sides, but the alterations did not interfere with the basic facilities which can thus be taken to have proved themselves both challenging and richly rewarding for the production of twentieth-century Shakespeare.

This evolution of a new style of Shakespeare production has been an artistic success beyond the dreams of the original founders. But it has also been a financial and audience success. That far-away first season played for six weeks to less than 69,000 persons. The tenth season produced three Shakespeare plays (and *Cyrano de Bergerac*) for fifteen weeks before nearly a quarter of a million.

In the interval the stage has been rehoused in a permanent theatre of impressive modern design, large capacity and lavish appointments—all of which has been achieved because the festival has paid for its running expenses from the start, the box-office gross this past year standing at approximately one million dollars.

In a sense the tenth festival was a miniature of what the festival now stands for and what it has accomplished. The three Shakespearian plays were *Macbeth*, *The Taming of the Shrew*, and *The Tempest*—one play aimed at students (*Macbeth* is a 'set' text), one at the tourists and one for the general public who might like to build up their repertoire of plays seen. The first of these was directed by an English director, Peter Coe, and was a failure; the second was directed by an expatriate Englishman, Michael Langham, and it was a great success; the third was directed by a native Canadian and it was competent only.

Coe, with that English passion for doing something new to stimulate the jaded appetites of Londoners, completely inverted the values of *Macbeth* and produced it as if Shakespeare did not believe in witches and thought Macbeth had no nobility. The whole production was full of Freudian overtones: Macbeth rubbed his head constantly into his wife's flanks to give the impression, as subtly as if it had been painted on a bill board, that he was trying to re-enter the womb; Lady Macbeth first entered with a milk churn full, one must suppose, of the milk of human kindness; she also tried to wash her hands clean in a well in the middle of the stage, and into this well Macbeth finally fell dead.

Altogether it was a strangely milk-and-water performance. For it was clear that the Macbeths, as Coe saw them, might get into a sea of troubles, but they would not at any time be strong enough to take up arms and end them. For when Macbeth was weak (in the first section and the last), Lady Macbeth was strong. And when Macbeth was strong (during the middle section), Lady Macbeth was weak, not being privy to his designs.

Given such rare opportunity to tear a passion to tatters and invent a new mode for each scene, neither Christopher Plummer, as Macbeth, nor Kate Reid, as his wife, could refuse it. Their performances were brilliant, ingenious and wrong. William Hutt, as Banquo, was funereal from the start and Bruno Gerussi's Macduff owed more to the Wild West than the gloomy north.

But this is not the first time that an English director has tried to blind the locals with his own brilliance and to dim the brightness of Shakespeare. Guthrie did it, notably in his 1954 production of *The Shrew*, and that may be why *The Shrew* was chosen for reworking (it is the only play to be given two productions as yet). The second *Shrew* was directed by Langham who, in the eight years that he has been artistic director of the festival, has emerged as one of the most sensitive, most resourceful Shakespearian directors now working in the theatre—and one of the most scholarly.

Not for Langham the obvious symbol, the cheap effect and the heartless cutting of lines to avoid a dramatic difficulty. He, indeed, added lines, for his *Shrew* was done as a play within a play and the irony of Sly (thrown out by one shrew and ready to be welcomed roughly in by another) was brought out by filching a final scene from the old *Taming of A Shrew*—a final scene which made the irony poignant: only on the stage do men wive it wealthily and/or happily.

On this tightrope between dream and reality, between dramatic illusion and audience absorption, Langham balanced his conception beautifully. Petruchio (subtly played by John Colicos) was false to his nature but true to his ideals. Hortensio and Lucentio, disguised, were false to their station and to their ideals. Bianca rightly, therefore, played her father fair and her lovers false. The pace being kept up, the illusion being deftly portrayed and sustained, the whole play was such a whirl of disguise, deceit and dishonesty that Sly's bewilderment at the end and his slinking away made us wonder which was foul and which was fair, much more than *Macbeth* did.

To achieve such reaction from what is often thought of as a fustian play is proof that a director of Langham's calibre can do more for Shakespeare than a library full of emenders, critics and scholars. It also proves that a stage like Stratford's, and the atmosphere of carnival and genial criticism which a summer festival properly mounted can produce, does wonders for actors, audience and author alike. What had been first shown in Langham's excellent 1961 production of *Love's Labour's Lost* was here triumphantly reaffirmed—that a director who moves away from his text (like Coe) does so at his peril and at the peril of his actors, whereas a director who moves, through a sensitive and comprehensive reading of the text, towards his author, can make old cloth shine like new satin.

The Tempest was not wrong, like *Macbeth*; nor was it gloriously right like *The Taming of the Shrew*. It was just *The Tempest*, a play beloved of Keats and Hazlitt for its poetry, but a play rather piously attended by veteran Shakespeare-goers who always try to find Trinculo funny, Caliban impressive and Ariel darling. And so the audience at Stratford reacted. The long second scene, though played with spirit and dash by William Hutt as Prospero, made us as seeming weary as Miranda, prettily played by Martha Henry. The gabardine antics of the clowns seemed vulgar rather than comic, and Gonzalo, though sturdily played and beautifully spoken by William Needles, could not stop from being as much of a bore to us as he was to the rest of the inhabitants of the island.

Ariel (tiresomely addressed as *Arriel* all through) was athletic but vapid and Caliban (Colicos again), though a proper monster, was a little *too* near to substituting 'Uhuru' for 'freedom'. Indeed, one had the impression all through that this island was not far off the Congolese coast.

As a baseball critic might say, Stratford in the tenth season was one hit, one run, one error. But it was all professional. The designs were superb; the music was new and, in some instances in *The Tempest*, enchanting; the acting was at a high level of competence; only the verse speaking was, as always, poor.

In other words, Stratford had yet again done what it has done regularly since it opened ten years ago, set a standard by which other drama in Canada must be judged. For Stratford has so set its mark on Canadian theatre, especially in matters of wardrobe design, property making, lighting and acting technique (the sword fights are *most* realistic) that it is difficult to remember that prior to 1953 the standards were either those of a touring company playing out an extra week or two at the end of an American tour, or those of the imported adjudicators to the Dominion Drama Festival—a festival at which, by invitation, the ten best amateur groups from ten provinces put on what was then the best in Canadian theatre.

THE YEAR'S CONTRIBUTIONS TO
SHAKESPEARIAN STUDIES

1. CRITICAL STUDIES

reviewed by PHILIP EDWARDS

Beginning, as we should, with tragedy, we have a remarkable book by John Holloway,[1] which asks us to be baptized into a new way of interpreting Shakespeare. *The Story of the Night* is contentious and choleric; it is not well planned, and has the air of being hastily written. If Holloway had delayed publication for five years, we might perhaps be welcoming the first real successor to Bradley. But, even as it is, the publication of this book is an important occasion in Shakespeare criticism. The introduction declares total war. The Enemy accepts it that literature exists to offer 'help to people perplexed over "how to live"'; consciously or unconsciously, he assumes that a work of literature is distinguished by its informativeness; he says that a play asserts or defines certain values. Holloway objects very strongly to a use of language which can make plays 'assert values' or 'obstinately question some of the things that are most deeply disturbing in human life'; it seems to him a muddled use, reflecting a muddled attitude to art. In any case, the values which the Enemy claims that Shakespeare asserts are trite and partial. 'When... critics give accounts of Shakespeare's explicating and defining which would convict him of being less well-informed about life even than I am myself, I am obliged to infer that they are casting not light but darkness.' The reason for the insufficiency is that critics 'have in effect made use of Shakespeare for preaching of their own, writing of his work but venting their personal moralities'. But even if the moral insights, for which the Enemy values the plays, were more rich and subtle, they would still be only peripheral in the experience of drama. 'Before it is a source of insight, great imaginative literature is a source of power.' Witnessing a play leaves us with a sense 'of having passed through a great experience'; moralist-criticism must give way to a kind of criticism which is capable of describing and accounting for the 'momentous and energizing experience' provided by the whole action of a play. Before going on to see what Holloway has to offer, we may glance at two other contributions relevant here.

In a difficult essay,[2] Hardin Craig seems also to think that we have had enough of theme- and concept-mongering, offered as descriptions of Shakespeare's plays. 'In Shakespeare scholarship, the region of the concept has been developed to what looks like a maximum degree, so that the issue has come to a point where there is only repetition and minor debate to occupy us.' Craig seems to want to lead us back to a very unfashionable and unfrequented territory, Shakespeare's knowledge of the human heart, and he writes of single speeches and scenes (like that of Hubert and Arthur) comprehending the states of life and 'the wear and tear of human existence'. J. C. Maxwell's review of 'Modern Shakespearian Studies'[3] covers a wide field and therefore shows Holloway to be much less of a John the Baptist than he makes himself. The short study

[1] *The Story of the Night. Studies in Shakespeare's Major Tragedies* (Routledge and Kegan Paul, 1961).
[2] 'Ideational Approach to Shakespeare's Plays', *Philological Quarterly*, XLI (1962), 147–57.
[3] *Talks to Teachers of English* (Department of Education, King's College, Newcastle-upon-Tyne, 1962), pp. 13–29.

is also a lesson in keeping one's temper. Though Maxwell is well aware that the different languages of criticism indicate totally different assumptions about what art is, he is protective and sympathetic to them all, believing there may be good in every method—even if he has to point to every practitioner as rather an extremist. Concerning a passage by one of Holloway's victims, D. A. Traversi, which says that the plot of *Lear* is an expanded image of the conflicting issues in the mind of the hero, Maxwell remarks (without endorsing Traversi's notions) that 'it does seem possible to say true and important things in this terminology....The type of centrality that Lear has in the whole structure, and the way he is related to his daughters, *can be brought out more easily than in a more literal account.*' I emphasize these last words because they light up one of the difficulties in Holloway's new approach. Holloway contends that the language of the current coin of Shakespeare criticism is metaphorical not literal, and is not recognized as metaphorical. Although he offers us (as we shall see) a new metaphor of 'ritual', he seems to me to underestimate the usefulness (or the necessity) of metaphorical language which is seen by Maxwell. 'It might conceivably be the case, in respect of these plays,' he says, 'that no critical comment whatever was possible unless it was expressed in metaphor. That suggestion, though grotesque, is not absurd.' Is it so grotesque? The only literal account of a play you can get is by listening to the play on tape. To discuss plays, to criticize them, is to employ the shorthand of analogy, and metaphor. As all art uses convention to reduce the complex litter of life to an appearance of tidy order, so all criticism uses convention to reduce the complex order of art into a simple order. Is not criticism the reduction of a work of art into terms other than itself? Holloway does it all the time. 'A part of Hamlet's experience...is to pass...from centrality to isolation.' Is this literal, or a figure of speech, conveniently representing something much more complex that is happening on the stage? Again, the action of *Hamlet*, we are told, *is* 'the progressive alienation of the dedicated protagonist from a society falling into chaos'. Literally, the action of *Hamlet* is nothing of the kind. These, and many other similar comments of Holloway, seem excellent; but they are couched in an analogical shorthand made familiar to us by the current coin of Shakespeare criticism which he disavows. There is no doubt about a man's failure to achieve the impossible: Holloway has not found a language capable of transcribing the all-inclusive action of a play.

To get the most out of Holloway's discussion of the tragedies, it is best to read first the final chapter, 'Shakespearean Tragedy and the Idea of Human Sacrifice', and Appendix B, 'The Concepts of "Myth" and "Ritual" in Literature'. Without these chapters, the criticisms of the plays, often very sound and very shrewd, are not revolutionary; in the light of them, the criticism shows itself as a rather noble failure to put into practice a theory of the criticism of the drama of the greatest importance. The analogy he suggests between sacrificial ritual and tragedy is too closely argued for summary. It is based on the idea of myth as something that 'works', stabilizing society, rather than enshrining concepts about life, exercising power and not offering statements; and the idea of ritual as something that sustains and strengthens the social bond between those who participate. A drama differs from ritual in that it takes its material from the common fabric of life, and, when it has made ritual of this reality, it returns us, somewhat altered, to the reality. 'This is an art which springs from reality, has its time of independence, and takes us back whence it sprang.' But our experience of drama *is* the experience of ritual. We are given, not the basic values of life, but 'a sense of how, at the most radical level, life works'. Rituals offer essential movements of the greatest possible emotional significance to a man, and tragedy embeds these movements in the material of our own lives. Holloway makes a particular case on the possibility of a partial resemblance—he does not put it higher—between tragedy and the sacrificial scapegoat rituals. The tragic hero, whether good or evil on balance, is gradually set apart from society, and moves towards the accepted death that brings new strength to the society; the audience is both the suffering individual and the society which demands community. I do not think that the scapegoat is a central necessity in Holloway's theory; but of the theory in general, I should say that, although a very great deal has been said before about drama, myth and ritual, we have now been given something that really must be followed up; we might be at the beginning of a much-needed 'new age' of Shakespeare criticism.

It is interesting enough that Eugene M. Waith should also publish a book[1] which seems to start, like Holloway's, in a dissatisfaction with the power of moralistic criticism to explain some of the heroes of sixteenth- and seventeenth-century drama; in particular, the 'warrior of great stature who is guilty of striking departures from the morality of the society in which he lives'; in Shakespeare, the examples are Antony and Coriolanus. What usually happens, in interpreting these heroes, is that 'we are invited to consider what a given author would have thought of the hero as an actual person, or how the author himself acted in regard to moral conventions'. Waith is doubtful if responses to life and to art are so much akin. He examines the figure of Hercules in literature, and finds a pattern of heroic strength, valour and fortitude in which inordinate pride or anger or cruelty is *not* treated as hamartia. Questions of right and wrong seem swallowed up in wonder at the vast heroism of the dedicated man, whose devotion to his ideal is a kind of enlargement of human power. Waith writes extremely well on *Tamburlaine*, and his researches on the Hercules figure enable him to point precisely to the kind of wonder Tamburlaine evokes. I do not think that the Herculean cap fits Antony or Coriolanus so neatly, but the book as a whole is invigorating; like Holloway's, it enlarges Shakespeare instead of confining him.

Both Waith and Holloway object to twentieth-century Shakespeares, and have done their best to elizabethanize themselves and us. John Lawlor[2] is another who wants us to get the image historically correct, but for him it is back to Chaucer rather than Sophocles. He awakens the dormant question—what really was the spirit of medieval tragedy? (*tragedie* he unnecessarily calls it). He suggests that we have oversimplified in thinking that it is just a matter of cruel and wayward Fortune demoting the prosperous. It is *Troilus and Criseyde* we must remember, not the Monk's Tale. 'Tragedie' is not a pessimistic surrender to death; the blows of Fortune make the victim understand that she has her task allotted to her from on high. The 'distinctive capacity' of Fortune 'is in fact the awakening to understanding of a greater good'. So, in *Romeo and Juliet*, the immaturity of the lovers blooms to real maturity in the storm of Fortune's blows, and the end is a triumph. Love, in a death which is not the end, transforms the world. The special interest of *Romeo and Juliet* for Lawlor is that it stands apart from the 'connective' drama of Shakespeare's tragedies, in which there is a clear relation between what men are and

[1] *The Herculean Hero in Marlowe, Chapman, Shakespeare and Dryden* (Chatto and Windus, 1962).
[2] '*Romeo and Juliet*', *Early Shakespeare: Stratford-upon-Avon Studies 3*, edd. J. R. Brown and B. Harris (Edward Arnold, 1961), pp. 123–43.

what they suffer. The relation of *Romeo and Juliet* is with the last plays, in which reconciliation and fulfilment depend much on the shocks of Fortune. (*Romeo and Juliet* is also studied in the light of contemporary conventions of thought and art by Paul N. Siegel,[1] who again sees the play rather as triumph than as tragedy.)

A fine essay by Sister Miriam Joseph[2] reopens the old question of what the Elizabethans thought of ghosts and what we should, therefore, think of *Hamlet*. Sister Miriam Joseph gives us a great deal to fill out and correct our notions about Protestant and Catholic beliefs. Doubts about the Ghost's origin, and words and actions to test his credentials—including the play-scene—all conform easily to a traditional Catholic caution about spirits. 'I believe it is fair to assert that the ghost scenes of *Hamlet* conform in detail to the centuries-old Christian teaching concerning the discernment of spirits, which was current in Shakespeare's time.' Reactions to the Ghost share a single 'othodoxy', and the Ghost himself is orthodoxly presented 'as a saved soul temporarily suffering the fire of purgatory until he be cleansed and admitted to heaven'. But what of the orthodoxy of such a ghost when he preaches revenge? Sister Miriam Joseph conducts a magnificent defence of the morality of the Ghost's commands (in the rather special circumstances of the case), in the light of traditional church teaching. No one who has read modern criticism of *Hamlet* can think such a defence unnecessary.

We all know the dangers of using our knowledge of renaissance ideas to 'explain' Shakespeare; none of the studies mentioned so far cuts Shakespeare down to size. I am not so sure that the use of 'intellectual background' by Terence Hawkes[3] really helps us to understand *Othello*. Hawkes surveys the history in western thought of *ratio superior* and *ratio inferior*, the opposition of the higher intuitive knowledge of spiritual truth to the lower ratiocination, which was all along a sign of man's sinful pride of intellect, until Bacon gave it status. Iago's reasoning and methods of demonstration are 'openly Baconian and scientific'. It seems to me that Hawkes is demonstrably wrong (or am I using *ratio inferior*?). His first example is Iago's speech:

> Even now, now, very now, an old black ram
> Is tupping your white ewe.

Can this be a 'rational and "scientific" explanation' of 'an affair of the heart belonging to a numinous world'? It *is* possible to describe coitus as one of the bleakest of the necessary bodily functions: see modern literature *passim*, especially Samuel Beckett. But Iago's highly-charged, metaphoric persuasion is hardly the sort of thing that would have appealed to Bacon. As Hawkes says, 'the effect [Iago] wishes to achieve is one of verity arrived at through a process of reasoning'. He *appears* as a plain man dealing with things as he finds them; he is in fact a consummate liar. For all I know, Shakespeare may, like Coleridge, have objected strongly to a world seen as a mass of little things, but what he seems to be denouncing in Iago is deception, malice, mis-representation and wholesale lying. If he is denouncing materialistic reasoning power, I do not like his methods; they are too much like Iago's.

Some other studies of the tragedies may be mentioned here. John B. Harcourt combs through the porter-scene in *Macbeth*[4] with a useful thoroughness, and wonders if the scene could (as well

---

[1] 'Christianity and the Language of Love in *Romeo and Juliet*', *Shakespeare Quarterly*, XII (1961), 371–92.
[2] 'Discerning the Ghost in *Hamlet*', *PMLA*, LXXVI (1961), 493–502.
[3] 'Iago's Use of Reason', *Studies in Philology*, LVIII (1961), 160–9.
[4] '"I Pray You, Remember the Porter"', *Shakespeare Quarterly*, XII (1961), 393–402.

as so much else) be an analogue of the medieval harrowings of Hell, with Macduff as a temporary Christ. F. H. Rouda[1] sees *Coriolanus* as the tragedy of the idealism of youth; the hero is 'a high-minded, emotionally untried youngster', who slowly learns of the universal frailty of man, and the mercy which this knowledge demands. This is a far cry from Hercules. There are several studies of *Troilus and Cressida*, the best of which, by David Kaula,[2] has a pleasant independence in questioning the godliness of the 'degree' speech, and in maintaining that Troilus has 'no other god to serve than self'. J. Swart's essay on *Hamlet*[3] finds fault with the prince for actions which can seem misdemeanours only to the author. H. R. Walley[4] argues that *The Rape of Lucrece* is a 'systematic and authoritative declaration' of the principles of Shakespeare's whole tragic practice.

The attempt continues to find in the comic forms and conventions of Shakespeare a perspective as interesting and as serious as the perspective implicit in the form of tragedy. Two valuable essays have been written by Harold Brooks and Frank Kermode.[5] Brooks' very careful study of *The Comedy of Errors* amply demonstrates that this early piece is 'extraordinarily finished work', 'more pregnant than has perhaps been supposed with Shakespearian ideas'. The heart of the matter is the treatment of mistaken identity, which wakes in the audience 'the ancient dread of losing the self or soul'. Mistaken identity, leading to loss of relationship, calls true identity into question, and the feelings of insanity and possession ensue. All this is so well discussed that it does not seem mere 'olatory' to talk of 'the large dramatic design' of the play. Kermode is also interested in philosophizing mistaken identity, in *Twelfth Night*, and in the confusions of *A Midsummer Night's Dream* (which he thinks Shakespeare's best comedy). His essay brings some sheaves from the rich harvest of renaissance mysteries, and he suggests that Bottom's dream lets us venture into transformations, by initiation, into a kind of love not comprehensible in the sober-sided world of Theseus.

It is a complaint against these essays that they make no attempt to find out why people laugh at these situations which they persuasively argue to be so serious, and make little attempt to show that similar situations occur in tragedy (loss of identity in *Richard II*, *Lear*, *Coriolanus*, for example) when no one is disposed to laugh. Comedy, like tragedy, is an energizing experience, and it is not enough to deal with the concepts in them without humanizing them. Brooks says that '*The Comedy* appeals first and foremost to laughter'. But how? Kermode talks of a 'comic equilibrium', but again, how is it achieved? It is not that Shakespeare plans a deeply serious life-attitude, and then pours it into a comedy; these plays are comedies because they are built upon the loss of identity. We still seem to be only on the fringe of understanding what comedy is.

John Vyvyan's *Shakespeare and Platonic Beauty*[6] is a more ambitious attempt to get at the

---

[1] '*Coriolanus*—A Tragedy of Youth', *Shakespeare Quarterly*, XII (1961), 103–6.

[2] 'Will and Reason in *Troilus and Cressida*', *Shakespeare Quarterly*, XII (1961), 271–83. See also F. Q. Daniels, 'Order and Confusion in *Troilus and Cressida* I, iii', *Shakespeare Quarterly*, XII (1961), 285–91, and W. M. Main, 'Character Amalgams in Shakespeare's *Troilus and Cressida*', *Studies in Philology*, LVIII (1961), 170–8.

[3] '"I Know Not 'Seems'"': A Study of *Hamlet*', *Review of English Literature*, II, 4 (1961), 60–73. See also R. T. Jones, '"The Time is out of Joint"', *Theoria* (University of Natal, 1961), pp. 54–71.

[4] '*The Rape of Lucrece* and Shakespearian Tragedy', *PMLA*, LXXVI (1961), 480–7.

[5] H. Brooks, 'Themes and Structure in *The Comedy of Errors*', *Early Shakespeare* (Edward Arnold, 1961), pp. 55–71; F. Kermode, 'The Mature Comedies', *ibid.* pp. 211–27.

[6] Chatto and Windus, 1961.

meanings contained within Shakespearian comedy. Vyvyan gives an account of the history of platonism and an exposition of the leading ideas of the Florentine neo-platonists, and then goes on to plead that Shakespeare's comedies show how, through love, earth's bond with heaven is made firm in the human soul. The author is an attractive pleader; he is very much convinced, he senses scepticism about him, and he appeals to us with great earnestness and humility: seeing these things in the plays, he asks, is it not true that Shakespeare knew of and believed in the ladder of the soul, and wrote his plays to illustrate it? Skilfully, Vyvyan steers for the awkward points in the comedies where 'psychological' explanations are unconvincing. Valentine forgives Proteus, and awards him Sylvia; psychologically, this is difficult, but it is a high point allegori-cally, for Valentine is presenting perfection to Proteus, giving him the ideal beauty which he had perceived. Bertram's rejection of Helena seems properly reprehensible only when we understand that Bertram is rejecting the principle of love in his life. Like Kermode, Vyvyan thinks that the confusion of the lovers in *A Midsummer Night's Dream* is capable of deeply serious interpretation; he sees it as Shakespeare's realization of the comic possibilities of the bewilder-ment of the searching soul. Vyvyan is very good indeed on the 'wild place' in Shakespeare as a testing ground in which people find themselves, on 'self-discovery' in general, and on the import-ance of happy endings in the earliest comedies. But the matter of intentional neoplatonic allegory is indeed a question. The importance of Vyvyan's book is in showing that neoplatonism is, over a large area, co-extensive with the perennial wisdom to be found in Shakespeare, and that the language of love in Shakespeare is often that of neoplatonism. The parable theory is a way of temporarily controlling the material of the plays; neoplatonism is a useful metaphor; it is hard to go much further in acceptance.

The Merchant of Venice was the subject of several studies. A very well-written essay by the late E. M. W. Tillyard[1] moves towards a single scene on a wide critical front. Portia knows that Shylock is going to be defeated by the legal 'quibble'; why does she hold it back so long? Not because she dislikes the quibble, not entirely because of the dramatic suspense, but because she is trying to save Shylock's soul by making him adopt mercy. 'Then must the Jew be merciful' is ambiguous: to the Venetians, he *must*, if Antonio's life is to be saved; to Portia (knowing Antonio safe) he *must* if his soul is to be saved. But of course she has to abandon the struggle. Undoubtedly this attractive theory makes the trial scene 'richer and more complex', but the problem of the audience's awareness of all this is not small. Tillyard says that the audience knew the outlines of the story, and 'they should recognize the other issue and watch Portia in her struggle to break down Shylock's obtuseness', ready to take her words in their double meaning. This seems doubtful, so that we are left with the difficulty of an element which is quite certainly 'there', but need not be, and probably was not, perceived by the audience. It is at times worth remembering the doctrine, though some have been burned in the market-place for professing it, that what Shakespeare has written can have a life outside the theatre as well as within.

This question of the legitimacy of 'free' interpretation, and the relation of 'meaning' to author's intention, so thoroughly dug over elsewhere, seems to occupy too little space in Shake-speare criticism at the moment. There are passing references, of course. Vyvyan writes, 'The notion of a definitive criticism is a death-thought, which withers the mind that entertains it'. 'The full meaning of a work of art—if that phrase itself is meaningful—is all that it can mean to

---

[1] 'The Trial Scene in *The Merchant of Venice*', *Review of English Literature*, II, 4 (1961), 51–9.

everyone who has ever beheld it or ever will, and so it is continually expanding.' This is rather generous; 'all it *can* mean' invites chaos, and the kind of criticism we have seen Holloway objecting to, which is well described by Maurice Charney in the work cited below: 'Critics are said to have a Faustian urge to replace the works they study by their criticism.' While we shall all be sceptical of a definitive criticism, we ought to be agreeing on the size of the area in which disagreement is allowed, rather than inviting a free-for-all, since the reading of Shakespeare provokes in critics far more hallucinations than the reading of other poets. Actors are critics of plays, and John Brown,[1] in his study of stage interpretations of Shylock, would seem to be with Vyvyan in pleading for liberty of interpretation in his hospitality to the different ways of acting the part; but he remains within the fold of Shakespeare's 'intention'; he feels that no actor's interpretation has soared beyond a creation ample and complex enough to contain them all. He argues the case well enough for Shylock, showing how wrongness and rightness, cruelty and humanity, do exist at the very same time in a single speech. This coexistence would not be accepted by J. H. Smith,[2] who suggests a developing and deteriorating Shylock, the earlier impression of humanity disappearing, until, at the end, he is a monster.[3]

The Histories do not seem to have provoked the same searching into fundamentals of criticism as the Tragedies and the Comedies; in a review of twelve months' work, this is perhaps only the luck of the draw. On the other hand, there has been some very sound and helpful exegesis. M. M. Reese's well-written and useful book[4] covers all the English histories. It does not break much new ground, but there is a great deal to be said for the man who comes after, and has no desire to construct grotesques. Although in some sense Reese has written a compendium, he is a critic in his own right, a very sane one—and he is also a very much better historian than most of those who have written on the Histories; he is always entertaining and instructive on the historical side, Elizabethan or medieval. There should be more books like this, but I suppose there are not many with the patience to produce a comprehensive, balanced and readable guide. J. P. Brockbank[5] gives a thorough and intelligent analysis of the Henry VI plays. Like Brooks and Kermode in the same volume, he speaks up for the young Shakespeare: 'the early histories too express stresses and ironies, complexities and intricate perspectives beyond the reach of the condescensions usually allowed them'. Gareth Lloyd Evans' study of *Henry IV*[6] keeps our attention firmly on Shakespeare rather than on the critic; Evans writes with sense and wisdom on the relations between Hal and Falstaff. If, like the other historians of the Histories, he is sound rather than explosive, he is certainly not tame; there is an excellent account of Hal in the scene with Francis the drawer, summed up with, 'In short, he is drunk'.[7] P. A. Jorgensen[8] makes the

[1] 'The Realisation of Shylock: A Theatrical Criticism', *Early Shakespeare* (Edward Arnold, 1961), pp. 187–209.

[2] 'Shylock: "Devil Incarnation" or "Poor Man...Wronged"?', *J.E.G.P.* LX (1961), 1–21.

[3] Among other essays on the comedies may be noted John F. Adams, '*All's Well That Ends Well*: The Paradox of Procreation', *Shakespeare Quarterly*, XII (1961), 261–70.

[4] *The Cease of Majesty. A Study of Shakespeare's History Plays* (Edward Arnold, 1961).

[5] 'The Frame of Disorder—*Henry VI*', *Early Shakespeare* (Edward Arnold, 1961), pp. 73–99.

[6] 'The Comical–Tragical–Historical Method: *Henry IV*', *Early Shakespeare* (Edward Arnold, 1961), pp. 145–63.

[7] Two further essays may be mentioned: P. G. Phialas, 'The Medieval in *Richard II*', *Shakespeare Quarterly*, XII (1961), 305–10; Leo Kirschbaum, 'The Demotion of Falstaff', *Philological Quarterly*, XLI (1962), 58–60.

[8] 'The "Dastardly Treachery" of Prince John of Lancaster', *PMLA*, LXXVI (1961), 488–92.

suggestion that the pressures of the Irish wars on old concepts of honour and chivalry made the victory by deception of Prince John a specially 'modern' problem for the original audience of *Henry IV*.

Criticism with a special emphasis on language is sparse. Perhaps, to encourage a backward trade, the Year's Contributions to Shakespearian Study might include a section on Language. F. P. Wilson's 'The Proverbial Wisdom of Shakespeare'[1] is perhaps not criticism, but in telling us about Shakespeare's employment of common and not-so-common sayings, which might formerly have been considered his own creations, he brings us nearer to understanding Shakespeare's art.[2] It is a temptation to say that, without language, there is nothing; that the rest is indeed silence; but there are critics in plenty to remind us that we have eyes as well as ears. Maurice Charney's pleasant book on the imagery of the Roman plays[3] pays tribute to R. A. Foakes' study of imagery in *Shakespeare Survey 5*, and insists that a study of imagery take account of what is seen and heard. An early chapter, differentiating the 'styles' of each of the Roman plays, is very good. Charney shows how the themes of a play are mirrored in repeated word patterns. In *Julius Caesar*, blood and fire are turned against those who use them. The collection of references in *Antony and Cleopatra* to eating, drinking, arming and disarming, being *up* or *down*, may sound rather dull, but Charney makes out a good case that the worlds of Egypt and Rome and the downfall of the hero and heroine are in part conveyed to us by such references. One has a warm-hearted feeling to books which increase one's respect for the richness of Shakespeare's workmanship.[4]

The only study of Shakespeare's rhetorical organization as a key to understanding a play is by R. F. Hill on *Richard II*.[5] This may be one of the most important ways into Shakespeare, but it is a hazardous road, and there are few signposts. Hill's analyses often seem personal.

> This battle fares like to the morning's war,
> When dying clouds contend with growing light,
> What time the shepherd, blowing of his nails,
> Can neither call it perfect day nor night.

The point of comparison...is weak since clouds and light do not actively *contend* as do the opposing forces in battle. Besides, the morning light must inevitably 'conquer' the clouds whereas the line of Henry's thought about the battle is the uncertainty as to the victor. The touch of the shepherd 'blowing of his nails' suggests an absorption in the prettiness of the simile rather than in the point of comparison.

But does not concentration on the 'point of comparison' remove some of Hill's objections? There is a point at dawn (the shepherd obligingly blows of his nails) when it is neither day nor night; there is a point in this battle when there is a similar 'equal poise', with neither side

---

[1] Presidential Address. The Modern Humanities Research Association, 1961.

[2] See also a useful review of work on lexicography by Gustav Kirchner, 'Zur Sprache Shakespeares', *Shakespeare Jahrbuch*, 97 (1961), 183–202.

[3] *Shakespeare's Roman Plays. The Function of Imagery in the Drama* (Harvard University Press, 1961).

[4] The importance of 'spectacle' is also emphasized by Julian Markels, in 'The Spectacle of Deterioration: *Macbeth* and the "Manner" of Tragic Imitation', *Shakespeare Quarterly*, XII (1961), 293–303. Only by concentrating on the visual, Markels holds, can we understand how the hero increases in depravity without losing our sympathy.

[5] 'Dramatic Techniques and Interpretation in *Richard II*', *Early Shakespeare* (Edward Arnold, 1961), pp. 101–21.

certainly on top. If we must speculate (and I think it is irrelevant to the 'point of comparison') on whether day or night is to win, we might at least look forward, not only to the inevitable conquest by the day, but to the equally inevitable conquest by the night a few hours later, continuing the see-saw of *this* 'battle'. Hill suggests that, in the early Histories, Shakespeare was suffering from an 'over-excitement about means' which may have 'checked an early development of that inwardness of experience felt in the plays of Shakespeare's maturity; it is equally likely that attention to language for its own sake was itself symptomatic of a thinness of tragic experience'. This is a vitally interesting subject. One might well argue that the only measure of profundity is the existence of the language which embodies that profundity, and that an absence of profundity means an absence of profundity. But are the implications of Hill's suggestion that for an artist to concern himself too much about verbal expression is to run the risk of starving himself of experience? I sense at the back of Hill's essay the notion (only most loosely to be called Romantic) that if the feelings are strong enough, the words will find themselves. Of an early couplet, he remarks: 'Shakespeare does not reach the expected inwardness. The language springs not from a hot imaginative centre, but is apparently organized dispassionately.' But perhaps I misinterpret the phrase, 'hot imaginative centre'. It may be that the direction of Hill's argument is that, as he grew older, Shakespeare felt more deeply about life and was able to control language more effectively in order to express these deepening feelings; on that point, I am sure we should all be in agreement.

A few studies call attention to special features of Shakespeare's craftsmanship. Max Lüthi[1] explores the means by which Shakespeare brings to life and makes real the immaterial: the inner world of fantasy, delusion and imagination. S. G. Sen Gupta, in *The Whirligig of Time*,[2] calls us back to the confusions in the references to the passing of time in the plays; there is purpose here, he claims. In the tragedies, as opposed to the histories, Shakespeare is not really interested in the passing of time as a factor in men's lives, but rather in the continuous flow of alteration of character; Sen Gupta firmly rejects the 'double time' theory. Horst Oppel,[3] like Sen Gupta, is opposed to a 'linear' view of Shakespeare's art, and shows how the 'polarity' principle, the dialectic of juxtaposing opposites, is basic to the plays, in plot, character and speech. Anthony Caputi deals with one play, *Measure for Measure*,[4] and draws attention to the frequency of long, slowly developing scenes between two characters, one representing civilized, the other natural man. The debates are not persuasions, because the distance between the two is greater at the end than at the beginning. The essay is an interesting attempt to let the play's structure declare its meaning. Finally, Patrick Cruttwell[5] observes that Shakespeare's plays contain all the symptoms of baroque—the ostentations, the blendings of tragic and comic, the fusion of real and unreal and so on—but he decides that after all Shakespeare is not a baroque artist. He shared to the full the uncertainty about the meaning of life and the nature of reality so characteristic of the late sixteenth and the seventeenth century 'but was convinced, in spite of this, that reality was knowable'.

[1] 'Die Macht des Nichtwirklichen in Shakespeares Spielen', *Shakespeare Jahrbuch*, 97 (1961), 13–33.
[2] *The Whirligig of Time. The Problem of Duration in Shakespeare's Plays* (Orient Longmans, 1961).
[3] 'Kontrast und Kontrapunkt im Shakespeare-Drama', *Shakespeare Jahrbuch*, 97 (1961), 153–82.
[4] 'Scenic Design in *Measure for Measure*', *J.E.G.P.* LX (1961), 423–34.
[5] 'Shakespeare and the Baroque', *Shakespeare Jahrbuch*, 97 (1961), 100–8.

2. SHAKESPEARE'S LIFE, TIMES AND STAGE

reviewed by NORMAN SANDERS

Although no comprehensive work has been published this year on Shakespeare's biography, a number of articles deal with various aspects of Shakespeare the man. Certainly the most immediate is Frederick J. Pohl's[1] review of the evidence for thinking the Darmstadt death-mask to be genuine. After summarizing briefly the features in common and the relationship between the Stratford bust, and the Droeshout and Chandos portraits, Pohl examines critically the twenty-six comparative measurements of the bust and death-mask made by Paul Wislicensus in 1911. He discards a large number of them and concludes that the two representations have ten valid measurements in common which are 'as much of proof as any reasonable person will require' that the mask is authentic. In a pleasantly written essay, Herbert Howarth[2] endeavours to see the man behind the mask by questioning what Jonson meant by 'gentle' when he applied it to Shakespeare. He suggests that Shakespeare would have been deeply influenced by his father's attempt and failure to obtain a coat of arms, and traces the ways his own pretentions to 'gentleness' are manifest in the style of the poems and plays. Thus *Venus and Adonis* is a 'deliberate first display of the gentle style', and *A Midsummer Night's Dream* the dramatic equivalent of it; the mature comedies show a movement from 'the brilliance of courtliness to the charity of courtesy', and the last plays a mastering of the toughness of the world by 'the purest and most ecstatic gentleness'. He claims that

by thinking of his gentleness as Jonson, Heminges, Condell, and Chettle appear to have thought of it, we can see it as a distinctive contribution to the Elizabethan stage; can see how it arose from his problems; how he transformed his problems into an art, and not one art but a changing art....

John Enck[3] queries the usual interpretation of another of Jonson's phrases, and suggests that the gibe about 'small Latine' was, in fact, a popular joke. He supports his opinion with some documentation and concludes that 'far from a cynical sneer at a competitor Jonson's "small Latine" praises Shakespeare in a way that would strike contemporaries as appropriate'. William A. Ringler[4] also bids us to take care in interpreting the words in which evidence of Shakespeare's life is couched. In a note on the words 'honour' and 'worship' in Spenser and Simon Robson he stresses that distinction in terms of address was scrupulously observed in Elizabethan times, and asserts that Chettle's claim that 'divers of *worship* have reported his uprightnes of dealing' means the reports of gentlemen only, and not of noblemen like Essex or Southampton. In the absence of new records having a direct connection with the poet, I suppose it is natural that attention should focus on those relating to his friends and possible acquaintants. Christopher Whitfield[5] has dug deeply into Midlands records to establish a degree of kinship between William Reynolds, Thomas Combe and Shakespeare. By means of interrelated family con-

---

[1] 'The Death-Mask', *Shakespeare Quarterly*, XII (1961), 115–26.
[2] 'Shakespeare's Gentleness', *Shakespeare Survey* 14 (1961), 90–7.
[3] 'A Chronicle of Small Latin', *Shakespeare Quarterly*, XII (1961), 342–5.
[4] 'Spenser, Shakespeare, Honor, and Worship', *Renaissance News*, XIV (1961), 159–61.
[5] 'The Kingship of Thomas Combe II, William Reynolds and William Shakespeare', *Notes and Queries*, VIII (1961), 364–72. See also 'Robert Dover and William Combe II', *ibid.* IX (1962), 51–2.

nections, he suggests that Shakespeare may have known the Bonners of Chipping Camden, the Savages of Broadway, and the Sheldons of Beoley, and also may have experienced the hospitality of Ann Daston, 'the most bountiful gentlewoman for hospitality of her degree in all England'. However, one does wonder just how much time a busy playwright would have spent attending weddings and christenings in the families of his friends' cousins, uncles and aunts.

Some interesting biographical speculations are indulged in by Alfred Harbage.[1] In a vigorously common-sense handling of the evidence for the date of *Love's Labour's Lost*, Harbage argues that the play was written for Paul's Boys in 1588–9 and suggests that such an early dating may throw light on some Shakespeare puzzles. For example, Aubrey's 'schoolmaster in the country' may mean no more than an older chapel boy imparting such Latin as he had acquired to younger boys; that the songs in Lyly's plays may have been written by Shakespeare;[2] and that 'our pleasant Willy' in Spenser's *Teares of the Muses* may refer to a Shakespeare who had written sufficient by 1590 to have commanded the older poet's respect. As he admits, Harbage proves nothing in his article, but it is full of stimulating suggestions. R. A. Foakes,[3] unlike Harbage, has no doubts about the traditional view of Shakespeare's emergence as a playwright in the 1590's. In an oddly titled chapter, he gives a most readable and well-balanced account of the Elizabethan theatres and their development during the period 1576–1600. While adding nothing new to our knowledge, the essay constitutes a well-illustrated introduction to a complex subject.

John W. Draper[4] usefully surveys Shakespeare's allusions to North Africa and its inhabitants and concludes that they show little accurate knowledge of the region's geography, history and culture. He contends, however, after analyses of the characters of Aaron, Morocco and Othello, that Shakespeare developed 'a realism of character' in portraying the Moor, and, in the case of Othello, one which agrees with 'the depiction of Moors by Leo Africannus, the chief authority available'.

An important document relating to the performance of a Shakespeare play has been discovered by Gustav Ungerer[5] at Lambeth Palace. In a letter to Anthony Bacon, Jacques Petit, a language tutor in the house of Sir John Harington (the cousin of the poet of the same name), describes the elaborate Christmas festivities arranged for some two hundred guests at Harington's house at Burley on the Hill in Rutland. He reports that on New Year's Day 1595/6 a professional company of players acted *Titus Andronicus*. Unfortunately, he does not specify the company or give any details of the performance, but does remark that 'la monstre a plus valeu q̄ le suiect'. G. A. Wilkes[6] also adds to the stock of contemporary allusions to the plays in noting an echo of the opening soliloquy in *Richard III* in Sir John Davies' satire 'Ignoto'. K. Muir[7] notes the

[1] 'Love's Labor's Lost and the Early Shakespeare', *Philological Quarterly*, XLI (1962), 18–36.

[2] G. K. Hunter has an extended treatment of this problem in his *John Lyly. The Humanist as Courtier* (1962), pp. 367–72.

[3] 'The Profession of Playwright', in *Stratford-upon-Avon Studies 3. Early Shakespeare* (Edward Arnold, 1961), pp. 11–33.

[4] 'Shakespeare and Barbary', *Etudes Anglaises*, XIV (1961), 306–13.

[5] 'A Performance of *Titus Andronicus*', *Shakespeare Survey 14* (1961), 102–9.

[6] 'An Early Allusion to *Richard III*, and its Bearing on the Date of the Play', *Shakespeare Quarterly*, XII (1961), 464–5.

[7] 'Blundeville, Wyatt and Shakespeare', *Notes and Queries*, VIII (1961), 293–4.

coincidence of the phrase 'remembrance of things past' in Sonnet 30, Blundeville's translation, *Three Morall Treatises*, and Wyatt's translation of *Quyete of Mynde*; and James G. McManaway[1] finds an echo of the Ghost's speech in *Hamlet* in Thomas Jordan's poem *A Speech Made to . . . General Monk* (1660).

Doubts about the possibility of an inner stage in Elizabethan theatres continue to grow, and the most-favoured alternative at present appears to be the curtained booth or 'tent', or a curtained canopy against the tiring house façade. In a turgidly written though important article, Lawrence J. Ross[2] postulates that a curtained booth projected from the rear of the stage throughout the performance of *Othello*, and was used for, among other things, Desdemona's bed, the 'bulk' from behind which Cassio is ambushed in v, i, and the 'discovery' of the Venetian senate in I, iii. He makes the point that

the most significant use of the booth in *Othello* may have been to provide a symbolic focal point for the central movement of the play by being connotatively associated with the marriage and the complex dubiousness gradually attaching to it.

William A. Armstrong[3] also favours the use of booths or tents, and, in a brief review of recent theories of the Elizabethan stage, brings forward evidence for their possible existence from *Edward I*, *Sophonisba*, *Bussy D'Ambois* and *The Poetaster*. In the course of reconstructing a possible contemporary staging of *King Lear*, George F. Reynolds[4] has a projecting curtain in front of a 'third middle door' at the rear of the stage, to which he gives a central symbolic function. He suggests that some of the difficulties in staging the play may have been solved by the existence of two, now obsolete, stage conventions: that of entry and re-entry through the same or different doors indicating a change of place, and the audience's acceptance of the non-existence of an actor who is on stage but not acknowledged as being so. Reynolds's argument tends to wander at certain points, but is backed by an obvious familiarity with the production of Shakespeare's plays on modern versions of the Elizabethan stage. Dieter Mehl[5] discusses one of the favoured devices of Elizabethan and Jacobean playwrights, the play within the play. In analysing the different uses made of it by Kyd, Shakespeare, Middleton, Jonson, Webster and Tourneur, he illustrates how it gave an extra dimension of reality.

A good deal of attention has been paid during the year to Shakespeare's contemporaries and the relationship between his work and reputation and theirs. T. J. B. Spencer,[6] in a polished and well-documented account, traces the early establishment of Shakespeare's supremacy, and its acceptance by subsequent ages for a variety of reasons, and contrasts it with the slow and comparatively recent promulgation of the works of his fellow dramatists. Arthur Brown[7] also looks at the period as a whole and provides an invaluable critical survey of work done on the Elizabethan and Jacobean drama since 1900. He sees the period as one of stocktaking with old ideas

[1] 'A *Hamlet* Reminiscence in 1660', *Notes and Queries*, VIII (1961), 388.
[2] 'The Use of a "Fit-Up" Booth in *Othello*', *Shakespeare Quarterly*, XII (1961), 359–70.
[3] 'The Enigmatic Elizabethan Stage', *English*, XIII (1961), 216–20.
[4] 'Two Conventions of the Open Stage (As illustrated in *King Lear*?)', *Philological Quarterly*, XLI (1962), 82–95.
[5] 'Zur Entwicklung des "Play within a Play" in elisabethanischen Drama', *Shakespeare Jahrbuch*, 97 (1961), 134–52.
[6] 'Shakespeare *v*. The Rest', *Shakespeare Survey* 14 (1961), 76–89.
[7] 'Studies in Elizabethan and Jacobean Drama since 1900', *ibid.* pp. 1–14.

being subjected to critical scrutiny in the light of new techniques and documentary evidence. In his five desiderata for the future he stresses the need for good modern editions, and bleakly observes 'To write about a man's work before being sure of what he wrote is a proceeding which in other disciplines would be regarded as bordering on lunacy; yet we have...come perilously close to regarding it as normal'.

Concentrating on the younger contemporaries, H. T. Price[1] takes us at a breathless gallop through the works of the University Wits. Claiming that 'drama is conflict and...the art of the dramatist is to repeat this conflict in different relationships while always keeping it focussed on the general idea', Price damns outright or with faint praise Lyly ('does not know what drama is'), Marlowe ('put together great plays, but he never achieved drama'), Peele ('cannot be said to have written comedy'), and Greene ('his plots...are only good plots for a novel, not for drama'). Only Shakespeare, he concludes, saw the necessity for pattern and dramatic unity, achieved a complex and controlled design and so created modern drama. Two writers consider the extent and nature of Lyly's influence on Shakespeare's comedies. Marco Mincoff[2] suggests that in *Sapho and Phao* and *Gallathea* Lyly had developed high love comedy of a delicate and subtle kind as far as he was able, and that it was left to Shakespeare to take it further 'not only because of his greater genius, but because he was *not* a court poet and was *not* drawn to the artificial code of love that ruled at court'. Mincoff sees Shakespeare reacting to the Lylian tradition in *The Comedy of Errors* and *The Taming of the Shrew*, but developing it in the direction of humanity in *Love's Labour's Lost*. He has, however, no doubts about Lyly's influence: 'Shakespeare's comic principle cannot be summed up in the phrase "comedy of courtship", it has been enriched with another principle, the discrepancy between appearance and reality. At least one aspect of that complex derives from Lyly.' G. K. Hunter[3] also takes up the concepts of appearance and reality in Shakespeare and Lyly. He points out that Lyly was evidently interested in the idea that his plays were 'unreal', as was Shakespeare; but for the older dramatist 'the court audience is reality...and the fount of truth; the play can only approach truth by mirroring the court's virtues, and can be at best but a shadow of that true perfection'. In contrast, for Shakespeare, the life inside his plays is one which is complete in itself, and the court and its values but a portion of the greater scheme of things to which he looks for his ultimate comic values. However, in spite of the great differences which Hunter sees between the two playwrights, his conclusion is similar to Mincoff's that 'The existence of [Lyly's] accomplished dramas... must have made much easier Shakespeare's passage across the middle ground of his comic development'.

Nicholas Brooke[4] turns his attention to the impact made by Marlowe on the early plays of Shakespeare. He claims that Marlowe's influence was a deeply disturbing one because of his obvious poetic power and because the Marlovian figure was a direct challenge to the Shakespearian ethos. Basing his opinion on analyses of plays like *Titus Andronicus*, *Richard II* and *Richard III*, Brooke sees the early Shakespeare treating Marlowe as 'the inescapable imaginative creator of something initially alien which he could only assimilate with difficulty, through a

[1] 'Shakespeare and His Young Contemporaries', *Philological Quarterly*, XLI (1962), 37–57.
[2] 'Shakespeare and Lyly', *Shakespeare Survey 14* (1961), 15–24.
[3] *John Lyly. The Humanist as Courtier* (Routledge and Kegan Paul, 1962), pp. 298–349.
[4] 'Marlowe as Provocative Agent in Shakespeare's Early Plays', *Shakespeare Survey 14* (1961), 34–44.

process of imitative re-creation merging into critical parody'. I. A. Shapiro[1] gives a beautifully concise account of the career of Anthony Mundy, which he uses as a starting-point for some provocative speculation. He suggests that Mundy's output of plays was large and probably contained some history plays, that *A Midsummer Night's Dream* shows the influence of *John a Kent*, that Meres' description of him as 'our best plotter' taken together with some of the payments in Henslowe's *Diary* and Mundy's known attempts at stage improvisation may indicate that he wrote scenarii for other playwrights. Shapiro is also convinced that Mundy wrote the original draft of *Sir Thomas More*, and casts doubts upon the validity of E. M. Thompson's paleographical evidence for Hand D's being Shakespeare's.

G. R. Hibberd's[2] book on Thomas Nashe gives a most thorough survey of Nashe's biography and valuable critical account of his works. Chapter 4 deals with the sole extant play from Nashe's pen, *Summers Last Will and Testament*, and gives a vivid recreation of an entertainment devised for a special occasion and presented in the house of Archbishop Whitgift by a professional actor, the young members of the household, and 'homespun rustics from the archepiscopal manor'. Hibberd makes some high claims for the excellence of the piece, comparing Will Summers' prose idiom favourably with that of the Jack Cade scenes in *2 Henry VI*, and opining that 'No earlier English comedy has anything like the intellectual content or the social relevance that it has'. There is an essay on the comedy of Greene and Shakespeare by Norman Sanders.[3] Harold Jenkins[4] eloquently contrasts Shakespeare's treatment of the revenge theme with Webster's. He argues that by means of the archetypal revenge plot Shakespeare in *Hamlet* reveals 'that larger pattern...concerning the good and evil which coexist in human life' which the hero comes to accept as the unavoidable condition of humanity. Jenkins believes that Webster shifted the dramatic focus from the revenger to the sufferers of revenge, in his two most important plays, because his imagination was engaged not by the contest between good and evil, but by the spectacle of life's victims as they reach out to passionate life, and progress towards inevitable destruction.

Two short articles deal with the responses to Shakespeare by two very different writers of later periods. R. K. Das Gupta[5] considers the references to Shakespeare in Milton's works and concludes that the epitaph *On Shakespear. 1630* is 'good judgement in good verse but is much less than a song of adulation...Milton did not intend it to be anything more than a set of verses addressed to a writer of high reputation'. Gordon C. Couchman[6] traces the growth of Shaw's animosity towards *Antony and Cleopatra* and suggests that in thus despising 'the modern romantic convention' Shaw himself fell a victim to 'what we might call the subjective convention'.

The most important work on sources to appear during the year is the fourth volume of Geoffrey Bullough's *Narrative and Dramatic Sources of Shakespeare*,[7] which deals with *King John*, *Henry IV*, *Henry V* and *Henry VIII*. As in the previous volumes, the selection of texts offered is

---

[1] 'Shakespeare and Mundy', *ibid.* pp. 25–33.

[2] *Thomas Nashe. A Critical Introduction* (Routledge and Kegan Paul, 1962).

[3] 'The Comedy of Greene and Shakespeare', in *Stratford-upon-Avon Studies 3. Early Shakespeare* (Edward Arnold, 1961), pp. 35–53.

[4] 'The Tragedy of Revenge in Shakespeare and Webster', *Shakespeare Survey 14* (1961), 45–55.

[5] 'Milton on Shakespeare', *ibid.* pp. 98–101.

[6] '*Antony and Cleopatra* and the Subjective Convention', *PMLA*, LXXVI (1961), 420–5.

[7] Routledge and Kegan Paul, 1962.

a generous one. For *King John*, for example, he prints not only the relevant passages from Holinshed and Hall, and the whole of *The Troublesome Raigne* (of which he has a higher opinion than most critics), but also a summary of Bale's *King Johan* 'because it started the dramatic tradition to which *King John* belongs', and Foxe's account of Peter the Prophet, John's submission, and his death 'because it influenced Shakespeare either directly or indirectly through *The Troublesome Raigne* or through Richard Grafton's *Chronicle*'. The sub-title of the volume 'Later English History Plays' gives a clue to Bullough's dating of this play: he rejects the 1590–1 dating of the New Arden editor 'after some vacillation' and believes that *The Troublesome Raigne* was written in 1590–1 and *King John* in 1596. His open-mindedness where the opinions of other scholars are concerned is illustrated by his printing of Coggeshall's account of the attempted blinding of Arthur even though he disagrees with Honigmann's conclusions about it.

Bullough's handling of the difficult source material of the Henry IV and Henry V plays is excellent; about these plays he claims 'There can be little doubt that Shakespeare conceived his Richard II, Henry IV and Henry V plays as a group and that he intended to follow out the fortunes of Bolingbroke and his son even while he was writing *Richard II*'. Of *Henry VIII* he fully endorses Wilson Knight's high opinion and sees the play as a rich chronicle pageant standing as a colourful finale to Shakespeare's treatment of English history. Nor has he any doubts concerning the authorship of the play: 'I agree with those writers who, perceiving more than one style in the play, believe that the differences are functional and that there is nothing there which could not have been written by the poet of the last comedies.' It is worth noting that all Bullough's introductions contain not only detailed and scrupulously documented analyses of Shakespeare's sources but also many searching critical observations. The first three chapters of M. M. Reese's *The Cease of Majesty*[1] are a valuable adjunct to Bullough's third and fourth volumes. They provide an excellent introduction to the theory and development of the Elizabethan view of history, and isolate the characteristics of the principal Elizabethan historians.

Some of the points made by Bullough have been discussed by other scholars. Leo Kirschbaum[2] argues for the anticipation of Falstaff's rejection in *1 Henry IV*, I, ii. He stresses the law and gallows references throughout the scene, by means of which 'iterated motifs, Shakespeare points to the imprisonment of the fat knight in *2 Henry IV* and his lonely demise in *Henry V*'. George B. Johnston[3] points out that while Shakespeare may have got a hint from Daniel's *Civil Wars* in making Hotspur a young man, both had the word of William Camden, who in his *Britannia* designates Hotspur 'iuvenis', to justify their choice. Marco Mincoff[4] disagrees with Bullough about the authorship of *Henry VIII*, and, on the basis of metrical, grammatical, lexical and stylistic tests, claims that 'every single test applied leads to the same clear division into two separate styles, and one of these styles always points to Fletcher'.

Using the study of sources as an approach to criticism, John Lawlor[5] compares the differences in plot and characterization between *Pandosto* and *The Winter's Tale*, with a view to assessing the characteristics of romance as a dramatic form. He gives a succinct account of the changes made

[1] Edward Arnold, 1961.
[2] 'The Demotion of Falstaff', *Philological Quarterly*, XLI (1962), 58–60.
[3] 'Camden, Shakespeare, and Young Henry Percy', *PMLA*, LXXVI (1961), 298.
[4] '*Henry VIII* and Fletcher', *Shakespeare Quarterly*, XII (1961), 239–60.
[5] '*Pandosto* and the Nature of Dramatic Romance', *Philological Quarterly*, XLI (1962), 96–113.

by Shakespeare, stresses the way Greene's sub-title 'The Triumph of Time' is invested with new meaning in the play, and illustrates by close analysis the 'complex unity' to which Shakespeare moved in casting the play from the novel. Allan Gilbert[1] examines the possible origins in Ariosto and Bandello of the inconsistencies in the Borachio-Margaret episode in *Much Ado About Nothing*. Giving an explanation anchored firmly to a superficial and somewhat old-fashioned view of the play, he depicts a Shakespeare who 'may disappoint frigid analysis but... seldom fails in popular effect'. Arthur M. Sampley[2] discusses two analogues to Shakespeare's treatment of the wooing of Cordelia in Dekker's *Old Fortunatus*, and in *The Wisdom of Doctor Dodipoll*. S. W. Wells[3] prints and discusses a version of Tom O'Bedlam's song from the commonplace book of Archbishop Sancroft, and suggests the possibility that, owing to Sancroft's title 'Blesse thy faire eyes from the foule feind', the song may have been used in a performance of *King Lear*. E. P. Kuhl[4] gives a reading of *The Tempest*, which he sees as a play distilling 'the spirit of the time of the Virginia colonization: its ideals of representative government, religious tolerance, prospect of trade'. In Kuhl's lively but debatable speculations about topical allusions in the play Shakespeare emerges firmly on the side of the Virginia colonizers (Prospero-Ferdinand-Miranda) against the Robert Cecil (Caliban) faction. Prospero's debt to Ovid, and many other borrowings by Shakespeare, can be studied in the handsome reprint[5] of Arthur Golding's translation of the *Metamorphoses*: it may be regretted that a new edition was not feasible, but the publishers are rather to be congratulated on making available again, even at a cost, the substantial edition of W. H. D. Rouse. Golding's solid labours have been lavishly repaid.

Related to source study, but more closely related to the neglected art of comparative criticism, is J. B. Leishman's *Themes and Variations in Shakespeare's Sonnets*.[6] Parts of the first section of this book, on 'Poetry as Immortalization from Pindar to Shakespeare' appeared in *Elizabethan and Jacobean Studies presented to F. P. Wilson*. The two new areas of criticism are 'Devouring Time and Fading Beauty from the Greek Anthology to Shakespeare', and '"Hyperbole" and "Religiousness" in Shakespeare's expressions of his love'. In the discussion of 'Time' Leishman remarks

We may perhaps perceive in modern poetry a tendency, beginning, as it were gropingly, in Keats's Odes and reaching full awareness and explicitness in Rilke's *Duino Elegies*, to accept transience (with no matter what heart-rending sadness) as the necessary price of uniqueness, whereas in Shakespeare's sonnets and elsewhere we may perceive a tendency, a willingness, to sacrifice uniqueness for the sake of permanence.

And he concludes on this point that while many modern readers equate 'love for love's sake' with being 'in love with love', Shakespeare seems to have felt differently; 'it is *because* his love

---

[1] 'Two Margarets: The Composition of *Much Ado About Nothing*', *Philological Quarterly*, XLI (1962), 61–71.

[2] 'Two Analogues to Shakespeare's Treatment of the Wooing of Cordelia', *Shakespeare Quarterly*, XII (1961), 468–9.

[3] 'Tom O'Bedlam's Song and *King Lear*', *ibid.* pp. 311–16.

[4] 'Shakespeare and the Founders of America: *The Tempest*', *Philological Quarterly*, XLI (1962), 123–46.

[5] W. H. D. Rouse (ed.), '*Shakespeare's Ovid*': *Golding's translation of the Metamorphoses* (The Centaur Press, 1961).

[6] Hutchinson, 1961.

is for love's sake that it can defy Time'. The distinction is far from being that between Eliza-bethan and modern sensibility alone. Leishman's main theme is put in question form:

Is it not that of the resemblances and differences between Shakespeare and other poets—or, rather, of the difference, the *differentia*, the *thisness* that becomes most strikingly apparent in and through the occasional resemblances?

This is the strength of the book; that through the comparisons with Greek, Roman, Italian, and French poets, with Shakespeare's predecessors, with Donne and Rilke, and through many necessary and fruitful digressions we never lose touch with Shakespeare's themes. Among them, that which Leishman calls 'compensation', 'The transfiguring and transubstantiating, redeeming and re-incarnating power of his love' is brought out with strong power as one of 'those great positive affirmations which are so characteristically Shakespearian and for which it is hard to find any real precedent in earlier poetry'.

There have been a number of interesting articles on Shakespeare and the visual arts. W. Moel-wyn Merchant[1] traces the visual image of *A Midsummer Night's Dream* as it is found in the works of engravers, painters and stage designers from the Restoration to the present day. While some artists, like Blake and Fuseli, have caught some of the disturbing moments of irrationality, treachery and demonic power which Merchant sees inherent in the play's fairy world, he finds that the piece 'has eluded authoritative presentation, in the theatre or on the artist's easel'. Marion S. Carson[2] and Hanford Henderson[3] consider early American pictorial and sculptured representations of Shakespeare, and James G. McManaway,[4] an engraving of the Westminster Abbey statue which was published in America in 1787, thus antedating the frontispiece to the Philadelphia edition of the works which has been accepted as the first American engraving of the dramatist. R. D. Monroe[5] has a note on the unique copy of an unfinished mezzotint by Abraham Wivell based on the Felton portrait.

A fascinating sidelight on Shakespearian stage history is provided by Carroll Camden,[6] who discusses a unique copy of *Songs and Chorusses in The Tempest* recently acquired by Rice Univer-sity Library and containing eleven songs, seven of which represent some version of the songs in the Folio, two of which are from Garrick's operatic version, and two which were printed apparently for the first time in Kemble's edition of 1789. Camden argues that the booklet was probably issued for free distribution in 1777, and that the two songs in Kemble's edition were written by Sheridan for his own version of the play in the same year. Equally fascinating, though no doubt tinged with the disagreement of contemporary theatregoers, are the contributions to current Shakespearian stage history as they are recorded in the many good review articles on the proliferating Shakespeare festivals.[7]

[1] '*A Midsummer Night's Dream*: a Visual Re-creation', in *Stratford-upon-Avon Studies 3. Early Shakespeare* (Edward Arnold, 1961), pp. 165-85.

[2] 'Shakespeare in Early American Decorative Arts', *Shakespeare Quarterly*, XII (1961), 154-6.

[3] 'Shakespeare in Marble in Colonial America', *ibid.* pp. 156-7.

[4] 'The First American Engraving of Shakespeare', *ibid.* pp. 157-8.

[5] 'Notes on a Unique Engraving of Shakespeare', *ibid.* pp. 317-22.

[6] 'Songs and Chorusses in *The Tempest*', *Philological Quarterly*, XLI (1962), 114-22.

[7] See J. R. Brown, 'Three Directors: a Review of Recent Productions', *Shakespeare Survey 14* (1961), 129-37; J. H. Bryant, 'The Phoenix Shakespeare Festival', *Shakespeare Quarterly*, XII (1961), 447-51; R. D. Horn, 'Shake-speare and Ben Jonson—Ashland, 1961', *ibid.* pp. 415-18; E. Hubler, 'Shakespeare at Princeton', *ibid.* pp. 443-6;

3. TEXTUAL STUDIES

reviewed by JAMES G. MCMANAWAY

Two more volumes of the New Arden Shakespeare are now in print. The earlier is *1 Henry IV*,[1] edited by A. R. Humphreys. The introduction deals admirably with the political and moral themes of the play, the sources, and the characters. Humphreys believes that in the composition of *Richard II* Shakespeare envisioned a series of plays extending into the reign of Henry V and that *Richard II* and the two parts of *Henry IV* were written in swift succession. Only thus could the name 'Oldcastle' have fixed itself so firmly in the public mind that, years after 'Falstaff' replaced it in the first quarto of *Henry IV*, theatregoers and even the members of Shakespeare's own company referred to Part 1 as *Oldcastle* and wrote of how 'the fat Knight, hight *Oldcastle*, Did tell you truly what this honor was'. It is Humphreys' belief that the play was probably written in 1596 and performed during the next season. William Brooke, Lord Cobham, a descendant of Oldcastle, was Lord Chamberlain from 22 July 1596 until his death on 5 March 1597 and was in a position to require an immediate change in the name if he felt anything touched the family honour: but there is a possibility that this action was left to his son Henry, who succeeded to his title but not to his office as Lord Chamberlain. In all likelihood the enforced change of Oldcastle's name was made before 17 March 1597, when Sir George Carey, the second Lord Hunsdon and, like his late father, the patron of the Shakespeare-Burbage company, became Lord Chamberlain. For under his protection Shakespeare felt safe in having the jealous husband in *The Merry Wives of Windsor* assume the *nom de guerre* Brook, a piece of impudence all the Court could enjoy when the newly elected Knights of the Garter (Lord Hunsdon among them) saw *The Merry Wives* performed during their festivities in May 1597. Another protest by the indignant Cobhams seems to have been effective in so far as Master Brook's name is concerned, because in the Folio he is called Broom. But Windsor and London had their laugh, and within three days after *1 Henry IV* was entered for publication (on 25 February 1598), the Earl of Essex in a private letter was referring jocularly to Sir Henry Brooke, Lord Cobham, as 'S^r Jo. Falstaff'. In his treatment of the text, Humphreys is conservative and sound. Rejecting the suggestion that Shakespeare wrote several versions of the play, of which only the latest survives as Q, he adopts as his basic text Q 0 in combination with Q 1. Evidence is cited to show that copy for the first edition was Shakespeare's foul sheets in which someone had made the necessary alteration of Oldcastle to Falstaff and had perhaps touched up other details that attracted attention. Later quartos and F have no independent authority: 'Emendations, therefore, are admitted only when evident errors can be evidently rectified' (p. lxxvii). At one point, II, iv, 240 the editor departs from his predecessors in reading 'elfskin' in the three copies of Q 1, for as G. B. Evans pointed out,[2] these all have *elsskin*. The 'elfskin' spelling appeared first in Q 3 any was retained in Qq 4 and 5 and thence taken over into F. Evans remarks that Hal is shortld

---

C. McGlinchee, 'Stratford, Connecticut, Shakespeare Festival, 1961', *ibid.* pp. 419–24; R. L. Perkin, 'Shakespeare in the Rockies: IV', *ibid.* pp. 409–14; R. Speaight, 'The Old Vic and Stratford-upon-Avon, 1960–61', *ibid.* pp. 425–42; V. K. Whitaker, 'Shakespeare in San Diego—The Twelfth Season', *ibid.* pp. 403–8.

[1] A. R. Humphreys (ed.), *The First Part of King Henry IV* (London: Methuen, 1960).
[2] 'Laying a Shakespearian Ghost: *1 Henry IV*, II, iv, 225', *Shakespeare Quarterly*, V (1954), 427.

called a 'dried neatstong' and that in *MND* Starveling is called 'you ellskin, you dried neats-tong'.

With *1 Henry VI*[1] the New Arden plunges more deeply than before into the treacherous waters of composite authorship. The editor, A. S. Cairncross, aligns himself with Peter Alexander in attributing the play wholly to Shakespeare and in dating it earlier than Parts 2 and 3 of *Henry VI*. Because of the very scanty external evidence, an intricate knot of problems, and a vast literature, the subject cannot be discussed here at the length it deserves. Comments on several of the chief points at issue may, however, be helpful.

From the wording of the title-page of the 'Bad Quarto' of *3 Henry VI*, it may be inferred that *2* and *3 Henry VI* belonged to Pembroke's men; and since the unauthorized texts of *The Contention* (1594) and *The True Tragedy* (1595) contain echoes of *1 Henry VI* (argued first by Alexander, who is joined by Cairncross—see his Appendix III), it may be assumed that this play, too, belonged to Pembroke's, who acted it often enough to mingle phrases of it in the reported texts of *The Contention* and *The True Tragedy*. Now the playhouses were closed by the plague in June 1592, and it seems probable that all three parts of *Henry VI* must have been written a considerable time before that date. Thus far Cairncross, who sets an earlier limit with his citation of borrowings from *The Faerie Queene* (Q, 1590). He might have narrowed the limiting dates of composition by using evidence provided by Alexander and supplemented by G. Blakemore Evans[2] that *The Troublesome Raigne of King John* (Q. 1591) contains reminiscences of *1 Henry VI* (and also *2, 3 Henry VI* and *Richard II*). Then it seems (unlike Hamlet, the investigator of these plays rarely knows greater certainty than *seems*) that Strange's could hardly have bought their *Harey the vj*, performed as 'ne' for Henslowe between 1 March and 19 June 1592, from Pembroke's, even though the latter company broke utterly on their provincial tour in 1593. *Harey the vj* must have been a rival to Shakespeare's play. And Nashe's allusion of August 1592 to the popularity of 'brave Talbot' may refer to either play or to both.

There is little agreement about the nature of the copy used by Jaggard in printing F. To Dover Wilson, it appeared to consist of the manuscripts handed over by the authors (Greene, Nash and Peele) to the first company that owned the play, to which their prompter had added occasional stage directions and notations for sound effects before a fair copy was made to be used as prompt-book (i.e. *1 Henry VI* is to be identified with Henslowe's *Harey the vj*). This manuscript, Wilson thinks, was divided throughout (or at least those parts of it attributed to Greene, the chief plotter) into acts and scenes. When Shakespeare was called upon to revise the play, he rejected certain scenes—the original v, i, for example—and displaced or rewrote others, producing a text in which only Act III has all the scenes numbered. This was transcribed in the preparation of a new prompt-book and survived to be used in printing F. Cairncross rejects all this. He postulates a Shakespearian rough draft containing inconsistencies[3] and even self-contradictions (e.g. Exeter's surprise at seeing Winchester in Cardinal's robes at v, i, 28, when he had certainly worn them in Exeter's presence at I, iii, III, iv, and IV, i). To this manuscript the book-keeper is sup-

---

[1] Andrew S. Cairncross (ed.), *The First Part of King Henry VI* (London: Methuen, 1962).

[2] In his review of J. D. Wilson's edition of *1, 2, 3 Henry VI* (New Shakespeare) in *Shakespeare Quarterly*, IV (1953), 84–92.

[3] In speech-prefixes primarily, but also in proper names (*Burgonie* as well as *Burgundie*), which Cairncross thinks may have been taken over from the various printed sources.

posed to have added some stage directions and sound effects, not always at the right point. At the same time, he indicated certain adaptations to be made in the cast—indicated them but did not actually mark all the changes (e.g. the 2 *Messenger—Lucie* confusion in Act IV). Then the rough manuscript was copied by a scribe who took liberties with the text, transposing words and phrases, 'improving' the diction, omitting many small words and inserting others, to the detriment of the metre. From this transcript a prompt-book was prepared and many years later it was used as printer's copy in F. The evidence is displayed persuasively, but doubts remain. Is there any other play in which Shakespeare carried over from his sources such contradictory details? Is the supposititious scribe an adequate agent to account for the a-metrical lines and the many other indications of heterogeneous copy? Did Shakespeare ever write blank verse as listless as some of that in *1 Henry VI*?

Cairncross relies heavily on H. T. Price's brilliant discussion[1] of the structure of *1 Henry VI* and his insistence that no other playwright than Shakespeare had such architectural skill. But granting all this, must one suppose that Shakespeare could not have salvaged scenes written by other poets and fitted them with others of his own composition in conformity to a plan of his own devising?

Acting upon his theory about the authorship of the play and the nature of the manuscript from which it was printed, Cairncross has felt unusually free to amend the text. Some of the changes are justifiable; others appear to go too far in smoothing the metre and improving the language. At III, i, 71, 'years' is unaccountably changed to 'tears'.

Conservative scholarship has resisted efforts to identify passages in Shakespeare's plays as insertions or revisions made by the author after the play took final form and was regularized for production. Now, reversing his earlier position, Brents Stirling adduces bibliographical, textual and aesthetic evidence that Shakespeare telescoped incidents in Act II of *Julius Caesar* in order to speed the action and increase the dramatic tension.[2] Revision also took place in IV, iii, containing the duplicate accounts of Portia's death. The starting-point of the discovery is the presence in a play with uniform speech-headings of certain passages in which the speech-headings are spelled differently. It has been claimed that in *Caesar* Shakespeare first learned how to write tragedy: by following Stirling step by step through his exposition, it is possible to see Shakespeare in the process of improving his art.

In two important essays, Marco Mincoff addresses himself to the criticism of plays of disputed authorship. The first[3] gives new evidence in support of the Bad Quarto theory but 'tries above all to show what problems any theory of the relationship between the versions must take into account, what can and what cannot be proved, and what methods of investigation must, in the nature of things, lead into blind alleys' (p. 274). This is a valuable reappraisal of the subject, and the clues it gives to further bibliographical studies of *The True Tragedy* should be followed up. In the second essay,[4] Mincoff reviews the problem in *Henry VIII* of single authorship *vs.* Fletcherian collaboration. In his summary (pp. 259–60), he finds many reasons for dividing the play into two parts, *A* and *B*; he can discover no evidence that satisfies him with Shakespearian

[1] Hereward T. Price, *Construction in Shakespeare* (University of Michigan, 1951).
[2] Brents Stirling, '*Julius Caesar* in Revision', *Shakespeare Quarterly* (1962), XIII, 187–205.
[3] Marco Mincoff, '*Henry VI Part III* and *The True Tragedy*', *English Studies*, XLII (1961), 273–88.
[4] '*Henry VIII* and Fletcher', *Shakespeare Quarterly*, XII (1961), 239–60.

authorship of *B*; and he concludes that, if Fletcher's participation be rejected, it will be necessary to find a new collaborator, for that there was collaboration he is positive.

The Taming of the Shrew lends itself to a variety of interpretations. It may be played as a boisterous farce in praise of the use of force to assert masculine superiority; or it may be acted as almost a high romantic comedy in which the principals, genuinely in love at first sight, must wage the eternal battle of the sexes before arriving at a joyous marital equilibrium. It is well known that Shakespeare's play, as preserved in the Folio, dispenses with Christopher Sly, the drunken tinker, *in medias res*, letting the play end with Katharina's assertion of wifely submission. Modern producers, particularly those who may feel twinges of guilt about Petruchio's crudity, avert unfavourable reactions by the audience by borrowing from *A Shrew* the dramatic epilogue in which the awakened drunkard, in his own guise, goes home to put in practice the lesson he has learned in a rare dream. 'Dramatic epilogue' is the term coined by Richard Hosley[1] to describe 'a short dramatic action following the play proper, normally performed by two or more actors, employing the same fictional situation as that of the induction, and concluding the dramatic action begun in the induction' (pp. 22–3). That is, to the kind of scene wanting at the end of *The Shrew* but present in *A Shrew*. Hosley names the forty-five Elizabethan plays beginning with an induction, grouping together the nineteen that end with a dramatic epilogue and the twenty-six that lack one. He observes that dramatic epilogues appear to have been out-of-fashion after about 1600. As to whether Shakespeare omitted the dramatic epilogue deliberately or whether it was left out of the Folio by accident, Hosley argues that Shakespeare did not write one. In the concluding scene, 13 (or 12), actors are on stage, not counting servants. Now Hosley assumes that some of these men doubled as Lord or Sly or Lady, and he points out that there was no time for the necessary change of costumes that would have been needed to bring Sly back on stage. It is his belief, furthermore, that Shakespeare would not have wished to blunt the edge of Petruchio's victory by bringing on Sly to point the moral.

It has long been suspected that *Macbeth* is an abbreviated text, and there have been many suggestions about missing scenes. Two discrepancies between the account of a performance seen in 1610 by Simon Forman and the play as printed in F are interpreted by Daniel A. Amnéus as proof that at one time there was an interval of one day between Banquo's murder and the Banquet Scene.[2] Forman writes in his *Bocke of Plaies*: '*The next night*, being at supper.... As he [Macbeth] did, *standing up* to drink a carouse to him, the ghost of Banquo came and sat down in the Chair behind him....' Amnéus finds confirmation that Shakespeare once used these details at III, iv, 78–80.

But now they rise again....

And push us from our stools

at III, iv, 71–3.

If charnel houses and our graves must send

Those that we bury back,...

and in Lady Macbeth's Sleepwalking Scene,

I tell you yet again Banquo's buried; he cannot come out on's grave.

[1] Richard Hosley, 'Was There a "Dramatic Epilogue" to *The Taming of the Shrew*?', *Studies in English Literatur* I, 2 (1961), 17–34.

[2] Daniel A. Amnéus, 'A Missing Scene in *Macbeth*', *J.E.G.P.* LX, 435–40.

Banquo, then, must have been buried before the appearance of his ghost at table. In a version with this time scheme, Amnéus says that III, ii, 8–22 must have been spoken after the murder of Banquo, not before as in F, for the crime that is without remedy is Banquo's murder; Fleance, who escaped, is the snake that was not killed. He suggests that the abbreviated text may have been performed at court in 1606, while the longer version was used on the public stage.

Since *Much Ado About Nothing* was printed from Shakespeare's foul papers, no one knows how some of the false leads (e.g. the naming of Hero's mother Innogen in a stage direction) and unreconciled details were handled in the final draft. Observing that Margaret really has two different roles, Allan Gilbert inquires whether this anomaly may not be a clue to revision.[1] Margaret is deeply though innocently involved in the betrayal of her mistress but is surprisingly absent from the wedding; later, when she should be anxious or contrite, she is witty. Gilbert suggests that late in the course of writing the play Shakespeare decided to rearrange the details as given in his sources so that Dogberry and his crew might solve the plot. This necessitated, perhaps, the dropping of Innogen and of Claudio's uncle, together with the details of Margaret's love-story. At this same time, he expanded the roles of Benedick and Beatrice. There are blemishes in the text as it has come down to us, but Gilbert accepts them cheerfully for the sake of Dogberry and the witty lovers.

After any period of exciting discovery and exploration comes a time for questioning: are the methods of exploration sound, have the discoveries been understood properly and evaluated truly, do late-comers follow docilely in old trails, or do they test all that has become orthodox and try new paths? In *A New Look at Shakespeare's Quartos*,[2] Hardin Craig, who has previously expressed dissent, challenges many of the assumptions of current textual study, particularly those associated with Bad Quartos. Three main propositions are advanced: (1) many of Shakespeare's plays are revisions—of plays by other men or of earlier versions by himself; (2) play texts were seriously corrupted in performance, and many of these corruptions were entered in the prompt-book as insertions or cancels; and (3) the First Folio was printed directly from the prompt-books. There are many things of smaller importance with which one might wish to agree or disagree, but space is available for no more than a few words about the chief propositions. Not content with reviving the thesis that *The Contention* and *The True Tragedy* are early versions of *2* and *3 Henry VI*, Craig asserts that Q I *Romeo* and Q I *Hamlet*, for example, represent Shakespeare's first handling of these plays and that later he rewrote them in the form preserved in the second quartos. My own reading of the evidence, in which I am not alone, is that the first printings of these four plays are memorial reconstructions of one kind or another. Elizabethan audiences can rarely have heard word-perfect performances of a play, for actors had to keep many roles in mind, there was little time for rehearsal in the modern sense, and a different play was on the boards every day. Undoubtedly they made verbal substitutions, introduced commonplace paraphrases when memory failed, and skipped lines. But is there any reason to agree with Craig that these accidental corruptions, or intentional minor changes of the same order, were noted down and that the prompt-book was made to conform to performance? Whose interest would be served? Who would ever have taken time? The doctrine of continuous copy encounters still

---

[1] Allan Gilbert, 'Two Margarets: The Composition of *Much Ado About Nothing*', *Studies in English Drama, Philological Quarterly*, XLI (1962), 61–71.

[2] Hardin Craig, *A New Look at Shakespeare's Quartos* (Stanford University Press, 1961).

another serious obstacle in the person of the Master of the Revels. This official was both con-scientious and fee-hungry. If he exacted payment for reading a revived play in search of new or profane material, would he have permitted promiscuous alteration of an allowed text? Objec-tionable lines might be spoken in performance without detection, or, if noted, with impunity, because guilt would have been difficult of proof; but such repeated tampering with the text as Craig assumes would not, I think, have been tolerated by Buc or Herbert. And surviving prompt-books bear no sign of such corruption.

The use by Jaggard of the official prompt-books in printing the First Folio is to me unimagin-able. As I have argued elsewhere, the licensed prompt-book was not only a valuable property; it was the company's defence against accusation. The prompt-book of *The Merchant* could apparently be sent to Stationers' Hall for entry without undue risk, but a manuscript much less precious to them (in Shakespeare's autograph!) was delivered in 1600 to James Robert for printing the first quarto. There is another and equally compelling reason for thinking that Jaggard did not give prompt-books to his compositors for putting the Folio in type. There is indisputable proof that this volume was printed from cast-off copy. That is to say that someone went through each play, marking what was to be put in print on each Folio page; then the two compositors parcelled out the leaves of text and set them.[1] Can anyone believe that the King's Men permitted their licensed prompt-books to be taken apart, leaf by leaf by a printer? Surely they supplied Jaggard with some unofficial manuscript or, lacking that, a transcript or the leaves of a quarto.

In a related study that can do little more than hint at what he has in mind, Craig indicates his belief that Shakespeare wrote the Lear story in about 1234 lines that appear with little difference in Q1 and F.[2] Then, deciding to incorporate the Gloucester story based on an episode in *The Arcadia*, he added about 270 lines of prose, some 120 lines of blank-verse embellishment, and 566 lines spoken by the Fool, Mad Tom, and the crazed Lear. Some 2500 lines are thus accounted for, leaving approximately 1000 lines to make up the full text. These, Craig says, include the passages that link the two plots, and in them are found the discrepancies between Q1 and F. He supposes that Q1 was printed from Shakespeare's foul papers. The fair copy of these, amended by Shakespeare in the process, cut for performance, and modified by stage usage, served as prompt-book; and Jaggard printed F from this manuscript.

Bad Quartos and memorial reconstructions are questioned in a different way by I. A. Shapiro,[3] who attempts to discover what Francis Meres meant in calling Anthony Mundy 'our best plotter'. Does it mean, perhaps, that Mundy, who had opportunity to see *commedia dell'arte* performances during his residence in Italy, made use of these experiences when he was acting 'extempore', and did he follow this by writing scenarios for playwrights and acting companies? Was there a Mundy scenario back of *The Famous Victories* or *The Troublesome Raigne* or *Leir* or *A Shrew*, all anonymous plays that have close links with Shakespeare? And do the hodge-podge texts of these short plays represent the clumsy tinkering of who knows how many poetasters

---

[1] See Charlton Hinman, 'Cast-off Copy for the First Folio of Shakespeare', *Shakespeare Quarterly*, VI (1955), 259-73.

[2] Hardin Craig, 'The Composition of King Lear', in *Renaissance Papers 1961*, ed. by George Walton Williams, assisted by Peter G. Phialas (Durham, N.C.: The Southeastern Renaissance Conference, 1962), pp. 57-61.

[3] I. A. Shapiro, 'Shakespeare and Mundy', *Shakespeare Survey 14* (1961), 25-33.

with Mundy's plots? This possibility seems more credible to Shapiro than the current explanation that they are memorial reconstructions.

Repeating with variation the title of the book in which F. P. Wilson challenged all-comers to prove that Shakespeare did not invent the English History Play, Alfred Harbage affirms his belief that Shakespeare wrote *Love's Labour's Lost* for a boys' company—quite possibly Paul's—in 1588/9 and explores the possibility that he spent his youth in a private household where he helped with teaching the children.[1] The engaging and witty essay brings into the open ideas that have been toyed with skittishly but never presented so adroitly. Shakespeare's numbers did not flow spontaneously about 1590 simply because the numbers came. He had learned the crafts of acting and play-making by appearing on the stage and by writing plays. And somewhere, very early, he had opportunity to observe and overhear people of education and social finesse. Beeston's comment to Aubrey about Shakespeare's having been a schoolmaster in the country has much to recommend it. Harbage's return to the identification of Spenser's 'pleasant Willy' as Shakespeare is heartening but would be more so if a reason could be assigned for thinking that Shakespeare interrupted a career as playwright for a considerable period about 1590.

J. J. Hogan introduces a very important consideration into the choosing between Q1 and F variants in *King Lear*.[2] Silently assuming that a copy of Q1 was used in printing F, he gives repeated instances in which the F 'printer' [sic][3] shortens the spelling of words or uses a different word than that in Q because his Folio column measure was so much shorter than the measure of the compositor of Q. This happens especially when the line must begin with a speech-heading or must end with *Exit*, and it occurs in prose as well as in verse. There are even a few stage directions that F may have curtailed in order to avoid overrunning a line. Hogan shows that the current tendency to prefer the F variant may be ill-advised. The First Quarto, in which a short measure is used on certain pages, plays tricks of the same sort occasionally.

The close study of how a play quarto was printed is a tedious but not necessarily unrewarding task. The first quarto of *A Midsummer Night's Dream* yields up to Robert K. Turner, Jr., not only the fact that one compositor set the play and very precise information about the order in which formes were set and printed, but strong confirmation of some of Dover Wilson's conjectures in 1924 about marginal insertions and mislineation of verse.[4] First Turner identifies and traces the pattern of the running-titles. Then he tabulates and interprets the use and substitution of certain key types of which there was a short supply. Finding no contradictions in his results, he is emboldened to speculate whether mislineation of verse and variation in the number of lines on a page in the Quarto were caused by faulty casting-off of copy or by the compositor's faithful reproduction in type of what he found in the manuscript. He concludes, as Wilson has suspected, that in important passages the manuscript contained mislined verse, inserted marginally or

[1] Alfred Harbage, '*Love's Labor's Lost* and the Early Shakespeare', *Studies in English Drama, Philological Quarterly*, XLI (1962), 18–36. Harbage allows for some revision by Shakespeare about 1597–8.

[2] J. J. Hogan, 'Cutting His Text According to His Measure: A Note on the Folio *Lear*', *Studies in English Drama, Philological Quarterly*, XLI (1962), 72–82.

[3] Unfortunately, Hogan ignores the fact that two compositors, B and E, worked on *Lear* in the Folio, and he makes no reference to readings in F that are shared by Q2 against Q1.

[4] Robert K. Turner, Jr., 'Printing Methods and Textual Problems in *A Midsummer Night's Dream*, Q1', *Studies in Bibliography* (1962), XV, 33–55.

between the lines. There is nothing, of course, to indicate whether Shakespeare added the lines at the time of original composition or later.

From his experiences in compiling his unpublished bibliography of Restoration drama and of editing the plays of Thomas Dekker and Walt Whitman's *Leaves of Grass*, Fredson Bowers formulates a statement of the theory of established texts and definitive editions.[1] After discussing the essential differences between editing a classical manuscript and an Elizabethan play, he considers the relative authority of original setting *vs.* reprint, then passes to editions revised by the author, with incidental comments on photographic and type facsimiles and related matters and detailed references to the textual problems in such plays as *Lear, Hamlet, Troilus, Richard III,* and *Othello.* Almost every essential point seems to be touched on except formal lists of faults escaped by the printer.

Since the publication of the *New English Dictionary*, it has been possible to gloss Shakespeare's text with an accuracy and confidence that would have aroused the envy of the great early commentators. This has led to a smugness that has been attacked more than once by Hilda M. Hulme, who has demonstrated that non-literary manuscripts contemporary with Shakespeare use many of his 'difficult' words in a sense that has been supposed archaic before his time or of much more recent origin. The result has been that a number of refractory passages have been explained satisfactorily without recourse to emendation. These individual notes have now been brought together as a small part of a book that 'describes a series of experiments to add to our knowledge of language in Shakespeare's time and attempts interpretions of some of the more difficult words and phrases of his dramatic text' (p. xi).[2] Following illustrations of her problems and methods, there are chapters on 'Proverb and Proverb-idiom', 'The Less Decent Language of the Time', 'Spelling Habits and Pronunciation Variants', and related topics. The problems are real, the methods sound, and many of the new explanations are palmary—cf. the discussion of 'brakes of Ice' (*Measure for Measure*, II, i). The author's learning leads her now and again into complexities of meaning that would have been impenetrable to all but the most erudite and agile-minded of Shakespeare's contemporaries, and it may be doubted that a writer for the public stage could have intended some of the subtleties that are expounded.

Scholarship now has as much reason as Industry and Labour to consider the benign and baleful effects of automation. Electronic computers hold out the promise, for example, of more and vastly better concordances.[3] There are attendant blessings, as S. M. Parrish points out:

If an editor can arrange to finish his collation and read proof on the text before proceeding to the rest of his task, he can be provided with a concordance in composing textual and critical notes, and the introduction to his volume (p. 12).

Consider how stylistic analysis may be speeded and made more trustworthy by the use of computers that can on demand produce all words beginning or ending with a given letter or combination of letters, or all lines ending in a word of one, two, or three letters, or can isolate

---

[1] Fredson T. Bowers, 'Established Texts and Definitive Editions', *Studies in English Drama, Philological Quarterly*, XLI (1962), 1–17.

[2] Hilda M. Hulme, *Explorations in Shakespeare's Language. Some Problems of Lexical Meaning in the Dramatic Text* (London: Longmans, 1962).

[3] S. M. Parrish, 'Problems in the Making of Computer Concordances', *Studies in Bibliography*, XV (1962), 1–14; Ephim G. Fogel, 'Electronic Computers and Elizabethan Texts', *ibid.* 15–31.

linguistic preferences. Fogel points out the current duplication of enumerative bibliographies of Shakespeare studies and suggests the inevitability of their abandonment in favour of one compiled electronically and printed within days after the end of a year. Such a product could, he insists, give far more precise guidance to readers, with enormous saving of time. And he envisages the publication of Shakespearian abstracts—in translation where necessary—by the use of text-reading machines that will encode on magnetic tape.

It is generally agreed that the modern approach to the study of Shakespeare's text began with Pollard, Greg, and McKerrow about 1909, and that the starting-point was the recognition of the differences between working with classical manuscripts and with printed books. Simultaneous studies by Alice Walker and Sailendra Kumar Sen now remind us that Edward Capell had apprehended a great part of the truth about first editions and reprints as early as 1760, when he chose an authoritative copy text for each poem in his *Prolusions; or, select Pieces of ancient Poetry*, and that by 1768 (his introduction to *Mr William Shakespeare his Comedies, Histories, and Tragedies*) his experience with quartos and folios had led him to a position that anticipates that of Pollard, Greg, and McKerrow. Sen[1] points out that on the evidence of duplicated passages of text, erroneous assignment of speeches, the naming of mute *dramatis personæ*, Capell set aside the first quartos of *Hamlet*, *Henry V*, *Merry Wives*, etc. as lacking in authority and accepted the other first quartos on to that of *Othello* as the equivalent of the author's manuscripts.[2] This was the distinction Pollard made between Good and Bad Quartos, and for many of the same reasons. Capell even suggested that some of the quartos had been printed from Shakespeare's manuscripts. He denied authority to the later quartos and to folios later than the first, except in particular cases where for undiscoverable reasons a reading might represent the author's intention. Malone, too, recognized the 'badness' of the first quartos of *Romeo*, *Henry V*, *Merry Wives*, and *Richard III* and of the First Folio for the plays first printed therein. The methods of Capell and Malone were, therefore, not eclectic in the older sense, and had their principles been accepted by later editors the modern study of Shakespeare might have begun more than a century before Pollard's *Shakespeare's Folios and Quartos*.

Miss Walker gives a brief account of Capell's life and a lively description of his personality and leads thence into an examination of his editorial theory and practice. Malone owed much to him, including the idea of approaching the study of Shakespeare as a literary artist by discovering the order in which his works had been written and thus tracing his development.[3]

Like *The True Chronicle History of King Leir* and *The Troublesome Raigne of John, King of*

[1] Sailendra Kumar Sen, *Capell and Malone, and Modern Critical Bibliography* (Calcutta: Firma K. L. Mukhopadhyay, 1960).

[2] Alice Walker, '*Edward Capell* and his Edition of *Shakespeare*', *Proceedings of the British Academy*, XLVI (Oxford University Press, 1962), 131–45, notes that Capell was aware of the possibility that erroneous readings would be found in even first editions because of the intervention of scribes and printers—that first editions have not the high authority of a holograph manuscript.

[3] In addition to the set of transcripts given by Capell to Trinity College, Cambridge, 'the only transcript that survives' (p. 137), there is a uniformly bound set of six volumes of Capell's holograph notes for the edition in the Folger Shakespeare Library (MS. S. a. 17–22). There is also his holograph transcript of *Edward III*, dated 3 October 1753 and 6 November 1753. At the end of the volume is an epitaph for himself in this own hand, with date of death supplied later. Below the epitaph, he wrote: 'Qui literas amas & excolis, tibi qui pro virili consuluit viveris huic consule et tu.'

England, The Famous Victories of Henry the Fifth—anonymous like the others—is inextricably linked with Shakespeare's plays. Certainly it was a source; possibly Shakespeare knew it so intimately because as a Queen's man he had helped perform it. Could he have written it, as is argued by Seymour M. Pitcher?[1] The evidence that is marshalled from examination of the language, the characters, and the supposed indebtedness to the Keen and Lubbock copy of Hall's *The Union of the Two Noble...Families of Lancaster and York* does not carry conviction. It is good, however, to have a purchasable reprint of this important play.

In his effort to solve some of the puzzles in *Troilus and Cressida*, Robert Kimbrough attempts with little success to refute Alexander's theory that the play was written for performance at one of the Inns of Court.[2] He may be correct in dating the play 1601; and certainly it was performed by the Chamberlain's Men, for it was their prompt-book that was conditionally entered to Roberts in 1603. But, as Greg remarks, there is nothing to show that it was acted on a public stage; in fact, the claim of Bonian and Walley in 1609 that it had not had public performance is entitled to very serious consideration.[3] Greg's conjectural reconstruction of the history of the two manuscripts lying back of Q and F and of the course of events from 1601 to 1623 appears to me to take the known facts more plausibly into account than Kimbrough's.

An interesting theatrical manuscript, never previously described, directs attention once more to the Witches' songs in *Macbeth*. It is a Restoration transcript of Davenant's adaptation of the play,[4] made, according to Christopher Spencer, the editor, from Davenant's foul papers, independently of the transcript that was supplied to the printer of the first quarto (1674) of the Davenant version. Reproductions of the title-page, the list of *dramatis personæ*, and three pages of text give an excellent idea of how the manuscript was prepared. The main scribe, *A*, left blanks for words he could not read; hands *B*, *C*, and *D* supplied missing words, made a number of interlineations and corrections, and wrote longer passages of revision on nine slips of paper attached by wax to the margins—five of these survive, and stains show where others were once attached.[5] Spencer is probably correct in thinking that the manuscript was intended for use in making the prompt-book. His attempts to show that Davenant had a pre-Wars manuscript of *Macbeth*, independent of F 1, and that a song near the beginning of II, v was written by Shakespeare rather than by Davenant are unconvincing.

> The worst of creatures fastest propogate
> Many more murders must this one ensue
> As if in Death were propogation too

reads to me like purest Davenant.

---

[1] Seymour M. Pitcher, *The Case for Shakespeare's Authorship of The Famous Victories With the Complete Text of the Anonymous Play* (The State University of New York, 1961).

[2] Robert Kimbrough, 'The Origins of *Troilus and Cressida*: Stage, Quarto, and Folio', *PMLA*, LXXVII (1962), 194–9.

[3] Kimbrough's interpretation of the cancel title-page and preface of Q is quite unacceptable (p. 197).

[4] Christopher Spencer, *Davenant's Macbeth from the Yale Manuscript: An Edition, with a Discussion of the Relation of Davenant's Text to Shakespeare's* (Yale University Press, 1961).

[5] Spencer suggests that *B* made the earliest additions and that *C* and *D*, whose hands appear only on the tipped-in slips, followed in that order. Each of them, in his opinion, referred to an independent text of Shakespeare in making his corrections. Hand *B* may have written the label on the cover, naming Mr Holden.

BOOKS RECEIVED

[Inclusion of a book in this list does not preclude its review in a subsequent volume.]

BEVINGTON, D. M. *From 'Mankind' to Marlowe* (Harvard University Press, 1962).

BULLOUGH, G. *Narrative and Dramatic Sources of Shakespeare*, vol. IV (London: Routledge and Kegan Paul, 1962).

CAPUTI, A. *John Marston, Satirist* (Cornell University Press; Oxford University Press, 1962).

CHARNEY, M. *Shakespeare's Roman Plays: The Function of Dramatic Imagery* (Harvard University Press, 1961).

FRASER, R. A. *Shakespeare's Poetics in relation to 'King Lear'* (London: Routledge and Kegan Paul, 1962).

GUIDI, A. *Gli Ultimi Drammi di Shakespeare* (Naples: Edizioni Scientifiche Italiane, 1962).

HIBBARD, G. R. *Thomas Nashe, A Critical Introduction* (London: Routledge and Kegan Paul, 1962).

HOLLOWAY, J. *The Story of the Night* (London: Routledge and Kegan Paul, 1962).

JACQUOT, J. (ed.). *Le Théâtre tragique* (Paris: Centre National de la Recherche Scientifique, 1962).

KNIGHT, G. W. *The Golden Labyrinth, a Study of British Drama* (London: Phoenix House, 1962).

REESE, M. M. *The Cease of Majesty, a Study of Shakespeare's History Plays* (London: Edward Arnold, 1961).

SEN GUPTA, S. C. *The Whirligig of Time* (Orient Longmans, 1961).

SHAKESPEARE, WILLIAM

(The Arden Shakespeare)

The First Part of King Henry IV, edited by A. R. Humphreys (London: Methuen, 1960).

The First Part of King Henry VI, edited by A. S. Cairncross (London: Methuen, 1962).

The Comedy of Errors, edited by R. A. Foakes (London: Methuen, 1962).

(The New Shakespeare)

The Comedy of Errors, edited by J. Dover Wilson (Cambridge University Press, second edition, 1962).

King Henry the Eighth, edited by J. C. Maxwell (Cambridge University Press, 1962).

VYVYAN, J. *Shakespeare and Platonic Beauty* (London: Chatto and Windus, 1961).

WAITH, E. M. *The Herculean Hero in Marlowe, Chapman, Shakespeare and Dryden* (London: Chatto and Windus, 1962).

WHITFIELD, C. *The Kinship of Thomas Combe II, William Reynolds and William Shakespeare* (Newnham: The Laverock Press, 1962).

INDEX

INDEX

INDEX

Grassilli, Raoul, 136
Greece, Report on Shakespeare in, 134
Greene, Robert, 167, 169–70, 173
Greg, Sir Walter W., 6, 180, 181
Guarnieri, Annamaria, 136
Guinness, Sir Alec, 27, 152
Gundolf, Friedrich, 63
Guthrie, Sir Tyrone, 18, 24–5, 26, 152, 153

Hai, Zafar, 135
Hakluyt, Richard, 77
Hall, Berta, 137
Hall, Edward, 169
Hall, Joseph, 98
Hall, Peter, 24, 27
Harbage, Alfred, 165, 178
Harcourt, John B., 158–9
Hardwick, Paul, 150–1
Hardy, Thomas, 16
Harington, Sir John (of Burley), 165
Harris, Augustus, 116
Harris, Bernard, 157 n.
Harris, Frank, 34
Hartop, Job, 77
Hauptmann, G., 10, 14, 134
Hawkes, Terence, 158
Heminge, W., 8
Henderson, Hanford, 171
Henn, T. R., 48
Henry, Martha, 154
Henslowe, Philip, 168, 173
Heywood, Thomas, 95, 96, 97
Hibberd, G. R., *Thomas Nashe* reviewed, 168
Hill, R. F., 162–3
Hinman, Charlton, 6
Hobson, Harold, 28
Hodges, C. Walter, 152
Hogan, J. J., 178
Holinshed, R., 169
Holloway, John, *The Story of the Night* reviewed, 155–7, 161
Holm, Ian, 151
Holtzmann, Thomas, 133
Honigmann, E. A. J., 100, 169
Hooker, R., 38, 125
Horn, R. D., 171 n.
Hosley, Richard, 175
Hotson, L., 30, 118–19, 152
Howarth, Herbert, 164
Hubler, E., 171 n.
Hugo, François Victor, 54
Hugo, Victor, 10, 14, 53–4, 70, 75
Hulme, Hilda M., *Explorations in Shakespeare's Language* reviewed, 179
Hulme, T. E., 34
Hume, David, 35

Humphreys, A. R., New Arden edition of *1 Henry IV* reviewed, 172–3
Hungary, Report on Shakespeare in, 134–5
Hunsdon, Lord, 172
Hunt, Leigh, 78
Hunter, G. K., 165 n., 167
Hutt, William, 153, 154

Ibsen, Henrik, 14
India, Report on Shakespeare in, 135
Ionesco, E., 19, 34, 70, 150
Irish dramatists, 62
Irving, Sir Henry, 21
Italy, Report on Shakespeare in, 135–6

Jackson, Sir Barry, 19, 25, 26
Jacquot, Jean, 56
Jaggard, William, 177
Jamois, Marguerite, 133
Japan, Report on Shakespeare in, 136
Jarvis, William, 135
Jefford, Barbara, 22
Jenkins, Harold, 168
Jesenská, Zora, 133
Johnson, Laurence, 100
Johnson, Richard, 27
Johnson, Samuel, 31–2, 33, 34, 51
Johnston, G. B., 169
Jonson, Ben, 4, 11, 77, 95, 96, 97, 126, 164
  Alchemist, 56 n., 138
  Volpone, 20
Jordan, Thomas, 166
Jorgenson, P. A., 161–2
Joseph, Sister Miriam, 158
Josten, Walter, 63, 66
Joyce, James, 34

Kállai, Ferenc, 135
Kaula, David, 159
Kean, Charles, 104, 110, 111, 112, 113, 114, 116
Keats, John, 10
Keller, Christa, 133
Kemble, Charles, 110, 112, 114
Kermode, Frank, 159, 160, 161
Khorava, 15
Kimbrough, Robert, 181
Kiss, Ferenc, 135
Knight, Charles, 32
Knight, G. W., 32–3, 50
Knights, L. C., 34, 43, 47–9, 59, 61
Knolles, Richard, 40
Köpeczi-Bócz, I., 135
Korat, Asuman, 137
Kortner, Fritz, 134
Kosintzer, G., 139
Koszul, André, 54

INDEX

INDEX

Place, P. A. de la, 53
Planché, James Robinson, 103–117
Planchon, R., 54, 56 n.
Plato, 125
Plummer, Christopher, 18, 153
Poel, William, 114
Pohl, F. J., 164
Poland, Report on Shakespeare in, 136
  Shakespeare productions in, 18
Pompignan, Le Franc de, 53
Ponelle, Jean Pierre, 134
Pope, A., 84
Porter, Eric, 144, 147, 150
Pound, Ezra, 34
Prévost, Abbé, 53
Price, H. T., 167, 174
Prokofiev, 15
Puget, Claude-André, 133
Pushkin, 10, 14, 17

Quayle, Anthony, 19–20, 25, 26

Racine, Louis, 53, 74
Rajz, János, 135
Ránky, Gy., 135
Redgrave, Vanessa, 144, 145, 146, 150–1
Reese, M. M., *The Cease of Majesty* reviewed, 161, 169
Reid, Kate, 153
Revenger's Tragedy, The, 90
Reybas, André, 54, 133
Reynolds, George F., 166
Rezepter, V., 138
Ribner, Irving, 44
Richardson, Sir Ralph, 20
Rilke, R. M., 170–1
Ringler, W. A., 164
Robertson, Forbes, 23
Robertson, J. M., 64
Robson, Frederick, 108, 115
Rolland, 10
Romei, Hannibal, 84
Ronsard, 12
Rose, George, 22
Ross, L. J., 166
Rothe, Hans, 63–5, 66–7
Rouda, F. H., 159
Rouse, W. H. D., 170
Rowell, George, 103
Rowland, Samuel, 98
Russell, Thomas, 118

Samoylov, Y., 15
Samploy, A. M., 170
Sancroft, Archbishop, 170
Sanders, Norman, 168

Santayana, G., 45
Sartre, J.-P., 19
Saudek, E. A., 133
Sbragia, Giancarlo, 136
Schalla, Hans, 134
Schaller, Rudolf, 63, 134
Schiller, F., 10, 14, 70, 134
Schlegel-Tieck translation, 63, 65–7, 70, 134
Schopenhauer, 34
Schröder, Rudolf Alexander, 63, 66, 67, 134
Schwarz, Hedwig, 63
Scofield, Paul, 18
Scoloker, Anthony, 99
Scott, Sir Walter, 10, 33
Seale, Douglas, 26, 138
Sen, Sailendra Kumar, 180
Sen Gupta, S. G., *The Whirligig of Time* reviewed, 163
Seneca, 37, 38
Seward, T., 31
Shakespeare, William
  plays: *see* N. Sanders, 'The Popularity of Shakespeare: an examination of the Royal Shakespeare Theatre's repertory', pp. 18–29: *and also* S. Wells, 'Shakespeare in Planché's Extravaganzas', pp. 103–17
  All's Well, 58, 83, 135, 138, 152
  Antony and Cleopatra, 15, 30–4, 56, 73–4, 80, 136, 138, 162, 168
  As You Like It, 72, 78, 138
  Comedy of Errors, 64, 132, 136, 159, 167
  Coriolanus, 55–6, 80, 83, 89, 92, 133, 135, 136, 159
  Cymbeline, 143–51
  Hamlet, 5, 11, 12, 13, 15, 16, 37, 47, 53–9, 65, 72, 74–5, 95–6, 99–101, 133, 134, 156, 158, 159, 168, 179
  Henry IV, *1 & 2*, 13, 42, 79, 80, 81, 132, 133, 136, 138, 161–2, 168–9; New Arden edition, 172–3
  Henry V, 43, 50, 56 n., 132, 135, 168–9
  Henry VI, *1, 2 & 3*, 80–1, 132; New Arden edition of *1 Henry VI* reviewed, 173–4
  Henry VIII, 168–9, 174–5
  John, 134, 135, 136, 168–9
  Julius Caesar, 13, 65, 80, 132, 133, 136, 138, 162, 174
  Lear, 13, 37, 38, 55, 56, 60–1, 64, 72–3, 74, 83, 88–9, 133, 136, 137, 156, 159, 166, 170, 177, 178, 179
  Love's Labour's Lost, 2, 4, 71, 72, 121–4, 129, 131, 165, 167, 178
  Macbeth, 12, 37, 42–53, 55, 58, 64, 73, 74, 81, 82, 83, 84, 132, 133, 137, 138, 143–51, 153–4, 158–9, 175–6; Davenant's version, 181
  Measure for Measure, 58, 83, 84, 93, 94, 134, 136, 143–51, 163, 179
  Merchant of Venice, 13, 38–40, 54, 55, 78, 82, 83, 132, 133, 138, 160–1
  Merry Wives of Windsor, 37, 54, 133, 135, 172
  Midsummer Night's Dream, 132, 133, 134, 137, 138, 143–51, 159, 160, 164, 173, 178
  Much Ado About Nothing, 13, 72, 133, 134, 135, 170, 176

187

INDEX

INDEX